COLD GROUND'S BEEN MY BED

COLD GROUND'S BEEN MY BED

A KOREAN WAR MEMOIR

Daniel Wolfe

COLD GROUND'S BEEN MY BED
A KOREAN WAR MEMOIR

iUniverse books may be ordered through booksellers or by contacting:

iUniverse
1663 Liberty Drive
Bloomington, IN 47403
www.iuniverse.com
1-800-Authors (1-800-288-4677)

ISBN: 978-1-4917-9038-0 (sc)
ISBN: 978-1-4917-9039-7 (e)

Library of Congress Control Number: 2016903624

Print information available on the last page.

iUniverse rev. date: 10/03/2016

Contents

Dedication

This book is dedicated to my late and loving son, David. Unfortunately he was not aware of my experience in Korea. I am sure he would have ingested, digested, and then cross-examined me about each incident. With the injection of his humor, it would have made this book a national treasure.

Prologue

The men who fought in WWII were called the greatest generation, yet the men who were facing the same bullets, the same grenades, and the same shrapnel were called participants in a forgotten war (the Korean War).

I can assure you that as a draftee in the Forgotten War, the men of Company L, Fifteenth Regiment, Third Infantry Division faced the same perils and the same heartbreak as the greatest generation.

As a draftee, my story begins with a report for a physical in order to determine whether I was fit to serve. All 126 pounds of me at 5' 7" was on the James Monroe High School varsity football team. I competed in speed skating, and a major part of my physical conditioning took place on the asphalt streets of the Bronx. Of course I was fit to serve. I was breathing.

Basic training, conducted by a cadre of callous Korean vets, was an ordeal of rigor, harassment, and laughs. The laughs kept us going.

When basic training was over, our sadistic master sergeant, Nokel Roach, extended congratulations to our men by handing us mimeographed sheets with Far East Command (FECOM) orders.

I arrived in Korea early in March 1952. Although I heard sounds in the distance from artillery, war for me was still in the movies. How did I go to war? A truck dropped me off about a mile from the main line of resistance (MLR). I was handed a Browning Automatic Rifle (BAR) by my sergeant and was introduced to a six-by-eight-foot hole in a hill called a bunker. This was my home for six months.

On the front line, I witnessed numerous incidents of misjudgment and errors of officers who were safely ensconced in tents and trailers far behind the MLR. We were outnumbered and outgunned by the Chinese infantrymen. There were endless periods of boredom broken up by nights of sheer terror. Oh yes, there were laughs too—plenty of them—especially when we went into reserve, where raids and patrols were placed temporarily on hold.

So here we were, Company L on the front line, looking at the powerful beacons from Panmunjom, where peace talks had been taking place since 1951. The beams were mocking us as we went out on our nightly patrols or raids and then returned with our casualties.

The Forgotten War is one that the military would like to forget because of the numerous errors made by high-ranking officers—especially General MacArthur, whose major miscalculation was to go all the way to the Yalu River, ignoring President Truman's order to go no farther than the thirty-eighth parallel.

General MacArthur refused to believe the evidence that countless numbers of Chinese "volunteers" were waiting to cross the Yalu and overwhelm a much smaller UN militia.

The war ended with an armistice on July 27, 1953. US battle casualties were 33,651 killed in action, 103,284 wounded in action, and 7,850 missing in action. How many suffered and are suffering from PTSD?

An Atypical Physical

"Okay. Bend over and spread your cheeks."

At 39 Whitehall Street, the induction center for the US Army, the proctologist was checking for hemorrhoids. The year was 1951. Draftees were going from station to station to determine whether they were physically fit for the Korean War.

Traffic was moving along smoothly as an amused and densely populated semicircle surrounded the doctor. The doctor was addressing Fridiholtz, a peculiar character we knew from high school.

"Let's try it again," said the frustrated doctor. "Stand here and watch how the next fellow does it."

The next draftee dropped his shorts, bent over, and spread his buttocks. With a mirror on his forehead and a tongue depressor in his hand, the doctor searched the interior. Satisfied, he then turned to Fridiholtz.

"You saw that, son. Now let's try it."

With his head making a U-turn, and with an eyeball on the doctor, Fridiholtz hesitantly bent over and spread his cheeks. As soon as the tongue depressor grazed his sphincter, he went into orbit, hurtling forward and scattering the men in the semicircle. The elderly doctor dropped his tongue depressor into a wastebasket, shook his head, and then placed his hands on his knees. Frustrated, he told Fridiholtz to move along to the next station but to return in half an hour.

What a profession! This doctor had seen more assholes than the pond at the bottom of a toilet bowl.

Following that hors d'oeuvre, the next stop, appropriately, was lunch—a harbinger of things to come.

Dave Sohmer, a friend since elementary school, accompanied me to the mess hall. Two corrugated metal garbage pails stood alongside the serving station. Inside one pail, clustered in a circle, were pale tan frankfurters floating like an island in an oily rainbow of a fatty liquid. It wouldn't have taken a rabbinical scholar to know that these franks answered to no higher authority. A kitchen helper fished out two wieners and slid them effortlessly into the entrée section of my metal tray. From the adjacent garbage pail, an ice-cream scoop of mashed potatoes was removed and plastered alongside the franks. Then some wrinkled and waterlogged pale green peas were added to a smaller section of the tray. A brown liquid they called coffee was accompanied by a square of yellow something for dessert. I later discovered it wasn't dessert but cornbread for the franks. After consuming this strangeness, we continued with our physical.

Glenn, a classmate, joined us as we approached the next station. Seated behind a bare tan Formica table with chromium legs was a friendly gentleman.

"Are you fellows next?" he called out.

By this time we were mindlessly following one another. We handed him our papers, he stamped them, and we moved on, chasing the stenciled green arrows on the wall. Glenn stopped and looked at his paper.

"Hey, that was the audiologist!" he shouted. He spun around and made a dash for the doctor.

"But I'm very hard of hearing!" we heard. "I had problems in school. I have a letter from my uncle, an attorney, declaring that my hearing is defective."

Physicals over, we accompanied a dejected Glenn to the subway station. He ran to a phone booth.

"They think I can hear! The doctor said I could hear!" There was a pause and then a despondent "Yes, I think so."

The subway ride home was not a happy one for Glenn. Dave and I had mixed feelings about being drafted. We would be occupied for the next two years, after being continually rejected for employment as a result of our draft status. On the other hand, who knew what would be in store for us while American troops were under fire in Korea?

Between March 13, 1951, the date of my physical, and September 27, 1951, the date of my induction, I futilely searched for employment, signed for unemployment checks, met friends, went on a rare date, and played softball and stickball on weekends.

On March 29, I received my Certificate of Acceptability: Selective Service number 50 30 30 243 was found acceptable for induction into the armed services. On September 7, I received my Order to Report for Induction at 39 Whitehall Street at 8:00 a.m. on September 27, 1951.

When the day arrived, I gathered socks, underwear, and shaving gear and stuffed them into a canvas satchel. I looked around to say good-bye to my uncle (he had come to my parents' wedding thirty-two years earlier and was still celebrating by living in our apartment). I received no good-bye from him; he had left for work. My parents stood by trying to free words that were wedged in their throats. What could they tell me? "Be careful"? They knew they weren't going to see me for a while. I dropped my satchel, we kissed and embraced, and then I left.

Take One Step

Leaving my grieving parents, I closed the apartment door and stepped across the familiar small white octagonal tiles composing the mosaic tenement floor. They surrounded a drab brown number two at the center of our floor that greeted anyone visiting or exiting the second floor of our building. As I looked at these little pieces of close-fitting tiles, I realized that I wasn't going to leave my footprints on them for quite a while.

Satchel in hand, I rushed down four flights of steps and passed the mailboxes on the ground floor. These were the mailboxes from which I had pulled my sheriff's badge out of a padded envelope when I was seven years old, and my checkerboard knife and secret decoder in exchange for Ralston box tops. For ten Planter's Peanuts cellophane wrappers, I had found a free paperback dictionary in that metal rectangle. My brother and I had waited at this mailbox for tickets to see the radio show *The Shadow* broadcast from a studio above the New Amsterdam Theater on Forty-Second Street in Manhattan.

I'd better get out of here, I thought, *before I cry.*

Thank God Mr. Tekula, our janitor, wasn't rolling his barrels to the end of the sidewalk for a Department of Sanitation pickup. He hated the tenants, but I got an occasional grunt acknowledging my presence. Had he been there, I guess I would have said good-bye to his grumble.

I jogged a block to our meeting place—Gitelson's Deli on Boston Road and East 173rd Street. Behind the wood-framed glass doors, the empty tables were stacked with upturned chairs. Here we boys had wolfed down pastrami on club sandwiches, frankfurters, sodas, and french fries after Sunday stickball games. Without Murray and Gene behind the counter, without the frankfurters sizzling on the grill, and without the aroma of hot pastrami wafting through the deli, it was merely a store like any other waiting to be opened.

Where was Dave? We'd agreed to be here at seven. I leaned against the locked doors, watching workers streaming toward the East 174th Street elevated subway station. I knew they were going to work; they had no idea where I was going. We had passed the physical. "Report for induction at 8:00 a.m.," said the letter. Dave and I were going to be employed for the next two years. There would be no more papers documenting our attempt to find a job, no more grilling at the unemployment office, no more rejections by potential employers, and no more unemployment checks.

Ah, there was Dave. I could easily recognize him in the distance. His tall, muscular frame was the envy of all the boys in the neighborhood. With satchel in hand and a smile on his face, he crossed Boston Road. We joined the working men and women on their march toward the el station.

"There's the first place I worked, Dave. It was a tiny watch repair store. It was so small and narrow it could only have been a place for watch repairs."

"What did you do there?"

"I was twelve years old. The owner gave me a small envelope of watches, and I roller-skated to a large jewellery store on Prospect Avenue."

"Yeah, I know that store. It's still open."

"The big store repaired watches. My boss's expertise was repairing gold chains."

Now I was on my way to Whitehall Street to add to my employment résumé.

We passed the Dover Bar. The bright blue-and-red flickering neon Pabst Blue Ribbon beer sign seemed to be in its death throes. Before my friend Jerry's sister bought a TV set, we'd watched *Friday Night Fights* from the street through this sign in the window.

Marching on under the marquee of the Dover Theater, I saw the sidewalk's terra-cotta triangles polka-dotted with tiny black mounds of gum expelled from the mouths of kids waiting for the early morning Saturday cartoons and comedies.

We stopped at the base of the el station where a World War II vet who had lost part of his an arm in Sicily owned a newspaper stand. My father always went out of his way to buy a newspaper from him.

"I haven't seen you since you left your job at the freight yard. What are you up to?" he asked.

"My friend Dave and I were drafted. We're on our way."

Pointing to his amputated arm he said, "Don't be a hero."

Onward we scrambled, up the subway steps and onto the platform. We had a job! We were going to work!

The doors opened. We squeezed in and gripped the white ceramic handles pivoting above us. The train was rattling toward 39 Whitehall Street, the launching pad for all New York City recruits heading off to the armed forces.

"What did you do for your last night as a civilian?" asked Dave.

"I met the boys at the bowling alley. We played a couple of games, said our good-byes, and called it a night. What did you do?"

"I had some beers with my brothers, Lee and Sonny, and then went to sleep. Not the kind of night we usually see in the movies before a draftee leaves for the army."

"No true girlfriends. No wild parties. Neither of us is a hotshot lover.

Our destination stood gray and tall, on time and waiting. Going through the doors and into a large hallway, we met most of the group who had taken their physicals with us six months earlier. A GI directed us to a drab tan room that competed with the building's depressing exterior. Standing tall, looking starched and military, a sergeant called out names from his roster.

"Does this guy ever sit down or bend his elbows? Look at that uniform. There isn't a wrinkle anywhere," whispered Dave.

Glaring in our direction, the sergeant thundered, "I want complete silence! After I read the following, you will raise your right hand and you will swear your allegiance to our country."

With our gym bags on the floor and our right hands in the air, we swore to whatever he rattled off.

"Take one step forward," he barked. "Congratulations. You're in the US Army!"

I didn't feel any different after the one-second conversion from civilian to soldier.

We were herded toward another sergeant and four corporals, who lined us up in front of the building. Five empty buses devoured about two hundred recruits. When we settled in our seats, Vinnie Intriglia shouted, "How many of you guys are going to Officer Candidate School?"

Lenny Silpe stood up to flaunt his military knowledge. "What are you, nuts?" he asked. "My brother told me second lieutenants are cannon fodder in combat."

That put an end to the military talk. Back to reminiscing, attempts at humor, and guessing what was in store for us. Murray Lichtman decided to contribute. "I wish they would send us south, where it's warm."

"Do you like sweat, insects, and snakes?"

"No."

"Then stay here and freeze your ass off," advised Vinnie.

An hour's ride brought our bus full of New Yorkers to the army reception center in Camp Kilmer, New Jersey. Cadre (the personnel at the reception center) escorted us to one-story wooden barracks, where we were assigned beds. Soon the processing began. We were quizzed on our medical history, were given vaccinations, took written tests, had our teeth inspected, and were given a "short arm" inspection by a medic. He checked for gonorrhea. Each man had to squeeze his penis; if a viscous white liquid emerged, he was sent to the post hospital to determine whether he needed treatment for gonorrhea. Once it was confirmed that we had a heartbeat and were still breathing, we returned to our barracks. Uniforms were to be issued in a few days.

It was October 3, 1951, the day of "the shot was heard around the world." With two men on base and the New York Giants losing by two runs in the ninth inning, Bobby Thomson hit a home run off Brooklyn Dodger pitcher Ralph Branca to place the Giants in the World Series. We were a New York crowd cheering or jeering, competing with Russ Hodges, the announcer, who kept repeating, "The Giants win the pennant! The Giants win the pennant!" *There must be something good about being drafted*, I thought.

After dinner, I collapsed on my bunk and didn't wake up until the following morning, when whistles and shouts reverberated off the windowpanes.

"Fall out! Fall out and line up!"

What does he mean, "line up"? I wondered.

"No, not like that, you meatballs! I want a line of nine men left to right in four rows. Don't you eight-balls know anything?" This frail corporal, who resembled Woody Allen and depended upon a uniform to identify his masculinity, screeched, "When I call your name, shout 'Here!' like you got a pair!"

Does he have them? I wondered.

If the name was not Smith or Jones, it was certain to be mispronounced. Sohmer was Shummer, Praver was Prohver, Wolfe was Wolfie, and the Italian names were completely macerated. We were to discover that this was the rule for the cadre rather than the exception.

"Quiet! Quiet! I want it so quiet I can hear a rat pissing on cotton!" A few guys chuckled.

"Laughing? If I catch the son of a bitch who's laughing, I'll stick my hand down his throat, grab him by his asshole, and turn him inside out!" Again there was a snicker.

"Laughing? Laughing? Do I hear laughing? The turd that's laughing is lower than whale shit, and that's at the bottom of the ocean!"

Paralysis set in. No one moved. *Two years of this? Is there an end to the script?* I asked myself.

"Okay. Stand tall. Give me a column of ducks; we're marching to the mess hall."

What the hell is this twerp talking about? What is this column of ducks?

Off we went for breakfast, scrambling about like bumper cars in Coney Island.

•

On the following day, my barracks was assigned KP at the battalion mess hall. Hundreds of men, perhaps a thousand, were to be fed. As KPs, we played a behind-the-scene role in the smooth operation of the mess hall.

"Espresso? Cappuccino? Tea? Or me?" (Dan on KP.)

Removing the eyes of the potatoes before they were placed into a peeling machine was my assignment. The mess sergeant cautioned me to remove the peeled potatoes' eyes with as little of the surrounding potato as possible.

As the hours passed, monotony led to dreariness and dreariness led to fatigue. Consequently, the potatoes became smaller as the eyes with their surrounding areas became larger. The mess sergeant stepped in to critique my surgery. He scrutinized a recently deformed potato. "If your work doesn't improve, I'll have you peeling these potatoes with your toes!"

"The potatoes we had for lunch tasted as if they were peeled with someone's toes," I replied.

"Oh, a New York wiseguy!"

He left. I continued butchering the potatoes until it was time to quit.

"Where are you going?" asked the sergeant.

"It's eight o'clock. KP is over."

"Not for you, smart-ass!"

I worked through the night. At 5:00 a.m. I walked out. I should have done it earlier—it was Saturday. I staggered to my bed and collapsed. My three-inch mattress felt like a top-of-the-line Beautyrest. At about 11:00 a.m., I was awakened by cries of "Wolfe! Wolfe! Private Wolfe!"

"Who wants to see him?" I asked.

"He's wanted at the CP [command post]".

Anticipating another KP assignment, I replied, "He left for the PX about half an hour ago."

The messenger left, and so did I, in the opposite direction. He returned to the command post; I double-timed it for the post library. I leafed through Norman Mailer's war novel, *The Naked and the Dead*—not recommended for a draftee. I looked up at the clock. *How could I have spent three hours here?* I wondered. It seemed as if I had just arrived. *That mess sergeant has probably forgotten about me. I can't take any more of this. I'm going to the barracks.*

The boys were still gabbing about Bobby Thomson's home run. Dave wanted to know where I'd been. I told him I'd been in the library, hiding from the mess sergeant. He seemed completely confused by my explanation, but I was too tired to pursue it.

Two months later, when I was home on my first pass, I related the potato episode. A brief period of silence followed. Then came the revelation: My father had schlepped for hours by subway and bus from the Bronx to Camp Kilmer to visit the day the messenger came looking for me. I felt so sorry for my dear, fragile father. I recalled the rainy days when I waited at the subway station for his return from work with an umbrella in my hand. I watched him rehydrate with a two-cent seltzer at the candy store before he wobbled home with me. I was consumed with guilt for his disappointing trip. I wanted to embrace him and tell him I was sorry. Why didn't I?

Indiantown Gap

Whenever I reached for the light switch at home, a weary voice would drift through the darkness.

"It's all right; it's all right. Leave it off; the cockroaches can see in the dark." This was Ma's attempt to save a few cents.

I was convinced my mother was the lighting consultant for the quartermaster warehouse where our uniforms were being issued. Upon entering the building, I extended an arm to keep from walking up the back of the GI in front of me.

"Let's see your papers," shot a voice out of the semidarkness.

The man behind a long counter checked my vital statistics.

"It's a thirty-eight jacket, a twenty-nine waist and thirty length for the pants, fifteen and a half for the neck, and seven and a quarter for the head."

His assistant threw two woolen Ike jackets, two pairs of matching pants, and two khaki shirts, also with matching pants, at me. I dropped them to the bottom of my empty duffel bag. As I moved along, two pairs of cotton fatigues, two pairs of cement combat boots, three pairs of woolen socks, two overseas caps, and an overcoat were added to my wardrobe. Next, two pairs of itchy long johns were draped over the counter.

"Keep them," I said. "Those things will never get close to my skin."

"You're signing for them. You'd better take them."

I stuffed them carefully into my duffel, hoping that their itchiness wouldn't corrupt the rest of the clothing.

With duffel bags on our shoulders, the company began the mile trek back to the barracks. The distant monotone of our cadreman's cadence lulled me back to James Monroe High School and Doc Wiedman, our football coach, warning the team: "Don't anyone dare show up without a suit and tie."

He was referring to the annual end-of-season football dinner. We earned a seat at the Chester House restaurant in the Bronx. The price we paid was Wiedman's bone-crushing daily practices on a field meticulously landscaped by the federal Works Progress Administration (WPA) during the Depression. Fringes of grass circled encrusted rocks breaking through the surface as if gasping for air.

A suit in those days was about as essential to my wardrobe as a pair of gray suede spats, but I wanted to attend the dinner and mingle with the football alumni and our boys who'd earned their letters.

My father and I entered Crawford Clothes in the Hotel McAlpin opposite Macy's on Thirty-Fourth Street. As a salesman approached, I leaned toward my father and whispered, "Pa, look at him. Do you think he knows what's in fashion.?"

"Knows? He knows nothing," he replied. "That's a suit he's wearing? The pants don't match the jacket. Ask me."

Rummaging through my size rack, we settled on a worsted blue sharkskin one-button lounge and a matching tie.

Spruced up in my suit, tie, starched collar, and foot-cramping shoes at the Chester House, I reminisced with the alumni and our boys who had suffered through the season with me. As the tedious speeches wore on during the dry chicken dinner, my collar began to shrink and my toes began to curl. *Where are my Keds sneakers? They are like pillows.*

Finally we said our good-byes. The Boston Road bus brought me home, where I could at last free my neck from the collar's stranglehold and my toes from the pinch of the shoes. I removed my suit and placed it in the closet. Lonely and limp, it hung there awaiting a call for another rare social event.

I was jolted out of my reverie when the front of Dave's shoe accidentally jabbed my Achilles tendon. While I was squeezing it to strangle the pain, our cadreman, who had observed the entire scene enfold, asked compassionately, "Can't you march in step? I think we'll have to send you Yankees to dancing school this weekend."

The barracks was a welcome sight. Out of the pile of clothing I shook out of my duffel, I selected a dress uniform, buttoned up, and then ran to the latrine. It was crowded with men, all in uniform, appraising themselves in the mirrors above the sinks. I squeezed in and saw a fit that was perfect but a color that could have been more flattering. Now we were soldiers. With my new dress uniform, I was in style with all the fashionable dudes from the Bronx, Brooklyn, Queens, and Manhattan.

When processing was completed, we boarded buses to carry us to our basic training camp. Conversation had reached a high pitch when someone from the front announced,

"I think we're going to Indiantown Gap in Pennsylvania."

Silence.

"Where the hell is that?" came from the rear.

"They said it's near Harrisburg."

"Harrisburg? Where's that?"

"In Pennsylvania."

"Are Abbot and Costello on this bus?" stage-whispered Dave.

A two-hour bus ride brought us through the gate of Indiantown Gap. Foreheads leaving oily streaks on the windows were soaking up the strange new neighborhood. Our bus came to a halt. A whistle from a cadreman waiting on a white-graveled path alongside the bus was our signal to disembark. He marched us to our new home.

The barracks had the appearance of abandoned buildings. They had been decommissioned at the end of World War II. Curled, peeling paint on the exterior revealed dull gray clapboards underneath. Each barrack sat on compacted clay soil interspersed with tousled tufts of weeds that had been browned by the autumn chill. In contrast to these sad wooden barracks and dying vegetation, imposing blue-green mountains framed the horizon—an impressive sight for city boys. Our beautiful sylvan panorama was disturbed by the sight of a capillary-marbled face mottled with scars and illuminated by a flaming red nose.

"Welcome, girls. I am Master Sergeant Roach. It's my job to change you eight-balls into men who are proud of their uniform. Now, step out!"

We hadn't yet mastered the art of balancing a bulging duffel bag on our shoulders, yet he was asking us to step out. Struggling with the weight of the duffels, we plodded behind Sergeant Roach until we arrived at our company command post. The company commander, Lieutenant Walker, came out to introduce himself and four sergeants, all Korean War veterans.

"My name is Lieutenant Walker. When you pass me or any other officer in this camp, salute them. It is your way of saying, 'Good morning.' These men will be your platoon sergeants. When your sergeant calls your name, fall into his barracks."

Each sergeant, holding a roster, called out the names of the men in his platoon.

"Kingsbridge! … Kingsbridge! … Kingsbridge, God damn it, where the hell are you, Kingsbridge? Kingsbridge, you're AWOL!"

"Do you mean Koeningsberg?"

"Kingsbridge? Kingsbridge? We don't get names like these in our army."

The next names were Winter and Smith. He called. They reported. Then "Wolfie? Wolfie?"

"Do you mean Wolfe?"

"That's what I said, Wolfie. What, do you have shit in your ears?"

When the roll call was over, there were still as many men on the street as in the barracks. Their names had been butchered and dissected to a point of nonrecognition. The men who could read solved this problem; they found their names on the roster and proceeded to their barracks.

Inside the barracks, there was a scramble for beds on both floors. Dave and I found adjacent beds on the upper floor. The blue-striped mattresses, resting on wire springs, were no more than three inches thick, but that was okay—I had no better at home. A metal locker for all our belongings stood to the right of our beds. There were no footlockers.

At the first opportunity, we introduced ourselves to the men nearby. Pitts and Gould, two black GIs from Detroit, selected beds to our left. Pitts warned, "I snore like a Mack truck with a broken muffler. But you'll probably be so tired you won't hear me."

Gould pierced through him with his steely eyes.

"Don't try it on me, Pitts, or I'll bury your head in that pillow."

With a smile, Dave turned to me.

"This is going to be fun."

A fellow from South Carolina walked over to introduce himself. His accent, I thought, had been invented for movies like *Gone with the Wind*. But the words rolled off his tongue effortlessly, unrehearsed. It was a genuine southern accent.

"Hi, boys. I'm Williams. I don't know anything about this war. How did you feel when you were drafted?"

"I wasn't happy," said Dave, "but I had no job; I was on a treadmill. How did you feel?"

"I'm no hero. Right now I'm as nervous as a cat in a room full of rocking chairs."

Uninvited, Iovino, whom we had met at Camp Kilmer, jumped onto my bed and shouted in his best Brooklynese, "Who's volunteering fur duh paratroopers?"

No response.

"What a bunch uhv joiks. Stay here and be ugly dogfaces."

He hopped off, shook his head, and ran to the first floor searching for someone to accompany him in volunteering "fur duh paratroopers."

Withdrawn from the buzz and chaos, slumped over and sunk into his mattress, head in hands, and ignoring the tumult around him was what appeared to be a very depressed soul. Dave and I walked over to ask him to join in the fun. He looked up and introduced himself as Harry Lapich. Through watery red eyes he said he had left his wife at the train station in Detroit three days after they were married. He missed her. Neither Dave nor I knew anything of marriage or the separation from a partner. Dave tried to comfort him.

"We'll get passes soon and—"

A screech of a whistle snaked its way through the barracks.

"All right, men, get your linen and blankets from quartermaster. Then come to the bathroom on the double."

The entire platoon of thirty-six men rushed to quartermaster, got their linen, dumped it on their beds, and assembled in the toilet.

"This is our bathroom. This is where you will piss, crap, shower, and shave. After you have done that, this bathroom will be as clean as it is now. Any questions?"

"Yeah. Who are you?"

"I'm Sergeant Bayliss, your platoon sergeant, and from now on you will call me *sir*. I know it's strange for many of you, but you will shower every day. Don't fall out in morning formation reeking from funk or with a day-old beard. And if you need a haircut, you will get it at the commissary."

What's a commissary? I wondered.

"Who cleans this bathroom?" asked Pitts.

"There will be a duty roster posted on the bulletin board at the entrance to the barracks."

If Bayliss spells names like he pronounces them, I thought, *this bathroom will really be a shithouse.*

Another whistle screeched. We assumed it was for us, so we ran out to the company street. It was Sergeant Roach, standing on the top step of the command post, told us to line up in a military manner and follow our platoon sergeant to the mess hall.

"Hey, Dave, how do you line up in a military manner?"

"I don't know. Let's follow the country boys."

Milling, bumping, and confusion reigned on the company street as the platoon stumbled toward the mess hall.

The battalion mess hall featured the Whitehall Street stainless steel tableware and the matching metal tray with depressed sections for entrée, vegetable, and dessert.

Dave Sohmer was in heaven. His mother was disabled. His father, a cabdriver, was rarely home. Dave and his two brothers had reluctantly made the meals. Now he was being served.

The aroma of the food in the huge hall was totally foreign to me. The men on KP dropped two now familiar brown-topped yellow squares and a serving spoon of lima beans into the small depressions of my tray. We moved along, and three thin, unfamiliar pale pink oval discs were deposited into the large depression for the entrée. Each slice was glisteningly uniform. They appeared to have been burnished by a fine steel wool pad. They lay there limply, waiting to be anointed with a brown sauce sporting an occasional clove and pineapple chunk. Dave told me these slices were ham—verboten in my kosher home. The yellow rectangles were the cornbread I had met at Whitehall Street. The lima beans had a strange flavor that followed me throughout my army career. I was hungry. I ate everything on the tray. Two weeks later, when I was on KP, I discovered the source of the mysterious taste and odor of the beans. There were ugly, bony brown masses called ham hocks that were were cooked with the beans. Welcome to basic training.

Hygiene in the Barracks

In sixteen weeks of basic training, an attempt was made to mold young men from farms, urban areas, slums, rural communities, and wealthy suburbs into a group of gun-wielding killers.

The Blue Mountain terrain of Indiantown Gap, Pennsylvania, was similar to the hills and valleys of Korea. It was a perfect setting for what lay ahead. Anyone who has gone through it will admit that infantry basic training is a combination of torture, harassment, and lots of laughs. I found the experience heavily weighted toward torture and harassment. The laughs kept me going.

The cadre at Indiantown Gap consisted of Korean War veterans. Using their sadistic temperament, they realized their goals of torment and oppression. But using their stupidity, we were able to cull many scraps of humor.

One day, during a break from the programmed agony, we were marched to view an instructional film. Still uncoordinated, our platoon, aching in stiff new boots, stumbled toward the instruction barracks.

"If you guys don't get it together and march in a military manner, I'll drop a hand grenade in your ass pocket," shouted Corporal Edwards.

His warning fell on deaf ears. Our platoon of draftees chuckled, stumbled, and swore as we lumbered toward the shed.

We missed the classic on venereal disease; however, awaiting us was a movie on personal hygiene. It met all the criteria for an Oscar winner in the short film category.

The film introduced us to the need for soap and how to use it. We were expected to shower at least once a day using soap. Many of the men didn't have a shower at home. Many of the men who did have a shower at home didn't shower. The narrator said that soap could also be used on wounds when there was no medication. We were told to use plenty of soap when cleansing a wound. It would prevent infection. Thus, with the simple vocabulary list used for training manuals and films, everyone was educated in the use of soap.

Finally, when the film ended and the lights went on, from a front seat rose a colonel. With pursed lips and a martial air, he declared, "All right, men. You saw the film. You paid attention. Let's see what you have learned. To the barracks for showers!"

We took off for the barracks. There were six showers for forty men. Men who had never passed the threshold of a shower were rubbing shoulders and buttocks with the usual patrons. There was no way I was going to be a player in this insanity. I sat on a bowl, watching a shower room that could accommodate six but was crammed with more than ten. It reminded me of the cabin scene in the Marx Brothers film *A Night at the Opera.*

As Williams, the draftee from South Carolina, squeezed out of the shower room, I sarcastically asked him if it was crowded in there.

"Crowded? Crowded? By God, it was so crowded I washed out six assholes before I got to mine."

How can anyone top the pithy humor of a southerner?

If the beds had been removed, our barracks would have appeared to be wood-plank floors, uninsulated walls, and a bathroom with six sinks and showers. The beds and the shelf above them upgraded it to the appearance of a sleepaway camp for underprivileged children. Our platoon sergeant had a room of his own.

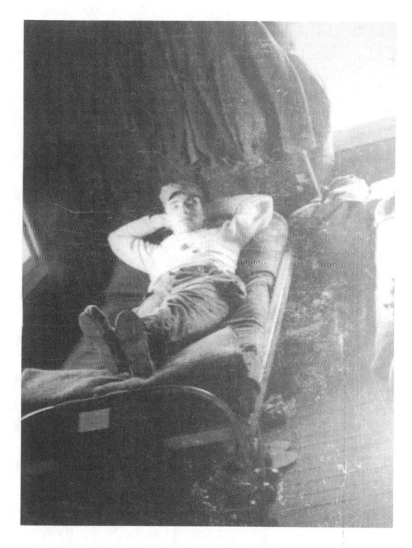

"Someday I'm going to murder the bugler.
Someday I'm gonna remain in bed."

There were no toilet stalls in the bathroom. A GI had a choice of five black-lidded toilet bowls facing the sinks. Sometimes, depending what was served for dinner, a trio or quartet would be performing for an uninterested audience of hand washers or shavers.

Before we could earn a weekend pass, we had a Friday night ritual—the barracks party. We began the celebration by organizing ourselves into groups, each with a specific detail. We dusted everything within reach, sanitized the bathroom and showers, and scrubbed the splintery wooden floors with brown GI soap bubbling from the stiff brown bristles of a brush. To end the party, each man polished his boots. Early the following morning, we tightened our bedsheets and blankets until they squeaked. The sinks and showers sparkled, their faucets polished and floors mopped.

After breakfast, Sergeant Bayliss carried out his rigid inspection. He checked the bed linen, the cleanliness of the floors, the shine and alignment of the boots resting at the side of our beds, and the dust on top of and under the shelves. The footlockers weren't checked, because we didn't have footlockers. The rest of our belongings were either in our locker or squeezed into our duffel bags.

Sergeant Bayliss appeared to be satisfied with the appearance and cleanliness of the barracks. His last check was the bathroom and showers. The shriek of his whistle told me we might be spending the weekend at Indiantown Gap.

"Everyone to the bathroom! Double time!" he shouted.

Forty men crowded into the bathroom, waiting for Bayliss's critique. He pointed to the ceiling.

"No matter what difficulty he had on the bowl," said Bayliss, "I want to see the athlete who could shit and leave his footprint on the ceiling. If he can't repeat that right now, nobody gets a pass."

Heads turned, but no one responded.

Our weekend was spent on toilet drill. On the command of a whistle, the men on the lower floor ran into the bathroom, raised the toilet seats, and then returned to attention alongside their beds. When the next whistle blew, the men on the upper floor ran down the steps to the bathroom, lowered the toilet seats, and returned to attention alongside their beds.

After many repetitions of this madness, the bathroom ceiling was cleaned bare. Subsequently, I learned that the footprint was the creation of a lower-floor resident who had stuck a broom handle into his muddy boot and then pressed the boot onto the ceiling.

The movie on personal hygiene had no effect on the GIs who had previously boycotted the showers. Their bodies formed an inseparable bond with their long johns, which soon became their second skin and probably were shed only as summer approached—if they hadn't decomposed by then.

Our government had spared every expense in building these simple two-story wooden barracks for the World War II GIs. But since their flimsy walls and floors had not yet collapsed, and their showers were still functional, they were deemed appropriate to accommodate the recruits for Korea.

Ref-you-jee Bucky

Bucky Praver was one of the many "ref-you-jees" (as Sergeant Roach called them) in the Fourth Platoon. Roach knew that these draftees had neither regard for nor training in military discipline. If most of them had no regard, Bucky had utter disregard. He just couldn't be bothered with it. He came to my attention during our daily calisthenics.

A corporal who looked like a wide receiver for the Green Bay Packers stood tall and flexing on a raised platform, shouting and demonstrating the way we were to contort ourselves for each exercise. He ended the exhausting routine with push-ups. We had to keep our bodies straight horizontally while lifting them off the ground with our arms to his cadence. Bodies were sweating, men were groaning, and arms were trembling while trying to perform one more push-up. From the corner of my eye, I saw Bucky lying flat on the ground, lifting only his head and grunting with the rest of the men as the instructor counted the repetitions. *This is a character worth investigating*, I decided.

On our return to the barracks, I found Bucky had a similar background to Dave's and mine. We Depression babies had grown up with a coin or two mingling with the dust and threads at the bottoms of our pockets. During childhood, one way we earned a bit of change was by waiting at the candy store for the phone to ring. When it did, we would run to call a building resident to the phone, and we would receive an empty milk or soda bottle as a tip, which we redeemed at the grocery for two cents. We lived in tenements and passed our leisure time playing ball on the streets. Now we were draftees in the hills and valleys of Pennsylvania.

Bucky was tall, dark, and handsome, but he was never a candidate for supernumerary (the sharpest-looking soldier assigned to guard duty—as a reward for looking the best, he is not assigned a guard post). Maybe he tried to look neat, but he just didn't get it. Bucky's nubby winter dress woolens never visited the dry cleaner. His tucked-in fatigue shirt billowed over his beltline. The first smears of polish that had dabbed his boots remained unburnished throughout basic training. When he bloused his pants legs, a small portion of the bottoms somehow escaped the tuck under the tied condom around the top of his boot. How did he get his overseas cap as flat as a beret? How did he get a weekend pass in that condition?

"You *will* look sharp before you get a pass," snarled Sergeant Roach.

In spite of, or because of, his slovenly appearance, Bucky was our gentle hero.

Bucky could have been a successful point man (the lead man on a patrol or raid). During a hectic morning at the confidence course, he managed to forge a trail through the woods in order to avoid all the stations. Mysteriously, he appeared as we were about to confront each next task, and then he dissolved. But he was promptly there when we lined up for our return to the barracks.

As a two-year English major at Long Island University, Bucky could have remained in school for two more years and then graduated, avoiding the draft. He said his art course in junior high school was more challenging than any of the courses he took at LIU. That was it for him. LIU's loss was our gain.

A Holiday in Harrisburg

It was different from all the others (just as he was different from all the others)—his whistle. Every sergeant in the cadre had the same shiny chrome-plated whistle, but somehow Sgt. Nokel Roach managed to elicit a distinctive piercing sound, alerting us with a shriek that was uniquely his.

"Fall in on me!" he shouted one evening soon after we returned from mess. Standing at the top of a short flight of steps leading to the command post, Sergeant Roach, the essence of ecumenism, growled, "Any Jew wanting to go to holiday services in Harrisburg, bring your ass and an overnight bag with clean underwear to the CP tomorrow before dinner. Some families in Harrisburg will take you to church. Then you can dirty their sheets overnight."

I knew Dave Sohmer wouldn't go. Although his father was Jewish, he identified with his mother, who was an American Indian of the Christian faith. His family had found its way into and adjusted very well to our ghetto.

Bucky was standing among the Fourth Platoon aliens. Perhaps he might go.

"Hey, Bucky. It's a day off. A day out of formation. A day of real food. Let's go."

"No, I don't think so. Einstein and I think alike: We identify, but we don't practice."

"What has that got to do with it? We won't have to look at Roach, and it's a day off from the mountains."

"Apparently I have higher moral standards than you."

One thing about Bucky—he was always good for a laugh.

About fifteen GIs, predominantly from New York City, were waiting on the company street for the bus. I had a nodding acquaintance with most of them, but that was the extent of our relationship. A creeping apprehension began to envelop me. I was on my way to get a snippet of a Jewish world outside my ghetto. For some strange reason, silence was the comversation among the New Yorkers. Perhaps they felt as I did about becoming acquainted with the outside Jewish world.

Harrisburg had a a prosperous Jewish community, judging from the group of people waiting outside their modern temple. An elderly gentleman holding a sheet of paper greeted us. When my name was called, a well-dressed middle-aged couple stepped forward, introduced themselves, and then led me to their Buick. The warm velvet feel of the seat was quite a contrast to the cold olive drab plastic on the GI bus. A cloying sweetness, apparently the wife's perfume, joined every molecule of breathable air in the car. I turned the knob and opened the window. The wife asked me politely to close it because she was cold. We pulled into a quiet residential neighborhood.

I had seen it in the movies and in my elementary school reader, but I had never entered a house occupied by a single family. I was shown the room where I would sleep and was then led into a dining room for dinner. In my family's apartment kitchen, we ate all our meals on an enameled metal table surrounded by a Quality gas stove with four curved spindly legs, a Kelvinator refrigerator beside it, and a utility sink near the window behind us. Before me now, a polished mahogany sideboard against a wall was lined with dining implements, dishes, and glassware I did not recognize. A massive dinner table with lace placemats was set with cutlery and china whose designs actually matched, unlike the *Yahrtzeit* glasses we used at home (short, thick glasses containing memorial candles; our household used them as drinking glasses when their original purpose had been fulfilled). The wine and water glasses on this table fired rainbows at me as I moved to sit down.

The ambiance of this elegant dining room was like a morgue. My hosts' daughter was away at college. Her parents had no curiosity about my hometown, my parents, army life, or my views on anything. Conversation was sparse. I couldn't penetrate their dense indifference, and I felt like an intruder. Today the scene reminds me of the classic Thanksgiving dinner in Woody Allen's *Annie Hall*. At the dining room table, Annie's grandmother, obviously an anti-Semite, gazes at Woody, envisioning him as a Hasidic Jew wearing long, curled *payes* (the sideburns required of highly traditional Orthodox Jews) and somber old-fashioned clothes. In my dress uniform, I was as uncomfortable as Woody would have been in that Hasidic outfit.

A few beads of green peas and a smear of mashed potatoes surrounded the lonely chicken breast on my plate. Where was the bread? At home Ma baked a large challah loaf for Friday night (the start of Jewish Sabbath) and holiday meals. Chicken on our earthenware plates rested next to a mound of green vegetables and Ma's homemade stuffed *derma*. I guess this was how my hosts kept themselves fashionably thin. After a dessert of tea and cookies, sundown was almost upon us. We left for the temple.

Everyone walked to synagogue on the Sabbath and holidays in my neighborhood. My hosts drove to their Reform temple, an unforgivable sin on this night, Yom Kippur (the annual Jewish Day of Atonement). The peeling yellow-gray walls of my synagogue paled before the smooth, sparkling white walls of this temple. I'd heard of Reform temples—considered mutations by the Orthodox. One was pointed out to me whenever our bus passed it on the elegant Grand Concourse in the Bronx.

The suits, dresses, and jewelry of this congregation left no doubt that it was an affluent group of worshippers. At my synagogue, prayer shawls as yellow as the aging walls hid the mismatched jackets and pants underneath them.

At front left, seated at a huge organ, was a desiccated woman whose austere face seemed to have crawled out of Grant Wood's brush. Covering her scalp were wavelets of silver-blue hair. I had never seen a Jewish woman with hair this color. I suspected the rinse was available only at church gift shops. She resembled my eighth-grade teacher, Miss Sanderson, whose annual day in the sun was leading the assembly in Thanksgiving hymns. While my classmates were singing "We Gather Together to Ask the Lord's Blessing," my friends and I sang *"Adon Olam,"* which ends the Hebrew Sabbath service.

Behind the organ, standing in a semicircle, was the choir, genetic clones of the blue-haired organist. They could have easily been mistaken for members of a Norman Rockwell New England quilting bee.

A long note was struck on the organ. The rabbi entered, stage right, solemn and hands clasped. He was wearing a flowing royal blue robe with sleeves billowing as he walked. His garment looked like a knockoff of one of the pope's outfits, except that the pope wore a *kippot* (skullcap) and this rabbi did not.

He stopped at the *bimah* (the dais from which services are conducted) and extended his arms. I didn't know whether to genuflect or run up and kiss his ring. This was the signal to start the service. The choir opened their transliterated *Kol Nidre* texts, which were covered with blue velvet, color-coordinated with their robes and the rabbi's. This ancient Aramaic chant, which appeals to God to forgive our sins, is the opening prayer of the Yom Kippur service. I can only describe their rendition of it as unintentional sacrilege; the magpies butchered it. Thank God the service was short.

That night I slept in a luxurious bed, which made up for all the discomfort I had endured during my visit. The next morning, I thanked my hosts for the delicious dinner, breakfast, and the opportunity to go to services with them. They did not observe the traditional Yom Kippur fast from sundown to sundown,

On the bus back to camp, I reflected on the unsophisticated, provincial life I'd led in my Bronx ghetto. I once again pictured the contrast of my host's coordinated dining room and the blue-and-white enameled-metal kitchen table with its four paint-laden chairs. I thought about my mother, who never sat down with us as she waited from the leftovers from her pot and our plates. We had two sets of silverware: one for meat, the other for dairy. Both "sets" had as many strangers as mates among them. Dishes that had once been part of a set now mimicked the silverware in their variety. The kitchen table featured a blue tablecloth on Friday nights and holidays. Sabbath candles in small brass holders illuminated this spare but joyful home.

Let my hosts live their version of the good life; I'll nestle in the warmth of mine.

An Outing to the Mountains

It was a day that challenged our strength, stamina, nerves, and reflexes. After breakfast, a three-mile march brought the company to the confidence course, a series of stations that dared the GI to exhibit his dexterity. Each acrobatic maneuver on the ground and in the air was designed by a sadist whose alleged mission was to instill confidence in the men.

As in any well-constructed exam, the early problems were easy. Everyone hopped from tire to tire without difficulty. Smith, the most uncoordinated man in the United States, had a smile on his face as he danced through the hoops. Everyone loved him. He was the company character. He always tried. On the other extreme, Phillips, who was always scheming for a discharge, feigned a stumble over the second tire and then sat alongside it squeezing his knee. Since basic training began, he had made no legitimate attempt to complete a physical task. I had no use for this conniver.

We managed the crawl through puddles under barbed wire fences without incident. Aside from mud-caked fatigues, we were ready for the next trial. From there, like Olympians, we took off to hurdle over a twelve-foot wooden wall. The next task appeared to be the same twelve-foot olive drab (OD) wooden wall we had just vaulted. Dave lifted me, and I grasped the top only to find myself hanging suspended in air as the wall leaned toward me. With great difficulty, I lifted myself up and over, and then I slid to the ground. As I followed the posted arrows through the woods to the next station, I tried to unscramble the difference between the two walls.

When we arrived at the next station, Dave and I looked up to find what appeared to be a stripped twenty-five-foot tree trunk suspended thirty feet above a stream. Surely they didn't expect us to crawl over that bulk of lumber!

Dave, who boxed at the YMCA, was a very well proportioned five-foot-ten-inch middleweight. Although he never played ball with us, he had the reflexes and aggressive attitude of an athlete. Whatever the sport was, I always gave a good account of myself in spite of my five-foot-seven frame. I was certain we would have no problem with this station.

"We can't go together, Danny, so why don't you go first."

"Okay. But you'll lead on the next one."

A ladder took me to one end of the long, round log. Terror replaced blood in my dilated vessels as I cautiously slid forward. Clutching the curved surface, I groped my way across, high above the stream. At the other end, I was revived by a deep inhale and a pause. The descending ladder stabilized my circulation. When Dave hopped off the ladder behind me, he asked, "Do you think we'll be better killers after this?"

"Maybe I'll get a *killer* [the Yiddish word for "hernia"] after this."

The next test took us to a wider part of the stream. I pushed Dave ahead of me for a climb up a twenty-foot ladder. We stood on a fifteen-foot platform, looking at a braided cable extending to the other side of the stream. A hanging handle was looped around the cable.

"Go ahead; it's your turn, Dave. Grab the handle."

He gripped the handle tightly with both hands, closed his eyes, jumped off the platform, took a knuckle-whitening trip over the stream, and landed on a strip of sand allegedly designed to absorb the impact. I followed. We left four deep scars in that "shock absorber."

On tender soles, we hobbled toward a sign announcing, "The Hard One." Below, in smaller letters the sign continued: "Proceed at Your Own Risk." I recalled the fight-or-flight reflex from Mr.

Donovan's high school biology class. A rush of adrenaline prepared me to engage the enemy like a hero or retreat like a coward. I decided to engage the enemy.

My eyes were riveted on a group of horizontal logs upon which some of our men were carefully inching forward. They were the same size and shape as the logs we had previously encountered, but these were spaced three feet apart. Dave said he would pass on this one.

Should I remain on the ground with most of the boys? Should I embarrass myself and climb up? I had just shown the cadre I could crawl on a log high above the ground.

I climbed the thirty-foot ladder to a platform, and there were the logs. I grasped, I scratched, and I squeezed to make the trip across, which brought me to the final insult: a braced six-foot ladder leaning up and out at an angle into space. From the top of this ladder, a thick hemp rope dangled to the ground. I had no choice. If ever I was to return to earth, I would have to climb up the ladder and then lower myself on the rope. My boots and trembling knees performed a pincers movement around the rope; my hands strangled it. I warily descended. Earth, soil, solid ground at last!

Rejoicing in my triumph but tempered by the lingering fear from this feat, I sat on the ground and looked up at that nasty ladder. It appeared to be leaning over and reluctantly nodding— "Well done!"

Bucky suddenly appeared when a jeep arrived with our lunch.

"Where were you, Bucky? I didn't see you on any of the platforms."

"Danny, it's not easy to explain when you're exhausted from climbing and crawling."

We jogged back to our barracks. Bucky couldn't fake this one.

After dinner, nearly every man in the barracks collapsed onto his cot, recovering from the confidence he had gained that morning. My last few ounces of strength were invested in tightly embracing my pillow as if some fantasy were stretched out on my pillowcase.

The tranquillity lasted no more than ten minutes. A screeching whistle echoed down my spine and onto every pain receptor.

We ran to the company street. Perched on the raised platform of the command post, his arms akimbo, his legs apart, targeting his menacing scowl at the men of the Fourth Platoon, stood M.Sgt. Nokel Roach. Highlighted by the glow from an overhead bulb, the jagged contours of his menacing face danced with shadows. It was a face that Humphrey Bogart would have yearned for in his 1930s gangster movies.

"Okay, men, double back to your barracks and get into your field jackets, backpacks, and helmets. You're going for an outing to the mountains!" He grinned. "I want you here and lined up in five minutes. Go!"

He knew we were spent from the confidence course. This was his diabolical scheme to further torment the troops.

Indiantown Gap was located in the foothills of the Blue Mountains of Pennsylvania. We saw these mountains daily from a distance but had no idea we would be intimately involved with their peaks and valleys.

Each squad leader reported to Sergeant Bayliss: "All present and accounted for, sir."

Of course we were accounted for. Where would we go? Where could we hide?

We left for parts unknown. Within ten minutes, I had built up a warm layer of air between my field jacket and my body. By the time we reached the base of the mountain, both my fatigue shirt and my T-shirt were damp with perspiration.

"Stop holding hands, ladies! Form a single file with a ten-foot interval!" shouted Sergeant Bayliss.

Typical of young mountains, these had no gentle slopes—just sharp vertical climbs to wherever we were going. The ten-foot interval could not be maintained on this terrain. We were either on top of one another or a greater distance apart. A GI in front of me pushed aside some saplings on his ascent. They responded by snapping back with a nasty whip to my face. Where we were going was anyone's guess. *Isn't there a top to this damn mountain?*

My body leaned forward with every step to avoid falling backward. To add to my fatigue, I had an unexpected burden—like the handicap of weights assigned to a favorite in a horserace. I looked over my shoulder to find Shorty from Cleveland. Spent from the morning's calisthenics, he kept a tight grip on the bottom of my field jacket.

"Damn it, Shorty, do you want me to carry you?"

"I'd carry you if I could," he replied.

How could I refuse him? I pulled him along until we reached the summit. Many of our men had not yet reached the top. This gave us a few minutes to recover.

The march along the crest seemed like virgin terrain. If there was a trail, we left it behind us by stomping down bushes, hummocks, and other underbrush. The walk along this horizontal summit had two redeeming features: I was able to stand upright, and Shorty stopped hanging on to my jacket.

Moving downhill wasn't as easy as I had anticipated. On the descent, I had to lean backward to avoid falling on my face, while once again getting tangled with every sapling in front of me. We assembled at the bottom of the mountain. The squad leaders took a head count to be sure no one had been left behind.

The spring in my gait was entirely gone. My buddy Dave was dragging alongside me, but we had neither the strength nor the inclination to talk. Shorty, bent over and breathing heavily, was ready to grab the bottom of my field jacket. This time I was taking no riders.

This exhilarating trek through the mountains induced deep breathing that cleansed my lungs of the city pollutants I had been inhaling for the past twenty-one years. The cement, bricks, and asphalt streets familiar to the big-city boys were supplanted by mountains, trails, and slopes dense with bushes and evergreens. The challenge added new fibers to our muscle tissue and improved our cardiovascular numbers. As a bonus to these benefits of a healthy night out with the boys, what greater comfort was there than to be greeted by a tenderhearted loved one on the company street? At 1:45 a.m., Master Sergeant Roach was on his perch at the command post platform for a "welcome home."

"If any one of you has any intention of leaving us, don't even think about it. We want you. We need you. We'll get you! Oh yes, we'll get you! And the division band will greet you at the gate, playing 'How in the Hell Did You Think You'd Get Away With It?' as two MPs dance you off to the stockade." He paused. "Now get me a shoelace!"

It was two o'clock in the morning. Barely standing, we were waiting to be dismissed, and Roach was asking for a shoelace! We made a dash for the barracks and up the steps for the other pair of boots under the bed. With Sergeant Bayliss watching, we removed a shoelace from a boot and returned waving it at Roach.

"I want a blanket! Get me one on the double!"

A sane person watching this would have thought it was a command performance at an insane asylum. Back to the barracks we went. We tore apart our beds and returned, waving a blanket at Roach.

"Show me your mattress cover!"

By the time we relaced our boots, replaced the mattress covers, made our beds, tucked the blankets tightly over them, showered, and shaved, it was nearly time to fall out on the company street to greet the new day.

Self-esteem from the confidence course followed by an outing in the mountains had prepared us city and country boys for an unforeseen future.

Tools of Our Trade

We were stumbling into the third week of basic training. Those who weren't fit were well on their way to becoming so from a daily concentration of hikes and calisthenics. We recovered with a few nod-offs during a scintillating instructional film. There were no options for the food. I found it foreign but tolerable. Dave loved it, but he usually fortified it with a snack to support his muscular frame. We learned to fall out, line up, and march in a military manner. Still, one thing was missing in our martial bearing: rifles. We couldn't play soldier without rifles.

The shriek of Sergeant Roach's whistle brought us into the company street. His grin above his starched khaki shirt told us we were to embark on a new adventure.

"How many of you have ever fired a rifle?"

A few southern and southwestern hands went up. Through his evil grin, he snickered, "I didn't expect any of the ref-you-jees from the Fourth Platoon to put up their hands."

This drew some chuckles. The majority of the Fourth Platoon consisted of Jewish and Italian boys from New York City. Roach subjected us to his bias and perverted humor sporadically during the sixteen weeks of basic training.

The smooth curves and tactile appeal of the rifles made them beg to be handled, but Sergeant Bayliss spoiled our sensuous moment. At the sound of his whistle, we were on the march to an instructional building. On long, gray tables, rectangular mats with outlines of disassembled M1 rifle parts lay at each seat. A corporal introduced himself, promising we would be completely familiar with the nomenclature of the M1 before we left that afternoon. *"Nomenclature"?* That hadn't been on the vocabulary list in any of my English classes.

We assembled and disassembled the rifle, placing its parts on the corresponding diagram. Finally we could do it with our eyes closed.

On our march back to the barracks, we began to assume a military bearing. The M1 was a nine-pound handicap whose web belt nibbled into our right shoulders. It was to be a witness to our every twist and turn during our working hours on the base.

But wait, I thought. *How does this thing work?*

Not so fast. First we had to learn to handle a rifle in a military manner. Sergeant Bayliss and two cadre had us on the company street making fools of ourselves for an entire day.

"I'm going to show you this once," he said. "Anyone who does it right is excused from the formation. Now watch me. 'Order arms' tells you to place your rifle on the ground alongside the right foot, trigger forward. With your right hand, grasp the wooden band around the barrel. Your left arm grabs the end of the rifle. Stand tall, look proud."

It was as if a well-lubricated tape recorder was connected to his tongue. The words, directly out of a training manual, flowed effortlessly.

"Let's see if you eight-balls can do it. Order arms! Damn, Phillips, can't you do a simple thing like that? Even Whitmire can do that. Homer, show him."

We went through right shoulder arms, left shoulder arms, order arms, port arms, and parade rest until the rifles had seemingly doubled in weight. When Sergeant Bayliss was satisfied with our performance, he marched us to the command post to perform for Sergeant Roach. We weren't exactly perfection, but I thought we did quite well for novices.

Sergeant Bayliss called out, "Order arms!"

Some of the overenthusiastic men hit their left thighs sharply as they snapped to attention.

"Look at them," shouted Roach. "Look at them slapping their asses like a bunch of faggots. Get them on KP tomorrow! And if I catch any one of you queers playing drop the soap in the shower, you'll be marching around the parade field with a sign saying, 'I Did It to Him Doggy-Style.'"

What next?

"Let's see how the fruits march with their toys."

Bayliss counted cadence as we tried to look sharp.

"Stop! Stop it before they hurt themselves," roared Roach.

We returned to the barracks and placed our rifles in the rifle rack. Another day of harassment and humiliation. *When do we start firing this thing?* I wondered.

In the evening, Williams, who was thoroughly familiar with rifles, had us gather around him. With his smooth southern drawl he went through the operation of the rifle. He warned us to be sure the safety was on and the chamber was empty except when we were firing the weapon.

The following day, we were introduced to the preliminary rifle instruction (PRI) circle, a neat circle about twenty-five feet in diameter. Along its circumference were approximately twenty-five firing stations fifteen feet from a small target at the center. Firing stations without fire. Not a round was fired. There were no rounds. It was all make-believe.

Lying in the prone position, we aimed our rifles at a small paper target. The GI aiming at the target adjusted his sight and then told the soldier when he was "zeroed in." Williams, about to become horizontal, called out, "Hey y'all, I never laid down in this position without a womam under me!"

Homer Whitmirer, lying alongside of him replied, "Yeah, any woman lying under you would be a lesbian or half-dead!"

"Firing without bullets at a paper target?" shouted Angelo. "I'll teach that to my kid when he's old enough to play cowboys and Indians."

We "fired." I don't recall how the direction the bullet would take was determined, but I do recall the little white gravel stones that dug into my elbow while I was supporting my rifle. We left with our elbows minced and our rifles as clean as the day they were issued.

"Dave, if I place my raw elbow on the ground, maybe I'll get an infection, and then I could get the hell out of here."

"It's no use. We're doomed to the infantry. Infections are not in the manual."

After a few days, it was good-bye PRI circle, hello firing range.

Whenever there was an outdoor instructional program, there were always bleachers for the troops. The safety officer stood in front of the bleachers, held up the M1, and asked, "How many of you are afraid of this weapon?"

I raised my hand. Very few men joined me. Maybe it wasn't fear. Maybe it was not knowing what to expect. But my hand was high in spite of the snickers from too many men around me.

Whether we were left-handed or right-handed, the officer instructed us to place the stock firmly into the crook of our right shoulder, aim, and then squeeze the trigger gently. We were to anticipate a substantial kickback when the rifle was fired. He repeated his warning to fire only when told to.

We were divided into two groups. One group was to do the firing; the other was to raise the targets from a cinderblock pit. The men in the pits rated the shooter by the location of hits on the target. A waving red flag (known as "Maggie's drawers") indicated a total miss.

The range officer gave the men at the firing stations the command to fire from the public address system. His voice blared, "Lock and load one round of ball ammunition." Pause. "Ready on the right. Ready on the left. Ready on the firing line. Commence firing!"

Dave and I were in the damp pit, supporting a target. I expected a sharper crack from the rifle fire. The hiss from the bullets whizzing overhead was unsettling.

"What do you think it would be like if the fire was aimed at us, Dave?"

"Don't even think about it," he replied.

When it was my turn to fire at the target, I was so tense that I pierced the target only once. The men around me scored no better. The red flags were fluttering at nearly every station. Maggie must have had a stockpile of drawers, or she was running around bare-ass naked.

As I was plunging the bore cleaner into my rifle that evening, I was bothered by my poor performance. What was wrong with me? Was I less coordinated than the men who had hit the target? They probably couldn't hit a baseball or catch a fly ball if it came right at them.

I soon realized that I gripped the rifle and the trigger too tightly; I had to relax. *I'll do better next time*, I told myself. And I did.

The M30 carbine was introduced after the rifle. It was a simple, lightweight weapon to which only a half-day of instruction was devoted. Compared to the M1, it was like a toy. The rest of the day was spent wrestling with gas masks.

The tear gas class was a challenge in how quickly and effectively we could get the masks over our faces. Its merciless straps had a tenacious grip on the few remaining hairs on my scalp. One by one, we walked into a tent wearing our masks. Every fold in the tent—the entire space—was suffused with tear gas.

"Take off your gas mask, soldier. What's the seventh general order?" asked the cadre man while wearing his gas mask.

I recited the seventh general order through the sourest, most asphyxiating mist a tongue could endure. The vile sweet gravy on the sliced ham that night finally loosened the grip of the remaining acidity in my throat. Good riddance. That was the end of the gas mask for basic training.

A few days later came a weapon I learned to hate. It was a twenty-pound BAR. Before we could fire it, we had to haul it to the instructional building for a lesson on its nomenclature. There were the mats again. Taking it apart was fairly easy, but reassembling all its parts was like assembling a Swiss watch. Everyone was checking his neighbor's progress but seeing very little. My first attempt ended with six extra metal pieces that didn't seem to fit or connect to anything. I couldn't find the parts on the nomenclature pad in front of me. It was a long day—a very long day. Finally I was able to reassemble the BAR without any spare pieces. When I returned the rifle, I asked a cadre man, "Does the BAR man carry this thing all day?"

"You don't have to worry about it, kid. It's given to the biggest men in the squad."

On a snowy, freezing morning, one man carried the tube and another the baseplate of a sixty-millimeter mortar. We sat uninterested and shivering in our field jackets as an instructor tried to impress on us the effectiveness of this hollow tube connected to a metal plate. A cadre man stepped alongside a demonstration mortar with an arc of base stakes (aiming pegs) embedded in the snow in front of it. Some of the chill fled, and our eyes opened wider when he dropped a round into the tube, which soon detonated near a target one hundred yards from our bleachers.

Under a cadre man's instruction, I pounded a few base stakes into the ground. Dave attached the sight and aimed the mortar. He dropped a round into the tube. Fortunately, it went off a distance in front of us. This brief exercise convinced me that it would take some serious work for the men to depend upon our expertise with the mortar.

Was the BAR heavy? It was balsa compared to the .30-caliber air-cooled machine gun and its partner, the tripod. We were divided into groups of three. One man was the gunner; another, the assistant machine gunner, carried a canister of ammo; and the third carried the tripod. Dave's huge biceps carried the machine gun as if it were a pistol. Our confidence was boosted by our performance with the machine gun. Directed by tracer bullets, we ripped the target bunker apart. That was it for the machine gun.

Grenades were next on the agenda. The war movies showed an infantryman biting the pin off a fragmentary grenade and hurling it at the attacking Japanese or Germans. How were we to know there were also phosphorus, smoke, thermite, illuminating, and who knows what other grenades? With a cadre man at our side, we removed the pin and threw a fragmentary grenade over a low wall; then we ducked.

Where did it go? I didn't care. All I thought was "Get me out of here."

Demolished tanks were our target for the bazooka. A freezing instructor, jumping from one leg to the other, shouted, "The round hits the tank, it melts the armor, and hot balls of steel bounce around the turret, wasting everyone inside. Stand clear from its rear when the bazooka is fired."

A round was placed in the bazooka. When its wires were connected, the triggerman was tapped on the helmet. With the bazooka on his shoulder, he aimed. He squeezed the trigger. A fiery blast rocketed out of the rear. We saw the round move slowly toward the tank.

Did the round hit? We didn't see anything penetrating the turret. *Did the round hit?* For all I know, it may still be lying on the training ground of Indiantown Gap.

The last tool of our trade was the .45-caliber pistol. Not yet. We had to wait for this one. Somewhere among the pines in the Blue Mountains of Pennsylvania, during bivouac, we were to get instruction at near zero degrees.

Of course we didn't get to be marksmen with any of these arms; nor did the army expect us to. But our chance was coming to reach a comfort level with these strange weapons.

A Crawl through the Mud

"Infiltration Course"—the words glared at us through our glass-encased bulletin board. Ponchos, helmets, rifles, canteens, and field jackets were the costume for the day.

"If I complete one more course, I'll get a degree in something," grumbled Dave.

"Yeah, you'll get a third degree, and it will be printed on toilet paper if you don't get your ass down on that infiltration course," replied Sergeant Bayliss.

Where did he come from? Where was he hiding?

We joined the boys at the mess hall table; they were muttering about the possible hazards on the course.

"All you need is one short round from that machine gun and you're dead."

"Thanks, Angelo. We are all very happy to hear from your stupid mouth." Sergeant Bayliss grasped every opportunity to berate Angelo. Angelo intimidated him. His diction was precise; he had had two years of college. He was a Yankee.

In preparation for the course, the boys stretched out on their beds, savoring every moment while awaiting the call. We'd hardly warmed our blankets and pillows when we heard Bayliss yell, "Fall out! Fall out!"

Dave Sohmer, who was losing his hair, vigorously massaged his scalp and repeated, "Fall out! Fall out!"

My hairlets, too, were quickly abandoning my head, but both of us had our chuckle for the morning. It broke the tension of anticipating crawling through terrain with bullets flying overhead.

On the company street, Sergeant Roach checked us over with his usual snicker and scowl.

"All present and accounted for," shouted Bayliss.

"Get them the hell out of here," replied Roach.

The company stepped out on a muddy, rain-slicked road. After one break for piss call, we finally came to a halt at an open field. *What's this?* I wondered.

Our calisthenics leader, who seemed to be fastened to the athletic field demonstration platform, was waiting. With helmets, rifles, canteens, and ponchos dropped at the end of the field, we went through the usual stretching, grunts, and groans, followed by the crawl we were to use in passing through the course.

"Up to the bleachers, men!"

We overlooked barbed wire suspended three feet above a wet field 150 feet long. Four water-cooled machine guns, about seven feet apart, secured into the ground by sandbags, faced the field. The range officer stepped up.

"You *will* crawl from the far end of the field, under the barbed wire, toward the machine guns. You *will* continue your crawl toward the bleachers. Look where you're going; keep your heads down. Your rifles *will* be clean at the end of the crawl. Let's go!"

Sergeant Bayliss kept our platoon together in the bleachers until it was our turn to go. We had front-row center seats for the show. The machine guns started blazing after the first squad had crawled about fifteen feet. Using alternate elbows, they reached out and pulled themselves forward. They covered the fifty yards without incident.

"No way. No way would I do that in combat. There isn't a chance in hell I would reach those guns in one piece," said Pitts as he watched the men from the First Platoon crawling.

Sergeant Bayliss overheard him. Glaring, he said, "Pitts, I want to see you when we get back to the barracks."

Pitts shifted nervously on the plank bench. As if infected by him, the men around him fidgeted uneasily too. The silence that followed magnified the rat-a-tat of the machine guns. We awaited the call that would snap the tension in the bleachers.

"Show them the way, Pitts. Show them how to do it," said Bayliss.

Pitts, alone, before the eyes of the entire company, crawled under the wire and under the machine gun fire. He moved smoothly. He had his head down. His rifle was clean, but the stark loneliness of Pitts moving on that bullet-buzzed field just added to our discomfort.

It was our turn. The mud, acting as a lubricant, allowed us to slither rapidly through the field. The whishes above let us know that bullets were overhead. We made it. We returned to the bleachers to watch the next two platoons perform. While shaving the mud off our field jackets and pants with our fingernails, penknives, or dog tags, we heard the PA system blast, "Cease fire! Cease fire!"

Smith, from the Fourth Platoon, was crawling while using his rifle as a plow. It was a shaft of mud. Even Pitts, shaken by his earlier trauma, joined in the laughter. There was an abrupt halt to the laughter when Bayliss reported that we had a small detail of incomplete business to attend to.

"Tanks are waiting to roll over us."

Within earshot of Sergeant Bayliss, Dave asked rhetorically, "Is this another course requirement for a degree?"

"Sohmer, keep your ass down, and stop trying to get educated."

We made another march, but a short one, to predug foxholes pitting an open field. An officer gave us a brief orientation to our final exercise.

"Get into the foxholes—two in each hole," barked Bayliss. "Once you get in them, stay down—all the way down."

Dave and I groveled toward the lowest part of the foxhole and assumed a fetal position. A tank came rumbling toward us. We squeezed together. A molecule of air could not have wormed between us. The loudest noise I'd ever heard came crashing out of the tank and dumping onto us. In a moment it was there; in a moment, it was gone. Dave and I crawled out of the hole and onto flat, solid, quiet terra firma. What a day!

The platoons returned to the company street with slimy government uniforms gripping their bodies. Pitts, trying to buffer his earlier remark at the infiltration course, addressed Sergeant Bayliss: "How are we going to have dry field jackets for tomorrow?"

"Just hang them up. The mud will dry, and then you can shake them off in the morning."

"But where are we going to hang them, sir? We don't have clotheslines."

"Hang them from the sides of your lockers. And if you can't do that, shove them up your ass. They'll dehydrate there, judging from those dry popcorn farts I hear blasting through the night."

Sergeant Bayliss had forgotten about the Pitts incident, apparently. It was just another day in the country.

Frozen in Bivouac

Platoon Sergeant Bayliss stomped around the barracks, lifting the beds of the GIs still in the sack. It was the fifteenth week of basic training: bivouac time. War games and a pup tent in the frozen tundra awaited us.

The yellow light reflecting from the barracks scarcely illuminated the company street. At 5:30 a.m., this dull glow created the proper prelude for a week in the mountains. While we stood shivering in formation, General Keiser, commander of Indiantown Gap, rolled out of his jeep and sucked in his gut, trailed by his group of flabby sycophants.

Meandering in and out of formations of frozen soldiers standing at attention on the company street, he stopped occasionally to make a random comment. I had shaved the night before, in order to avoid the morning assault on the latrine.

"Did you shave this morning, soldier?" he asked when he got to me.

"Yes, sir!" I replied.

"Well, let's say that your face didn't get close enough to your razor."

All the lapdogs yelped hysterically. Fortunately, he moved on to the Fourth Platoon.

A large number of New York City boys and a heavy dose of country southerners populated this platoon. A fair description of them is "good-natured eight-balls." They were the butts of compassionate Sgt. Nokel Roach's nasty jokes whenever the opportunity presented itself.

Smith, was one of the rejects in this platoon. He was pleasant and friendly but mentally challenged. General Keiser stepped up to Private Smith and asked how he liked being a soldier. A reply to an officer calls for snapping to attention, staring straight ahead, and speaking out loud and clear. Private Smith casually leaned on his rifle, smiled, extended his hand to the general for a handshake, and replied, "I like it fine, General. How about you?"

General Keiser and his toads croaked with laughter.

The march to the bivouac area began immediately after inspection. It was a relief to get under way after the morning freeze and a visit by the group of flabby fawns.

We had a ten-mile march to our new home. Whenever there was a choice between selecting a level road or one that snaked over a mountain, the army would always opt for the latter. After a mile into the march, we stopped for breakfast.

The freezing winds penetrated my field jacket and thin fatigues. Dave and I decided to jog around the mess area while waiting our turn for food. Everyone thought we were out of our minds, but while they were thinking and shivering, we were slowly generating a warmth that would maintain us until the march continued.

Dense stands of trees stunted by their proximity to one another made it difficult and sometimes painful climbing over the mountains. Experience taught us to hold the thin, whiplike branches as we passed the trees. Hadn't we been whipped on our march a few weeks earlier?

The topography was like that in Korea: up one hill and down another. Finally the company reached "home." After lunch, we cleared the undergrowth to set up our pup tents. Lieutenant Walker, our company commander, gave an orientation for the next few days. We were to learn to fire a .45-caliber pistol. (Why couldn't we have done that back at the firing range?) A few days would be devoted to preparation for the major event—the company attacking a hill with fortified positions.

Dinner arrived, accompanied by total darkness. The arctic winter in the Blue Mountains of Pennsylvania is for penguins, polar bears, and ice cubes. I would never have imagined I could ever be this cold. How was dinner? It was warm. Immediately after, Dave and I crawled into our sleeping bags in the pup tent. He whipped out a hidden pint of Canadian Club and poured some into our aluminum canteen cups. Horrible! Awful! This burning, bitter liquid in a cold metal canteen cup could have encouraged the most committed alcoholic to go cold turkey. With spinning heads, we zipped up our sleeping bags and were transformed into the world's greatest comedians. Any syllable we uttered elicited hysterical laughter. Shouts from the surrounding tents telling us to shut up did not stop the giddiness.

The following morning, while shaving with ice water on frozen faces, we reaped additional harassment from Sergeant Bayliss, who wanted to know who had played the girl in our tent the night before. Homer Whitmire asked if he could change places with Dave this evening. Finally breakfast arrived to interrupt the inquisition.

After breakfast, a long march led us to a small section of lonely bleachers on a mountain ridge. It was positioned to catch every arctic blast that whistled through the mountains. Our teeth chattered while we waited for instruction on the nomenclature and use of the .45-caliber pistol. Our field jackets were useless against the howling winds. Maybe it would have been worth suffering the itch from the long johns. Overcoats? Overcoats were for sissies.

A warrant officer pulled up in a jeep. After securing some flapping charts to an easel, he began his lecture to a group of GIs who shared only one interest—warmth. He withdrew a pistol from his holster. As soon as his hand touched the barrel, it stuck to it as if it were covered with Krazy Glue. His driver sped him to an aid station. That was the end of .45-caliber pistol instruction.

On the final day of bivouac, we were to carry out the company-sized attack on a fortified position. Of course, this required a march of considerable distance. Good. It kept us warm.

Dave Sohmer, Murray Lichtman, and I found a predug bunker. Dave and I had left our blankets in our pup tent. Fortunately Murray had brought his. In the evening, we huddled together, covering ourselves with the single blanket. I sat in the middle. Throughout the night, Murray pulled on his side of the blanket and Dave pulled on the other. Whether it was Dave or Murray who had most of the blanket was of no consequence; I was covered (but still frozen) throughout the bitter night.

The following morning, our company successfully overran the enemy's fortified position. To celebrate our victory, we were herded to the bleachers for a critique. It was like sitting inside a refrigerator. A colonel congratulated us on our victory and quickly returned to his waiting jeep. Dave and I went back to the comfort of our pup tent and warm food.

All good things eventually come to an end. It was time to return to the barracks. We broke down our tent, rolled each half with our blanket inside, and tied it around our backpacks. Bob Anderson, whose father was an officer in the Studebaker Corporation, offered Dave ten dollars to carry his backpack for the ten-mile trek back to camp. Dave refused. I guess Bob had never been denied anything in his life. He stood in the snow, dumbstruck by Dave's rebuff.

From the day he had come to the Third Platoon, Phillips had been scheming to be discharged from the army. As the company began the march back to camp, he decided that this was a propitious moment. A half mile into our march, he unbuttoned his field jacket, unbuttoned his shirt, grasped his throat, and began gagging loudly. The rasping and retching continued until he sat down in a culvert and refused to move on. A jeep following the troops picked him up and brought him back to the barracks.

The barrel of a water-cooled .30-caliber machine gun was resting on Murray Lichtman's shoulders. With or without water in its jacket, this barrel is quite heavy, especially when the soldier carrying it is trudging ten miles over frozen, hilly terrain. At one point, Murray stepped and then slid into an icy rut. The barrel went flying backward, and so did Murray. He hit his head on the ice-hardened path. Unconscious, he was evacuated by ambulance.

Sergeant Roach was ecstatic as we dragged ourselves onto the company street.

"I want to congratulate my boys. You did a good job. You did such a good job that I'm happy to give you your shipping orders, which begin this weekend."

He passed out mimeographed sheets indicating that all the men in the company received FECOM orders. Yes, unless we were kept in Japan, we would be on our way to Korea.

Phillips had worked hard during basic training—very hard—to be found undesirable for service. He was rewarded for his effort with a discharge when the rest of the company received our FECOM orders. Murray returned to the company in two days, just in time to receive his invitation to FECOM.

On Jackson Heights, a hill occupied by Company L, Fifteenth Regiment, Third Infantry Division, in Korea, an exploding mortar round killed Murray Lichtman.

Last Home Leave

Murray was sitting comfortably in the front seat alongside Shelly while I was wedged between Bucky and Dave in the tapered back. This was our good-bye trip from Indiantown Gap. Shelly's lead foot had us speeding home in his father's Buick. I was determined that my FECOM orders were not going to destroy my two-week "delay en route" (a pass to go home before a GI is sent to where his orders indicate). I was to be a civilian for two weeks! There would be no more chow lines, no more freezing on the company street, no more of Roach's repulsive grin and nasty remarks. I was to have two weeks with the boys, two weeks home on Seabury Place with Ma and Pa, two weeks of real food, before I started soldiering again.

We passed Langhorne, Pennsylvania. The bright Saturday afternoon brought an overflow crowd to the high school football stadium.

"It's probably their last game—a playoff game," Bucky keenly observed. "If they don't get a college football scholarship, they'll enlist in the army."

"What makes you so sure?"

"Look at our company. Except for myself, I don't think anyone went beyond high school. In fact, many men in our company are enlistees who didn't finish high school."

"The three of us didn't go beyond high school, but we didn't enlist."

"Well, of course—there are unexpected results in any experiment. But we who went to college have a superior view of our surroundings."

"Stop the shit, Bucky. You're a college dropout."

"The college didn't live up to my standards."

Our laughter put a stop to Bucky's observations about himself, the football players, and us.

In a half hour, we were nodding off as the car passed over a bridge and under a sign reading, "What Trenton Makes, the World Takes." I guess we were catching up from that sleepless week of bivouac. But Bucky noticed that Murray was having trouble falling asleep.

"What did the medics say about your head?"

"They said I'm okay. But I still get headaches, so they gave me a bunch of pills."

Shelly, who had been quiet during the entire trip, contributed.

"They'd give you those APCs [a drug related to aspirin that we called all-purpose capsules] and send you off even if you had a heart attack."

We passed through the Lincoln Tunnel, turned left onto the West Side Highway, and sped on to the Bronx. Buildings abandoned by landlords were vandalized. They stood like hollow memorials to a vibrant borough.

Bucky was the first to leave the car. I stepped out a few blocks from my apartment. Walking the streets I had run through and tripped over for twenty-one years brought back memories of all the street games I'd played throughout the years. Over there, at the sewer lid, how many hours did we sweat away playing pitching in? How many hours had we played roller hockey using the sewer lids as the goals? The entire street had been cleared for our Sunday stickball games. There was Nick the Shoemaker's store—still open. He'd aided and abetted a thievery by giving us clippers to remove the corn fibers from a broom appropriated from a fire escape, so we could use the broomstick for playing stickball. But these weren't the same streets. On my first pass home in early autumn, there weren't any teenagers playing stickball or hockey on the chilled asphalt. The sidewalks, once busy with housewives rushing home from the Jennings Street Market to prepare dinner, were as vacant as an alley. Danger had replaced safety on the once friendly blocks of Seabury Place. The slow transformation that had taken place before I went into the service had dramatically accelerated within a matter of four months.

I was looking forward to reminiscing, to playing evening basketball at PS 61, and to having a few laughs with the boys. What had happened to them?

Krebs had been the first to be drafted. We had chipped in, bought him a gold ring, and thrown a farewell party the day before he left for Whitehall Street. Mysteriously he turned up the same afternoon, a civilian. Why?

Alvin, being the only child of a widow, had received a hardship discharge from the army. Herman had received a medical deferment. Why? Mutt was another who'd been rejected by the Selective Service. Why? Marv, stationed at Camp Detrick, Maryland, had planned to come home on the weekends to his fiancée, Annette. Jones, aka Resinhead, was married to Naomi, and Peanzy was married to Elaine. Was that why they hadn't been drafted?

Winkler was a case study. When he and Alvin went to Whitehall Street for their physicals, he discovered a stale roll in his jacket pocket. He knew this was an amulet deposited by his father in the hope that his son would be designated 4F–unacceptable. Winkler was livid. Cursing at no one, he sent the roll flying over the draftees' heads to hit a wall and fall into crumbs. He was designated 4F– unacceptable for military service.

Rock was already in the army. Jerry, Peb, Bob, and Julie had recently been drafted and were at their basic training camps.

So here I am, I thought, *with the Far East awaiting me, and there will be no Friday basketball games and no pastrami on club sandwiches at Gitelson's. What was I thinking? With whom was I going to play basketball?* Alvin was going steady with Harriet, Marvin was going steady with Annette, and Herman was soon to be married to Vivian; Peanzy and Jones were old married men. It wasn't like the good old days. The boys had been growing up while I was still lost in my predraft years.

Mr. Tekula, the janitor, stepped up onto the street from his basement apartment. He couldn't avoid me. I nodded; he grunted. Compared to his hostile relationship with the tenants, this was a warm "Welcome home!"

When I opened our apartment door, Ma raced Pa to join me in a loving threesome. Food? Of course it was hot and on the table.

What can I tell them? I wondered. *That our company successfully captured a fortified position somewhere in the Blue Mountains of Pennsylvania?* They could see that I was a healthy specimen in spite of the food I'd learned to like. My FECOM orders were resting in a pocket of my Ike jacket. How would I tell them I was going to Korea? I decided I'd tell them we hadn't been told where we were going. *So where do I say I'm going when I leave? I'll tell them we're going to Japan—which is true.* I knew my father would know what that meant, but he didn't say a word.

The rest of the week I read newspapers and said hello to a few neighbors. Neither a TV set nor a phone would occupy our home until I was discharged from the army. I visited Nick the Shoemaker's store. We reminisced about his clippers and broomsticks. He told me about his army days in France during World War I. Ma sent me to Jennings Street. It, too, wasn't the memorable bazaar of the good old days. They called it urban decay. Many stalls were closed, the characters behind them gone. Jake the Pickleman, in his white apron, was still behind his barrels. I bought pickles for the week and then looked for Miller's fruit stand. Rotting pieces of wood covering a canvas was the tombstone for that former crown jewel of the market. I went to a small fruit stand and headed home.

At the end of the second week, my friends' wives and fiancées planned a party for me. Naomi asked me to call her friend Elaine, whom I had met before I was drafted. Alvin, Marv, Herman, Peanzy, Jones, and Krebs were there to cheer me off.

Elaine was slim and cute, but I wasn't ready for any type of relationship. We spent the evening searching through our biographies. After our brief conversation, I realized that her interest in clothing and my interest in sports were headed toward a minor disaster. The only thing we had in common was our vital organs. The evening ended with a peck for a kiss and a promise I would write her as soon as I knew my address.

The next day, Dave Sohmer and I had lunch in my apartment. Rolls from Litroff the Baker with either cream cheese or scrambled eggs was the choice my mother offered.

"Wait a minute, Mrs. Wolfe," said Dave. "Where's the SOS?" This was our abbreviation for Shit On a Shingle, a breakfast food that consisted of ground beef floating in a gray sausage gravy (the shit) poured over a slice of toast (the shingle).

"What's SOS?" she asked.

"It's what we sometimes get for breakfast," replied Dave.

"Is it kosher?" Ma asked.

"Ma, we call it Shit On a Shingle."

"Very nice talk you learned in the army."

We laughed. She was always available for a chuckle, whether she got the joke or not.

"Now, how about the party? Was it okay? How was Elaine?" asked Dave.

"Do you know her?"

"I think I saw her once. She's not from our neighborhood, is she?"

"It doesn't matter. She's very nice, but she gives me heartburn when she talks about clothes. I'm not for her."

We spent the afternoon together over pizza at the Dover Bar, reminiscing about Sergeant Roach, basic training, and our junior high school down the block. I halfheartedly nursed a beer as Dave downed a few.

"I'll see you tomorrow at Penn Station. Sonny's taking me. Do you want a ride?"

"No, thanks. My parents aren't taking this too well. I want to be with them as long as I can."

In the evening, Ma looked at me as if this were my last meal before going to the gallows. I looked at Pa, whom I had unwittingly disappointed at Camp Kilmer. How much longer would I have him? Ma was not her cheery self but was as vigorous as ever. She baked her delicious challah and made my favorite browned chicken with vegetables, highlighted with stuffed derma. Honey cake, apple cake, cookies, and tea tempered the spicy entrée.

The following morning, Ma and Pa watched me dress, waiting like mourners at a funeral. What could I say to soothe them?

"I'll write in Yiddish," I promised.

Ma kissed me. Pa sat in his chair, hardly able to squeeze out a good-bye. It wasn't that he didn't care. I guess he didn't know what to do. Shrolleh, my father's brother, who came to their wedding and had lived with us for twenty-one years, was an uninvolved spectator—another body that didn't know how to react.

I looked at my parents and asked, "What kind of good-bye is this?"

With flowing tears, we stood and hugged near my convertible bed. I picked up my duffel and left for Pennsylvania Station.

Dinner in the Diner

Pennsylvania Station was the launching pad for New York GIs shipping out to the Far East. On the lower level, a troop train was waiting to absorb the soldiers crowding the platform. Although I pretended not see them, I glanced with envy at the GIs who were fused to their girlfriends before they parted. For a moment, I was distracted by Bucky, who had predicted that the war would be over by the time this train had reached the West Coast. By now his statements held as much water as cheesecloth. My attention returned to the couples. Weren't the GIs in the World War II movies all sent off with tears, kisses, and tourniquet embraces? Where was mine? Something must be wrong. I found some comfort in Dave, Bucky, and Murray, who, like me, stood alone.

The train we boarded was not the *Cannonball Express*. It was more like the *Little Engine That Could*. Since we were accustomed to bottom-of-the-line dormitory accommodations from basic training, the upper and lower sleeping berths created from the seats and something that folded out of the ceiling seemed deluxe for the four-or five-day trip. In addition, we had the elegance of dinner in the diner, but the reasonable cuisine was tempered by long lines, miniportions, and exhortations to "leave quickly because men are waiting."

Confined within the rectangular boundary of a Pullman coach, how long can one endure? We tried playing cards. My maximum was two games before my bored rear end told me to move on. What was there to see? There were GIs "crapped out" (sleeping) over their seats, GIs writing letters, and more GIs playing cards. This GI returned to his seat to review his list of addresses. I crossed out those who did not deserve a letter, leaving me with no more than five names. What next? Bucky had the solution: sleep whenever possible. Dave was engrossed in a story in *Good Housekeeping*; Murray was relating his tale of the water-cooled machine gun that had landed him in the hospital. On my way to the bathroom, I excused my way down an aisle cluttered with GIs. Of course there were two men in front of me, waiting. For me this was merely a time killer, so I returned to Dave, who was still absorbed in the magazine. Bucky awoke from his nap. With eyelids at half-mast, he anxiously called out, "Did I miss lunch? Why didn't you guys wake me?"

No, it wasn't time for lunch. What was it time for? Time to go home?

There were no stops for this train. No one was getting on; no one was getting off. We were chugging along somewhere in the Midwest when a streamlined train slowly passed us as we approached the Denver station. Its passengers, our contemporaries, were dressed in ski outfits designed to make them appear tall, affluent, and handsome—and they were. On the side of a window, bold white letters announced Aspen.

"Where's Aspen? What's Aspen?" was the buzz throughout the train.

Finally a conductor passing through told us it was a luxury ski resort. Murray wasn't very happy at the sight of those beautiful people.

"Why aren't they in the army?" he asked.

Bucky had an answer to all queries. Whether he was right or wrong didn't matter.

"They're very rich, but they're not healthy. They all have medical deferments."

With no mail and no newspapers and the aisles still cluttered with GIs, we were distracted by a sergeant who came through the cars shouting, "We're in Denver, and you *will* get out. Make sure your uniform is neat and your fly is buttoned. No sweaters, no jackets. When you get off, stand tall and look proud."

The train came to a halt. As if they were preparing for inspection, GIs were combing their hair, adjusting their belts, tucking in their shirts, rubbing their shoes against the backs of their pants legs, and running their fingers along their flies. The boys bunched up at the doors, expelling three days' worth of stale Pullman air from their lungs and anxious to meet admiring females. On the platform, we were told to line up and stand tall beside our car. An officer with a booming voice perched above us on an open cart led us through a series of calisthenics. It did get the kinks out of muscles that hadn't been tested in days, but where were the girls? And what was I going to do with them if they were there? What had I done with Elaine? Back onto the train. Fresh Denver air, yes; females, no.

Did he own all the essential kitchen tools? Dave Sohmer was back into *Good Housekeeping*, taking a serious exam to answer this question. Bucky fell asleep as soon as his pants made contact with the seat. Murray was playing pinochle with Serge, a GI who'd latched onto our group on the train. Everyone seemed busy with nothing. I couldn't find anything to do, so I disrupted Dave's test to reminisce about junior high school. But in spite of our laughs, the underlying anxiety of my loneliness at Pennsylvania Station still lingered. Why shouldn't I have a girlfriend? Why shouldn't I be one of them?

The rich, dark, evergreen mountains of Oregon gave me time to reflect on the beauty of our country. But how long could I reflect when the scenery kept repeating itself, bringing me back to the midnight hikes and the deep freeze of the evergreen mountains in Pennsylvania? The boredom was finally relieved when we arrived at Seattle. A chain of buses brought us to Fort Lawton, a camp perched on the top of a mountain overlooking Puget Sound. The barracks were the usual two-story wooden rectangles. The beds were neatly fitted with tightened blankets until we deposited our duffels and lay down on top of them.

It came time to explore the camp. We found the same architecture, the same parade grounds, in a different place. Bucky was feeling the effect of the portion-controlled meals served on the train.

"Where's the mess hall? It's dinnertime. If I don't get something to eat, I'll wipe out the candy bars at the PX."

Serge, who had attached himself to us on the train, pointed to a large building that could have been a hangar for a couple of B-29 bombers. Serge was one of the GIs at Pennsylvania Station who had been plastered to his girlfriend on the platform. I detested, or perhaps envied, him when he showed us letters from her telling him that lefty missed him and righty ached for him (referring to her breasts).

The Bronx boys at Fort Lawton.
Standing, left to right: Serge, Murray Lichtman, Dan Wolfe, Bucky Praver.
Kneeling: Carl Fogel.

The mess hall was a megastructure. It was wall-to-wall olive drab. How could they feed so many men? As we moved along the food line, a red mountain of Delicious apples was losing height below a sign reading, "Take What You Want, But Eat What You Take." The chicken was just the way I liked it—slightly well done. The apple was a novelty. Delicious apples never appeared in apartment 11. I determined to get some when I returned home. A sergeant stood at a barrel where we were to dispose of our leftovers. He was taking the names of the men who had left good portions of their meals on their trays. They were doomed to KP.

"They won't get me," said Bucky as he gave his empty tray to a GI on KP.

In the evening, a detail for KP with our names appeared on the barracks bulletin board. This was followed by the arrival of an officer and two cadre men who chalked large numbers onto the backs of our fatigues.

"A bus will pick you up tomorrow at 5:00 a.m. for KP duty. You *will* be up and ready!"

No I won't, I thought. *We're going overseas.* What could they do to us?

Bucky, Dave, and Murray joined me for a visit to the latrine. With a few shakes and a few rubs of our fatigue shirts, the chalk numbers disappeared. The big city guys had outslicked the military! But was it worth falling asleep on a cold, damp, and pungent concrete floor? Was it worth the aches the following morning just to avoid the pots, pans, and grease pits? It didn't matter. We'd beaten their system. That was what counted.

Two days later, our journey continued.

Level One, Section Three

U. S. NAVAL SHIP GENERAL SIMON B. BUCKNER

January 1952: A fog-shrouded gray Seattle pier turned to olive drab as thousands of pairs of combat boots scuffed its cold surface. Anchored in the harbor, hovering over us like a threatening cloud, the Military Sea Transportation System (MSTS) *General Simon Buckner* was a massive gray backdrop for this somber scene. Foghorns blared; boat whistles responded. Out of the haze, a jeep carrying a captain pulled up to the pier. He stepped out, climbed onto a podium, and shamelessly announced, "God bless you, soldiers. You are the best-fed, best-clothed, best-equipped, and best-informed army in the world. Complete your mission, and I will be here to welcome you home."

Yeah, I thought, *when I return, I'll wave to you.*

The captain then climbed into his jeep and disappeared into the morning mist as we stepped onto the ramp of the *General Simon*

Buckner. This huge troopship was to carry us across the Pacific to Japan.

The "best-fed, best-clothed, best-equipped, and best-informed" GIs leave for the Far East.

"Wolfe, Daniel, 5118844, sir."

"Level One, Section Three, soldier."

The weight of a swollen duffel bag on my shoulder unintentionally pushed me down three narrow flights of metal stairs to Level One. Three tiers of cots rose toward the ceiling. Like prospectors seeking the mother lode, GIs were buzzing around trying to find a choice bunk. A duffel bag deposited on it staked a claim in the hold of the ship. That was okay; I didn't expect a stateroom.

The uppermost bunk, tier three, was most desirable. If a seasick soldier liberated a previous meal, which occurred frequently, the victims in the bunks below would be pelted with his undigested contents. But the climb up to tier three was too much for many of the GIs. Neither Dave Sohmer nor I had that problem. Claiming our top bunks, we stretched out on the tight canvas sheets that were to be our beds for the next twenty days.

Dave Sohmer and Dan Wolfe on their first cruise.

A few blasts from the ship's horn had us scrambling up to the crowded deck. By now the mist had lifted, so we could see our ship leaving the shoreline. The men from our basic training company were mingling with thousands of strange faces—faces that would eventually join us on assignment in Korea. Where was Bob Anderson, the prima donna whose father was one of the principals in the Studebaker Corporation? He probably was dissolved into the SOS (shit on a shingle) at our last meal in Indiantown Gap. Or was he one of the dandies on the ski train going to Aspen?

"Level One, Section Three, line up for the mess hall," blasted the PA system.

The lines moved rapidly up the narrow stairs. It took a while before we reached the mess. The food bore no relation to the food thrown at us in basic training. It was edible, and we could have as much as we wanted. The decor was gray enamel, the seating plan was standing room only. With one hand, I held the coffee cup and anchored the tray against my chest on a metal counter. With the other hand, I foraged with my eating utensil.

"Keep the troops busy and you keep them out of mischief"– this basic training credo followed us up the gangplank and onto the *Simon Buckner.* Within fifteen minutes, after we returned from lunch, an officer arrived announcing the details (work assignments) for our section. Jobs were distributed by last name in alphabetical order. Since all the details were exhausted by the time he reached the Ws, I spent leisure parts of the voyage with either Dave or Murray, pretending to be on a detail in their group.

The assignments were KP, cleaning the decks when the weather and the waves permitted, and helping in the laundry. Most of the men were assigned to KP, which consisted of cleaning giant pots and pans, helping the cooks before meals, mopping the floor, and general cleanup after the meal.

Early in the trip, the Pacific was pacific. Water and sky were the high points of interest on the voyage. A group of albatrosses followed but found the trip as boring as we did. They soon left, searching for excitement. I found myself wondering how they stayed in the air so long without flapping their wings.

In spite of fairly rough weather, we were permitted on the deck after breakfast. On the third day, I noticed a group of men hunched over near a wall. A line was forming behind them. *I'd better get in that line*, I thought, wondering what goodies were being distributed. As I neared the head of the line, I saw three corrugated metal barrels receiving the last meals these men had consumed. The soldiers collapsed over the barrels, retching and heaving into them. In the line behind them, seasick GIs were bent over, preparing for their turn. This was not my problem, but it was worthy of a photo, so I clicked and moved on. More seasick soldiers, tightly compressed in the fetal position, littered the deck. There weren't many of us alive and well.

"Hurry up and barf, or you'll miss dinner!"

Bucky became seasick as soon as the anchor was lifted at the Seattle harbor. He couldn't roll out of his tier-three cot. He was cursed by having a PA system speaker projecting from the wall right near his ear. The directional horn of the speaker was funnel-shaped. No matter how he tried to stuff a T-shirt into the horn, within a minute or two it slipped out. Whatever medication he was given for seasickness did not work. Finally he gave up, collapsed on his cot, and lay prone for the entire trip.

What seemed to be a giant troop transport at the dock in Seattle turned out to be a bobbing cork in the middle of the ocean. What do you do on a mlitary transport heading for Japan when pounding waves are battering the hold of your ship? It's too early to go to sleep. It's movie night. Why not try it?

We were clustered like peanuts in brittle in the hold of the ship. *Romance On the High Seas* was the featured attraction. I didn't own a phonograph but was fond of Doris Day when I heard her sing on the radio. Well, there she was, with her starched golden-blond hair, her tiny nose, and her mechanical smile, singing her heart out. I lived in a neighborhood composed mostly of immigrants: Italians, Spaniards who had fled from Franco, and Jews. No girl in either public school or in the neighborhood bore the faintest resemblance to Doris. She appeared as if she had stepped out of a page from a Talbots catalog and was programmed to walk and sing. The crash of the waves against the hull of the ship was blunted when a mass of GIs helped Doris at the conclusion of her song. Baritoners, tenors, and listeners crowed, "It's Magic."

A raging storm developed to a point where I thought the waves would turn the *Buckner* over. The furious waves colliding against its sides sounded like pounding sledgehammers. The vessel plunged down and then soared up like a ride in an amusement park. The well-trodden paths to the toilets were slick with vomit. Handrails were caked with undigested residue. Seasick GIs, sprawling on the floors, slid in rhythm with each crashing wave. We were not permitted on deck for three days. I climbed up to my bunk for my edited edition of *Leave Her to Heaven*. What a bitch! Leave her to heaven? Leave her to the morgue!

No matter how I tried to keep the annoying woolen blanket from attacking my neck, it always found a way to let me know it was there. I might as well finish the book.

"Now hear this. Now hear this. There will be a show given by the Armed Forces Entertainment Unit at the center hold of the ship at eight o'clock."

Once again, the passengers assembled in the hold. There was buzzing from the GIs when they wondered if the entertainers were the men among us.

A black GI stepped up and sang some popular songs. Then he sang *Harbor Lights*. With tears flowing from his eyes, he crooned,

I watched those harbor lights
How could I help if tears were starting
Goodbye to tender nights
Beside the silvery sea.

I wondered why I didn't have tender nights. I knew Shirley in my senior class at James Monroe High School was interested in me. While she waited for her mother to drive her home, she sat in the chilly stands watching me practice with the football team. But the fun in the candy store didn't teach me how to approach her. High school football, softball, and speed skating isolated me from my maturity.

At last the storm let up. We lounged on the deck once again, but the barrels were still there, with their usual patrons.

One might think we would have been apprehensive or nervous as we neared shore, but everyone was eager to see Japan without thinking of it as a staging area for Korea.

A Japanese pilot climbed aboard at a distance from the shore. He steered the ship past bunkers that were burrowed into low cliffs surrounding the port. They would have been used for defense against an American invasion in World War II. The US casualties would have been staggering had we invaded Japan.

Laden with a full backpack, a duffel bag on my shoulders, and a rifle somewhere alongside the duffel, I went cautiously on rubbery legs down the gangplank. Waiting buses carried us to Camp Drake, the reception center for all troops visiting the Far East.

Processing began immediately. Dress uniforms and fatigues were exchanged for two pairs of new olive drab fatigues. Why new boots? They reminded me that breaking in new boots during basic training had cost me a painful Achilles tendon. Fortunately I received the softer World War II roughout boots. Rifles were exchanged, and helmets were also issued. *Are we really going to use them?* I wondered.

Our arms were punctured with vaccines; our minds were punctured with orientations. The reality of war still hadn't settled in.

We devised schemes for escaping assignment in Korea while we cleaned the Cosmoline from our newly issued rifles. Dave Sohmer, who'd had some boxing experience at the Y, looked for the coach of the boxing team. Mel Winter went on sick call to display a couple of breast tumors, and Bucky Praver went to personnel, telling them his experience of living next to the Bronx Hospital, where he absorbed a good deal of medical knowledge. At 126 pounds, I foolishly went to the coach of the football team with my high school résumé.

Mel struck pay dirt. He was sent to Tokyo Army Hospital to have the tumors removed from his chest and then was assigned to the hospital after he recovered from surgery. Bucky returned dejected. He claimed that the clerk only pretended to make a note of his medical expertise. Dave and I were rejected outright. The coaches had the pick of the best amateur boxers and outstanding college football players; why should they fool with us?

Scanning my threatening 126-pound physique, the football coach said, "I'm sorry, son; you've got to go to frozen Chosin [the Japanese name for Korea]."

"An Orientation to the Far East" was the lecture given from a stage by a distinguished-looking colonel. He began his dissertation with the variety of foods available to GIs remaining in Japan. He held up a copy of a sign that should appear in the window of an approved restaurant. We were warned against eating any root vegetables, such as carrots, radishes, beets, or turnips. In a scholarly manner, he expounded, "The Japanese have many pathogenic microorganisms in their digestive systems. The Japanese farmer uses human feces as fertilizer—commonly known as shit."

He nearly blew me out of my seat. The academic air he projected did not prepare me, or anyone else in the auditorium, for "shit."

The Korean weather was next on his agenda. "Summers are hot and humid," he said. "Winters are cold and wicked. How does your government prepare you for these winters?"

A GI dressed in skivvies and a T-shirt stepped out from a wing of the stage.

"First the long johns."

The GI pulled on the bottoms and tops of the long johns.

"Next your fatigues. Over the fatigues, you will place the OG woolen shirt and OG pants." The OG shirt turned out to be a woolen olive-green flannel shirt similar to today's Polartec. "On top of all this, the pile-lined field jacket and pile-lined hooded parka."

The GI slipped into all the clothing with ease.

"To warm your hands, you will get lined mittens with a separate finger to fire your weapon. For your feet, the new thermal boots over your socks."

His model stood on the stage, motionless. He resembled an immobilized, overdressed child insulated against the bitter cold.

"Now you are prepared to face the coldest weather Korea has to offer," assured the colonel. "But you have one problem: what happens when there is a need to urinate? How do you get two inches of penis past seven inches of clothing? You're on your own."

It was a fun orientation, but that was where the fun ended. When we returned to the barracks, orders came to pack our gear. We busied ourselves by rolling our clothing tightly and placing it into our backpacks and duffel bags. We wound up our shelter half with a blanket inside and strapped it around our backpacks.

While this was going on, I caught sight of Bucky. He was fully recovered from seasickness and sitting on his bed, leisurely reading a magazine while a houseboy to whom he had given a pack of cigarettes was preparing his gear.

In the morning, a column of buses carried our group from Camp Drake to the port of Yokohama. The MSTS *Sadao S. Munemori* was bobbing at the pier. The *Munemori* was as ordinary as the *Simon Buckner* had been imposing; this was an aging utilitarian tub with mottled patches of rust melding with its battleship-gray exterior, giving the impression of camouflage for combat. Put simply, it was a no-frills transport. We boarded the ship, and without any fanfare, we were underway.

U.S NAVAL SHIP PVT. SADAO S. MUNEMORI

Korea:
Land of the Morning Harm

"Korea", at times is referred to as
The Land of the Morning Calm.

With rifles on one shoulder and duffels stuffed with their few
wardrobe items on the other, the men scrambled up to the deck
and then down into the bunk-stacked guts of the ship. Below the
lowest berths, puddles with scattered with debris—candy wrappers,
cigarettes, and empty cigarette packs—ebbed and flowed in cadence
with the gentle rocking of the docked ship. In spite of the difficulty
in scaling to the desirable top bunks, Dave and I bagged two where
we wouldn't be vulnerable to an undigested deluge from upper
berths.

Although everyone was dressed alike, it was akin to a party
on a leisurely Day Line cruise up the Hudson River. The tranquil
sea kept lunch and dinner inside our digestive systems. With
adolescent shoving and horsing around, we spent a good part of
the day without the word "Korea" passing our lips. It was almost
as if we knew and accepted the notion that "Korea" means "The
Land of the Morning Calm."

The PA system announced, "Breakfast is being served to
Level One."

A napkin? We had never had one in basic training. I should
have joined the navy. Breakfasts on both ships were haute cuisine
compared to the cud and guts we received in basic training.

The *Munemori* was headed for Inchon, Korea. A chilly dampness crept under my fatigues and lodged in my bones. *Maybe if I climb up to my bunk and get under a blanket, I'll thaw out.* I had just crawled to the top bunk and crept under my blanket when a blare of static unwrapped me.

"Now hear this; now hear this" boomed into the sleeping quarters. "On the port side of this vessel, our gunners will direct their fire at a white sleeve being towed by a Piper Cub," the PA system announced. "There will be a firing exercise by our ship's naval gunners on the port side in ten minutes."

Where is port? Convinced that port would be where the GIs were assembled, I climbed two flights of stairs to the deck.

A crowd of GIs were on the left side of the ship.

"Everyone on deck, and fix your eyes on the target."

A single-engine plane flew by pulling a long, white tubular sleeve—the target. We could easily judge the accuracy of the fire by the streaking tracers and the visible black bursts of the antiaircraft shells. Not a single round exploded within twenty yards of the target.

"If these guys are getting off this ship and joining us, I'm going home," quipped Intriglia.

In the evening, while I was stretched out on my bunk, listening to the soothing sounds of the waves lapping against the side of the ship, my thoughts went back to Pennsylvania Station, where I had left without an embrace and without a good-bye. Elaine suddenly became a candidate for the space between my arms. I quickly reached for my pad and pen. "Dear Elaine," I began, but then thought, *How will she interpret "Dear"? Is this too intimate? Do I really mean it? Crap. How do I get involved in a relationship when I don't know how to start?*

I tried "Hi, Elaine," and then the pen flowed smoothly over a few sheets of paper. The sealed envelope remained in my writing kit until we received our new address. The rocking of the ship as waves gently crashed on its sides quickly put me to sleep.

The *Munemori* skirted the south coast of Korea on the third day. Moving north, we passed a few uninhabited islands in the Yellow Sea. We waved to fishermen on our approach to the port of Inchon. I wondered why we laid anchor at such a distance from the port. Later I learned that the port has a thirty-foot variation in tides, and we had arrived at low tide.

All the troops were lined up on the deck. Why were cargo nets lowered along the side of the ship?

A string of Higgins boats (landing craft infantry) approached and circled us.

"As you climb down, grab the vertical ropes and put your boots on the horizontal ropes," shouted an officer.

"What in the hell is 'vertical'? Where in the God damned hell is 'horizontal'?" asked Williams, a Nobel Prize candidate from South Carolina.

Climb down? Of course. We couldn't walk through doors and step into the ocean. Without a previous exercise, we placed a leg over the rail of the boat, grabbed two vertical ropes of the cargo net, slipped our boots into the horizontal squares formed by the ropes, and carefully descended to the landing craft. One GI froze halfway down the net. With the help of two adjacent GIs, a lasso was secured around him. He carefully climbed down to two sailors who helped him into a rocking Higgins boat.

Darkness had fallen by the time everyone was on shore. Hundreds of GIs were milling around the pier. Where was my buddy, Dave Sohmer? I knew he was somewhere nearby. I shouted into the darkness, "Sohmer! Sohmer!"

Somewhere from a distance, he replied, "Wolfe! Wolfe!"

Within a few seconds, a chorus of GIs had picked up the chant, and I was surrounded by shouts of "Wolfe," "Sohmer," "Wolfe," "Sohmer." Meanwhile, Dave dissolved into the night.

It was about midnight. We climbed onto trucks to be taken to a repo depot (replacement company) opposite the University of Seoul. Here I became property of the Third Infantry Division. I stumbled into a squad tent to find an empty cot among sleeping

GIs. A few miles to the north, the pounding of 155 mm cannons and 105 mm howitzers still didn't register that this was a war zone.

The next morning, while gathering my shaving gear, I beheld an obscure neighborhood character I hadn't seen in years.

"*Rahchmuniss* (pitiful in Yiddish) What a place to meet!"

"Shh, shh! Don't call me that! I'm Arthur. What are you doing here?"

"The same thing you are," I replied.

"No you're not. I'm going home. You're going to the front line."

"*Bastard.*"

A nearby blast had us streaking out of our tents. Soon an ambulance with red crosses painted on its sides, back, and roof came speeding by with its gaping rear doors flailing. It opened a path through a swelling crowd and came to a halt. I saw a frantic Korean dash toward the ambulance carrying a limp and bleeding child draped like fabric over his arms. The girl had stepped on a land mine on her way to school. The parents accompanied her to a nearby medical unit.

What became of her? I wondered. *We're moving up soon. What will I do when I am faced with such a horror?*

After breakfast, I was wandering around the repo depot when I came across a group of boisterous veterans being processed for their return stateside. Something about their grimy, rugged, rumpled appearance caught my attention. Their fatigues were more wrinkled, worn, faded and filthy than the fatigues I or the repo depot personnel were wearing. No matter how Hollywood tried, they couldn't duplicate this shabby look. I enviously watched their horseplay and wondered if or when my day would come.

"Attention! Attention! Tomorrow will be the first day of Passover. There will be services tomorrow in Seoul. Jewish soldiers wishing to attend will meet after breakfast at the command post. Trucks will be waiting."

Bucky and Murray joined me for the Seder (the ceremonial dinner celebrating Passover). Seoul had been liberated from the

North Koreans about eight months before we arrived. Vestiges of street-to-street fighting were everywhere: wrecked jeeps and three-quarter-ton trucks were lying on their sides, and other trucks were completely burned and overturned; most were rusted, with gaping, jagged holes. Shells of buildings and craters littered the surreal landscape. One structure towered above the ruins—a government building. Its dome, probably once a miniature version of our nation's Capitol, was so pierced by shells and bullets that only its naked metal frame could be clearly distinguished, resembling the working end of an eggbeater.

Along the dusty unpaved roads stood the pathetic shacks of the residents. From a distance they looked like tall cardboard cartons. Up close they resembled tall cardboard cartons. Their roofs were made of anything the tenants could find. Corrugated metal sheets with scraps of tires were the predominant roofing materials.

The Seder was a Bronx high school reunion. Many of my classmates from James Monroe High School were there. We spent some time reminiscing about our carefree school days. Lenny Silpe asked, "When Dr. Hein handed us our diplomas four years ago, who would have thought we would be at a Seder in Seoul?"

"The only thing I knew about Korea was they had very good long-distance runners in the Olympics."

"Korea? Maybe I should have listened to Mrs. Todrus [our junior high school geography teacher]," added Murray.

A short, slight chaplain, lost within the folds of his blue-striped tallith (prayer shawl) conducted the Seder. After a brief reading of the Haggadah (the book telling the story of Passover), we were served a generous menu of sweet kosher wine, chicken soup, gefilte fish, chicken, horseradish, the obligatory sponge cake for dessert, and coffee. If my mother had been there, she would have said, "Feh! Who eats gefilte fish that comes out of a jar? Don't eat it. Give it back! This is sponge cake? This is straw!"

When the Seder ended, we had an hour of free time. Murray and I accompanied Bucky in search of his friend Stan Distenfeld. Which way to go? Which way to turn? The streets were unfamiliar, the buildings were shells, and the homes were patched shacks. Serendipity! Within five minutes we ran into him. He had been wandering the streets, lost, looking for the Seder, and here we were—we had found one another in the middle of Seoul!

Stan was a gifted speaker with a resonating bass voice. He reported the news to the GIs on the Far East Network. While the truck was waiting to take us back to camp, he told us Bucky's mother had made a temporary home for him after his parents passed away, and then we relived basketball games in Crotona Park.

"Come on. Get your ass up here!" shouted the driver.

On the ride back, I thought about my military occupation specialty (MOS). Why hadn't I been able to get a rear-echelon assignment like Stan? I guess I had nothing to offer the military except a healthy body and a weak mind.

The following noon, after being sorted and graded, we were crated onto a train heading north. Bucky was standing on the boarding steps as the train slowly pulled out of the station. He was distributing Ex-Lax to the children running alongside the train. "Make sure you give a piece to your friend," he shouted. "You there, don't hog it all! Share it! Share it!"

The Japanese trains were like toy Lionels compared to the Korean trains. These were US-size cars running on US-gauge tracks. The barren landscape—with its geometric, sun-baked abandoned rice paddies—was as stark as the cement squares of the sidewalk in front of our Bronx tenements. As the train headed farther north, the lifeless, barren plains evolved into hills. It wasn't long before we were moving through a green valley between low mountains.

From the moment in Seattle when I'd climbed up the steps of the *Simon Buckner,* the reality of war had been as remote to me as the port of Inchon. Now a train was carrying me toward the front line, where there was only a space between the United Nations forces and the Chinese military.

How does one go to war? I wondered. *Will we get out of the train and march to our unit? Will a jeep bring us there? Once we get there, what will we do?*

My musing was interrupted when the train came to a halt about five miles north of Seoul. On a dirt road adjacent to the tracks, a jeep was waiting. Bucky picked up his backpack, duffel bag, and rifle and accompanied an officer to the door.

"Where are you going?" I asked.

"They need medics," he replied.

"You're not a medic."

"I told them in Yokohama that I lived near the Bronx Hospital and absorbed a lot of medical expertise, so they assigned me to an evacuation hospital."

Although Bucky defused the tension with his humor, a combination of anger and envy consumed me: anger that he could joke while I was heading up front toward a rifle company, and envy of his wile in avoiding combat. I subsequently discovered from his letters that he had been assigned to the 121st EVAC, the hospital that would receive my company's seriously wounded and evacuate them to Japan or the United States. We said our good-byes; the train continued north.

What was wrong with me? Why hadn't I fabricated a story? Why wasn't I clever enough to avoid assignment as a rifleman? And where was Dave?

Sundown swept in a driving rainstorm. A scenic designer could not have created a more perfect setting for this production.

The train came to a halt.

"Grab your duffel and put on your ponchos before you get off the train" came thundering through the cars.

Viscous puddles of mud greeted my boots as I disembarked. Trucks were waiting to carry us to battalion headquarters, about a half mile behind the main line of resistance (MLR)—the front line. Standing in the downpour, we were asked to leave everything we owned in our duffel bags except what we were wearing. Our rifles, the soaking fatigues on our backs, and a small OD canvas backpack containing a change of underwear, fatigues, and a shaving kit were the only possessions we were to bring with us. Our duffels, we were told, would be stored in a squad tent to await us when we rotated back to the United States. (We never saw them again.)

"Welcome to the Third Battalion. The MILK Battalion of the Cream Regiment (it consisted of Companies M, I, L, and K)— the Can-Do Regiment, the Fifteenth Regiment. In our regiment, instead of saying, 'Yes, sir!' we say, 'Can do, sir!' and if you are especially on the ball, you will say, 'Have done, sir!'"

Is this junior high school? Am I really hearing this? Is he serious?

Thus spake a rotund major, squeezed like the contents of an Italian sausage into a slick poncho. He was perched under a glossy helmet liner with a Fifteenth Regiment decal appliquéd onto it. His congregation, supersaturated from the March deluge, awaited the ark to ferry them to their final destination. This was a fine reception to the Third Battalion, Fifteenth Regiment, Third Infantry Division.

Approaching darkness added to our discomfort. My back began to itch from the new, drenched fatigues, and naturally the itch was out of reach of my fingernails. I rubbed my back against the spare tire of a jeep. Oh, it felt so good! I wondered whether I had the same orgasmic expression I'd seen on pigs rubbing their backs against an inside door handle of a freight car at the Seventy-Second Street freight yard, where I had once worked.

We stood. We waited. Where were we to go? Finally there arrived a truck with slits like cat's eyes for lights. Climbing into the truck with me were Oscar Konnerth, Russell Wirt, Murray Lichtman, and John Hollier, fellow graduates of Indiantown Gap. Harry Lapich was sent to Company K. We were on our way to our new home. Sitting in the back of the truck, I remembered the cadre who had told us in basic training, "The best camp in the army is the one you just left and the one you're going to." Where was I going to? He was full of shit.

Will I Ever Walk
on Asphalt Again?

The sun had just dipped below a craggy wall of mountains to the west. A bumpy ten-minute ride from battalion headquarters brought us to Company L's position on the MLR. The rain let up. My body, warming my wet fatigues, itched wherever the cloth chafed my skin.

Sergeant Springer, a World War II veteran, greeted me on the reverse slope of our position–the side of our hill away from the enemy. I envied the comfort of his dry, worn, soft, faded fatigues. My stiff, dark OD uniform labeled me as a newcomer. He introduced himself as my squad leader. The distant chatter of machine gun and rifle fire accompanied us.

Thoughts raced through my mind. *What have I come to? Will I be out there–part of that noise? Will I ever walk on asphalt again? Should I squat as I walk through the trench? Springer isn't squatting. I'll need a friend, and he seems like someone who would listen.*

Like a calf following its mother, I anxiously followed him to my new home. He pulled aside a limp and filthy OD blanket–the door to a hole in the ground called a bunker. On its roof, I could see brittle, pale weeds twisted among scattered rocks and soil. I entered onto a slick floor of earth tamped down from months of traffic. Jagged earthen walls conspired with the floor to radiate a chilling cold and dampness. Before he left, Springer introduced me to Jesse, who was sitting on three stacked grenade boxes next to a wall.

Am I expected to sleep here? Will this be home? Until when? I had been raised in a humble home in the Bronx. I slept on a convertible couch in the living room whose piercing springs were covered by a thin fabric, over which Ma placed a blanket. This had been my mattress at home. But wrapped in my clammy fatigues, I was totally unprepared for a sleeping bag rolled out over my poncho on a damp, slick floor.

My new home on the MLR

"Jesse," I said, "don't tell me you can sleep through the night in this miserable damp box."

"Through the night? No more of that. You're not stateside. You're not in the artillery. You're not in the tanks. You're a dogface. We take guard duty every two hours." Pointing to his rolled-out sleeping bag, he said, "When I'm not on guard or on a patrol, this is my innerspring mattress."

Then he sung lines from a blues song by Brownie McGhee:

> Rocks has been my pillow,
> Cold ground's been my bed,
> Blue sky's been my blanket,
> And the moonlight's been my spread.

These words resonated within me for a few days. Soon they became my way of life.

On top of two grenade boxes at one corner of the bunker rested .30-caliber bandoliers (belts with pockets for magazines containing rifle ammunition). Near Jesse's OD backpack, a flickering candle lit the opposite corner. Outside, a telephone (EE8) was connected to our command post—the company commander's bunker.

Jesse offered me the empty grenade boxes as my club chair. He straightened the blanket door, so that no light would escape, sealed the firing hole, and then lit a candle. We spoke about home, his girlfriend, and his experiences on the line. Jesse was a black from Detroit. He said he was going stateside in a few days, but he was not looking forward to returning to his drug-infested neighborhood. He said that he and his girlfriend planned to move to North Carolina, where his parents had been born. Then the conversation turned to the usual—women.

"Do you remember the first time you got laid?" he asked.

"Of course," I replied.

"Tell me about it."

"I was in Montreal, Canada, sixteen years old. My friend Peter took me to a whorehouse somewhere downtown. The madam directed me to a room with a bed in it and told me to wait. In the room opposite me, I could hear lashes from a cat-o'-nine-tails whistling through the air, followed by groans as the strands sliced into a body. I wanted to leave. I was scared shit. I sat on the bed listening to my heart pounding. Soon a fairly attractive blond in a robe entered the room. She opened her robe. I was trembling. What was I supposed to do? What would she do if I touched her?

"The glow of the bulb suspended from the ceiling reflected off her pubic hair like the sun's rays reflecting off a golden wheat field—a golden wheat field like you've seen in a bank calendar. She was my introduction to the reality of my teenage fantasies."

"Like a golden wheat field in a bank calendar! Wow!" repeated Jesse.

Maybe, I thought, *I too will eventually develop his upbeat attitude.* But now I was exhausted from a wet, physically and emotionally draining day. It seemed as if I had just shut my eyes when Jesse poked me.

"Wolfe, Wolfe … it's time for your two-hour guard. If you see or hear anything suspicious, wake me. If it's serious, there's the phone. Call the CP right away. If they ask you, tell them we're Fox 3."

I slipped a bandolier over my shoulder, placed a magazine of ammo into my rifle, and rested it on the front lip of the trench line outside our bunker. I scanned the deformed shadows of trees and projecting rocks. Sounds I never heard in the Bronx assaulted me— whishes from overhead artillery and sporadic rifle and automatic fire rattling in the distance. Occasionally an exploding artillery shell muffled the clatter of the small arms. Like two ghostly towers, far off to the left, two spotlights from the Panmunjom peace talks pierced the night sky.

Welcome to Korea! Incoming white phosphorus rounds.

How am I going to tell the boys at home about this? War was for the World War II vets or the movies. Small arms fire? Exploding artillery rounds? Seabury Place and James Monroe High School had not prepared me for this. Having fun had been at the beginning, middle, and end of our daily program there.

After two hours, Jesse came to relieve me. Two hours later, I peered into the night once again to a somewhat quieter darkness.

Tour of the Line

In the morning I awoke, stretching and scratching, to a typical Korean vista. Mountains pitted by craters of yellow clay soil looked down upon hills and knolls dappled with patches of vegetation. Like ghostly scarecrows, dwarfed, jagged, leafless trees with amputated limbs stood upright in the valley before me. Traveling east to west, an endless serpentine gash defaced the forward slope of the hill where Company L was deployed. It was our trench line. Interspersed were camouflaged bunkers. A free lane (paths where no mines had been laid) led a patrol to the enemy.

Sergeant Springer asked me to join him for a walk along the trench line to introduce me to the other members of my platoon. I was happy to find the familiar faces of Oscar Konnerth, Russell Wirt, and John Hollier. Murray Lichtman was with the mortars in the Fourth Platoon.

Moving along, Springer said to be careful at the next bunker. There was a bent sapling forming an arch alongside it. George Whitefeather, like many men in Company L, was a wild paratrooper reassigned to our company. He had created the arch by connecting a string to the top of the young tree's trunk, bending it back, and tying it to a stake in the ground. Dangling from the branches by their nearly straightened firing pins were fragmentary grenades. He claimed that when he cut the string the tree trunk would snap forward, releasing the pins from the flying grenades and sending them in the direction of the assaulting Chinese. I took note of this and assured myself that I would never visit that bunker again.

"Move only in the free lanes," warned Springer. "Our front lawn is scattered with land mines."

A low barbed-wire fence designated the lanes to be used when leaving on or returning from a raid or patrol; no land mines were embedded along these trails. These were the free lanes.

"The day before you arrived, a sergeant who was due to rotate wandered off the free lane, stepped on a Bouncing Betty (land mine), and was blown apart."

At the base of the forward slope, about 150 feet from our bunkers, aligned with the thirty-eighth parallel, was a continuous six-foot double barbed-wired fence traveling east to west, parallel to our trench line. This was the Smith Fence, extending from the east coast to the west coast of Korea. In front of this fence was a long, broad valley—the Chorwon Valley. It was blanketed with tall reeds, dismembered trees, bare soil and scattered hills. Three miles north, toward the far end valley, were the permanent Chinese positions: Hill 317, Breadloaf, Cheeseburger, and Sugarloaf.

I was assigned to the second squad of the Second Platoon. An intact rifle squad consists of nine men: two BAR men and six M1 riflemen, directed by a squad leader. Sergeant Springer, my squad leader, replaced my M1 rifle with a twenty-pound BAR.

"Keep the magazines clean, and fire in short bursts. Because of its rapid fire, the enemy can easily spot you. Move after you've fired a few bursts. Bring plenty of ammo. You can quickly run out. Carry it by the handle after you fire it. The barrel gets as hot as melted metal."

Thanks, I thought. *In my next letter, I'll tell my parents how concerned my sergeant is about my safety.* This was my initiation to the weapon. There was no test fire—no review of the nomenclature. Ideally a tall, strong man who can easily handle its length and twenty-pound weight was assigned the BAR. I was five feet seven inches and weighed 126 pounds. I had seen this weapon only two days in basic training. At that time, I had felt insecure with it, as if it controlled me. I recalled how, when I complained about its weight in basic training, a cadreman had told me not to worry about it, because only big men were assigned to it. Now it was in my hands, with the rest of my squad depending on its firepower.

In reserve, Russell Wirt with his M1 rifle, and me with my BAR.

When I returned to the bunker, Jesse told me that the BAR changed hands as frequently as a replacement arrived. I had arrived; it was in my hands. I soon learned that because of its rate of fire (about 650 rounds per minute), it was a prime target for the enemy. For the survival of my squad and myself, I soon became thoroughly familiar with it.

Neither my poncho nor my sleeping bag spread out above it were a barrier to the bunker's cold, damp ground, but once I crept outside my sleeping bag, I was able to reacquaint my muscles to their bones.

On my second day in the trenches, our squad was assigned to clear an area where a firefight had taken place the previous night. I flipped the BAR's switch to lock, hoping there would be no need to flip it to automatic. We patrolled through the reeds, cleared some hills, and then came to a bunker. With a very tight asshole, I went to the high ground with my BAR as the rest of our squad surrounded it. Charley Kauneckis approached the bunker from its side and threw a grenade into it. We waited, it detonated, and then he crawled in. It was abandoned. On the ground at the side of the entrance was a beautiful brown enameled canteen. An embossed red star glowed in the center. Charley bent over to collect his souvenir.

"Don't touch it!" shouted Springer. "It could be booby-trapped."

Charley was embarrassed. He, the veteran paratrooper, had made an ass of himself in front of the green draftees. I returned to the MLR armed with another life-saving experience.

This small operation relieved some of the initial tension about the unknown that had started to curl my intestines when I'd realized there was nothing but space between us and the enemy.

Listening Post

In the evening, Russell Wirt and I were assigned to a listening post, a wide shallow foxhole that accommodated two men, a third of the way down the Free Lane. The Free Lane led to an opening in the Smith Fence which led to the Chorwon Valley in front of our position on the MLR. A phone (EE8) enabled us to keep in contact with the command post where Captain Smith, our company commander had his hideaway.

Russ and I kept twisting to find a comfortable position in the foxhole. Soon, a platoon passed by. They nodded then quietly moved down the Free Lane and through the opening in the Smith Fence. I could see that Russ was extremely agitated. In near panic he told me that his brother was killed in the Battle of the Bulge during World War II. We were to alternate sleeping, two hours on, and two hours off. I told him that I'd take the first watch.

In fifteen minutes, the crack of rifle fire and the buzz of burp gus interrupted the eerie silence. A phone call from Captain Smith told one of us to assist the patrol that had passed by earlier. They'd been hit by the Chinese and were bringing back their casualties.

I was immobilized with fear.

Can I handle this? I can lift a litter, sure, but I've never aided a wounded person. How can I help? What if the Chinese are there? Will I fire my BAR?

I was a product of America in the 1950s, where real men were ostensibly tough, or at least had a veneer of toughness. We didn't express our feelings. We never spoke of fear. My best audience was myself. Maybe this helped me to maintain my sanity at the beginning of this insanity.

Russ was asleep. His teeth were screeching and grinding. I awoke him to say that he was to remain in the foxhole. A patrol was returning. I rushed down the free lane and into the field to assist the litter bearers, the KATUSAS (Koreans Attached To the US Army). They were carrying our wounded men. The Koreans were exhausted. One GI was wriggling like a cut worm. Off the side of a litter, his hemorrhaging foot was encased in a shredded boot that was dangling like a pendulum. A medic ran over and applied medication to his wound. A mixture of powdered plasma dissolved in sterile water was injected into him, followed by a morphine syrette (a single-dose injection device). He wrapped a bandage as a tourniquet around his ankle. Within a minute, the specter of anguish on the wounded man's face was transformed into a dreamy vision of tranquility. I helped a Korean carry him to our aid station. Russ was still sleeping fitfully when I returned.

How will I explain what happened last night to my future wife, to my grandchildren, to my children, to my friends? Briefly it was a nightmare, and I had no idea how Korea would affect my life. What surreal events in my past helped me get through this night?

We returned to our bunkers at daylight. Jesse greeted me. "Well, what do you think of Korea?"

Was a reply necessary?

"Where's the toilet, Jesse?"

"Grab your entrenching tool and dig a rut on the reverse slope."

"Where's the reverse slope?"

It's on the backside of our hill. You don't want the Chinks to see your shiny white ass, do you?"

"Okay, where's the toilet paper?"

"We don't have toilet paper."

Jesse handed me *Stars and Stripes*, our army newspaper.

"Tear off a page. That's our toilet paper."

My entrenching tool left a scar on the slope of the hill. There was no seat; I just squatted and began to read.

"The Yankees are still in Florida for Spring Training," the paper stated.

Eddie Fisher joined the army and is coming to entertain the troops in Korea. My dear little father loved him when he sang. "Oh My Papa."

"Our airmen shot down 2 MIGs … Rumors about peace talks continue."

All done. There was no more *Stars* but plenty of stripes. I was a toilet rookie, but in a few days I became a veteran.

Sergeant Springer came to tell us that the cooks had brought hot breakfast. "After breakfast, go with Wright and bring back a couple of barrels of water from the pond."

Very few faces on the chow line were familiar. Charley, whom I recognized from my first patrol, turned to Whitefeather. "George, you still here after last night's raid? I thought they got you."

"Naw, I'm too mean to die. You're the one they're looking for."

Just like my unfaded OD fatigues, I was a newcomer. I wanted to be one of them. I wanted to wisecrack with them. I couldn't yet. I hadn't paid my dues. I joined Wright in a jeep. The trip was like traveling through the remains of a once lush forest. Bare trees and tree stumps were littered around us. Scraps of grass made a meager attempt to recover and return to the original greenery.

Russ couldn't bear it any longer. The night, the tension, and the specter of his brother were too much. He was reassigned to an honor guard unit in Seoul. My temporary bunker buddy, Jesse, and Sergeant Springer rotated home a week later. The glue to secure me to the close-knit platoon hadn't quite set.

Four days later, our platoon was assigned to patrol a mile into the Chorwon Valley. Recalling the night when I guarded the free lane, my head became entangled in a web of what-ifs.

What if we meet the Chinese and I freeze? What if one of our men is hit—do I leave him for the medic, or do I tend to him? What if I get hit? Will our medic see me, or will I be abandoned in the valley? What if I'm taken prisoner? What if I return up the free lane? Will I remember the password? What if my parents get the telegram, "I regret to inform you …"?

So if you were wondering how one goes to war, this how I went.

Life on the Line

I gradually became acquainted with the details of ordinary life on the MLR. Those details centered around the bare essentials of existence: food, clothing, shelter, and survival.

•

As for style, it couldn't turn a head in our crowd. It would not have merited an ad in a throwaway insert from *Gentlemen's Quarterly*. All the boys wore exactly the same one in exactly the same color and exactly the same size: our armored vest. Whether the soldier was slim or stout, tall or short, the vest was one-size-fits-all. Unlike most women, the men considered the sameness to be of no consequence. We warmed to its embrace and wore it with gratitude.

Its state-of-the-art fabric was a synthetic compressed into hundreds of wafer-thin sheets. Like most of our garments, the style was casual. There was no satin-buckled belt in the back—no matching buttons. Instead, heavy industrial-steel snaps ran down the front. After a month of wear, the vest blended perfectly with the surrounding terrain. Not to worry; a gentle rinse from a canteen of water brought it back to a showroom glow.

Comfort? Although it began to follow the contours of the body somewhat after a few weeks of wear, it was as hard as a shield. It did not bend. This vest was an excellent conductor of heat in the summer and a superior conductor of cold in the winter. No, it was not user-friendly in that respect, but what do you expect from synthetics?

Our vests and our helmets occupied the space between the enemy and us. Did we wear them with the frequency that we wore our fatigues? Of course not. When we went on an adventure or anticipated incoming enemy fire, most of us glued our vests to our fatigue shirts and our helmets to our scalps. But some men wore neither helmet nor vest regardless of the situation.

One vest made it onto the front page of *Stars and Stripes,* the army newspaper. Modeling the vest was our medic from the Third Platoon, Rogers. He was pointing to what appeared to be a zipper running at an angle across his vest. But our vests didn't have zippers; they closed with snaps. Was this a custom-made garment? Of course not. Rogers never carried a weapon; he was a Mormon. The previous week, however, he could have used a carbine when his platoon was engaged in a firefight. While attending to one of the wounded, he was struck by a string bullets from burp guns, which fire seven hundred to nine hundred rounds per minute. Fortunately the layered sheets of the vest had stopped the bullets. The embedded shots had left a metallic line across the surface of his vest.

After soldiers reported frequent injuries from shrapnel ricocheting off the vest and piercing necks and jaws, the army updated the vests to canvas-covered models with armored collars. Was the initial grainy, plastic-covered vest an experiment? The canvas-covered vests that followed persisted through Korea, Vietnam, and Desert Storm. Iraqi Freedom featured the state-of-the-art Kevlar vest. Will those follow the path of the Ike jacket and the field jacket and become civilian political statements?

•

Who is he? Where is he? He could have been on a shopping spree in Milan or surfing off the California coast. I knew he existed. His rank told me that the US army had commissioned him. But he was a name without a body.

He was Captain Smith, commanding officer of Company L. I didn't know of any man in the company who had ever seen him; I hadn't. His bunker was the command post. Without ever laying eyes on him, the men christened him CP Smith ("Command Post" Smith). Instead of leading a raid, he was safely ensconced in his bunker (command post), contacting his underlings by radio. Meanwhile, the men of Company L carried out their assignments as if they had a leader.

It was a quiet early April morning. Oscar Konnerth, Ken Brockett, and I had just thrown our empty C-ration cans into a sump when a few whishes broke the silence. We dived into Ken's bunker. His flying helmet landed outside, in the trench.

Boom! Boom! With each burst, we curled up tighter. Then there was silence. We waited. It was over. Truman Bastin, who shared Ken's bunker, returned from wherever he had taken shelter. He picked up a bent steel helmet lying in the trench and shouted "Ken! Ken! Ken Brockett, where are you?"

Shaken and trembling, we crawled out of the bunker. Ken, stunned from the rounds, called out to Truman, "Get rid of that helmet, and get me an entrenching tool. I'll shit in my pants if I don't dig me a hole."

With the tool in hand, he ran over the reverse slope to relieve his trembles and clear his colon.

Jungles and Lancaster's bunker had received a direct hit. Fortunately Benny Hoover and Gus Chobot's bunker was nearby. They ran over, cleared the debris, and helped them out.

Sergeant Jeffries repairing his mortared bunker.

That afternoon, Sergeant Jeffries assigned Ken and me to clear Lancaster's collapsed bunker with a shape charge. Massey, our armorer, gave us a powerful explosive device shaped like an automobile oil can but rounded on the top. Ken was from Joliet, Illinois. As a lifelong resident of New York City, I assumed that the key to handling tools and explosives was anyone with a southern or Midwestern accent. But Midwestern Ken knew nothing about shape charges. To me it looked like an innocent metal device from our army's vast assortment of such devices. *How could this benign thing explode?* I wondered.

It couldn't explode as long as it was in Ken's or my hands. We didn't know which side was up. Along came Charley Kauneckis. Charley, a wiry six-foot-two blond paratrooper, had come to Company L from the paratrooper 187th Regimental Combat Team. Six-footers intimidated me. They had a military bearing that a man my size could never achieve. Charley's interest in my confusion made me stand just a bit taller. Anything that blew up provided him with as much nourishment as two eggs or a can of C-rations. Seeing our dilemma, he left and then returned quickly with wire, a gadget with a handle, and some other wiry things. He connected wires to the thing with the handle and then attached wires to a primer on the shape charge. He buried the charge at the bottom of the collapsed bunker and then told us to join him in a trench with our helmets secure on our heads.

"When I yell 'Fire in the hole!' get down."

We waited.

"Fire in the hole! Fire in the hole!" shouted Charley.

A boom resonated from the collapsed bunker and bounced off the surrounding hills. Considering our distance from the explosion, I waited a few seconds, stood up, and removed my helmet. A shower of shards, pebbles and earth came down on my head. Charley nearly collapsed with laughter. After this incident, he christened me "Reilly, the New York Irishman." To Charley I was no longer Danny; I was Reilly. He was my first buddy in Company L.

•

George Whitefeather, a rotund, rugged American Indian, was another ex-paratrooper. His was the last bunker at the far left of Company L's sector. Among his numerous bizarre activities, George collected fingerlike, finely serrated shiny leaves from bushes scattered throughout our area. He soaked his harvest in aftershave lotion for a day or two; then he laid them out to dry on his poncho. With his bayonet, he chopped the leaves into fine pieces and tamped them into his corncob pipe. In the morning, after an evening of puffing, he would say, "Man, I wasn't sitting in that free lane last night; I was floating over it."

A corncob pipe? Aftershave lotion? Where did we get these luxuries? A three-foot crate made of thin wooden slats held together by wires—called a 101 pack—was sent up to the MLR, allegedly full of treats for the fighting men. However, as the crate made its way toward the MLR, the boys in the rear had the pick of the litter. By the time it arrived, we had a choice of a few cans of shoe polish, some bottles of aftershave lotion, corncob pipes, and a couple of crushed packs of Chesterfields, which the southern boys called Chesterweeds.

What does one do with shoe polish or aftershave lotion on the line? Mickey Spillane would have said, "Live fast, die young, and have a good-looking corpse." Maybe we should have polished our boots and doused ourselves with aftershave lotion before we went on a raid?

•

My language was being enriched by the colorful expressions thrown at me.

"Who's covering the free lane tonight?" I asked.

"You don't know, do you?"

"What's the sign and countersign for today?"

"You don't know, do you?"

To raise the dialogue to a higher level, there were the following responses:

"Did you see my helmet liner?"

"I got your helmet liner; I got it hanging!"

"Did the mail come in yet?"

"I got your mail; I got it hanging!"

At first I thought these brilliant replies were snide responses to legitimate questions. Then I realized that I should avoid questioning the mentally challenged.

●

Our "Orientation to the Far East" lecture had not mentioned the presence of the anopheles mosquito, the carrier of malaria. In response to this parasite, Friday, after lunch, we lined up in a grove for "dessert." With arms spread, we filed past a medic who sprayed us from head to toe with a dense, white mist. *DDT?* I wondered. This was followed by a chloroquine tablet. Large and white, it was the most bitter object that ever passed a human's lips. It was supposed to mask the symptoms of malaria. Upon our return to civilization, we were told, we would be issued pills called primaquine and the familiar chloroquine. Allegedly these would treat the disease if we had it.

Did they ask me if I wanted to be sprayed? Did they ask me if I wanted the pill? This is the army, Reilly.

Another serious disease was hemorrhagic fever. According to Sergeant Jeffries (Springer's replacement as squad leader), a bacterium or a virus living on rats' fur transmitted it. Its symptoms were uncontrolled bleeding of the internal organs, then a high fever, and finally death. I knew we had the furry visitors, because I noticed that they had dined on the crackers in the C-ration can in my bunker. In order to keep the rats away, the medics dusted lye powder in the trench lines and bunkers. They said that the rats absorbed the lye through their feet; it would then get into their bloodstream and kill them. The success of this procedure was questionable, since a large hemorrhagic fever ward in Seoul was filled to near capacity.

●

The weaponry of an infantry company at this time was vintage World War I and World War II. The riflemen carried the M1 semiautomatic .30-caliber rifle (World War II). Some had smaller .30-caliber carbines (World War II). The .30-caliber BAR was a holdover from World War I that had been modified for World War II. We also had the air-cooled World War II machine gun. Everyone carried World War II fragmentary grenades. A thermite grenade, which produced an extremely high temperature, was attached to a thin, classified RCA radio used by our commo (communications) man. In the weapons platoon, there were sixty-millimeter mortars, a fifty-seven-millimeter recoilless rifle, and .50-caliber air-cooled machine guns, all of World War II vintage.

Almost all combat took place at night. Precision was not essential; firepower was. With a semiautomatic weapon like the M1, the small capacity of the clip (only eight rounds) made it almost impossible to hit targets we could not see. The Chinese had an inexpensive Russian pressed-metal burp gun, named after the sound it made as it expelled seven hundred to nine hundred rounds per minute. Burp guns sprayed the combat area with a dense output of low-caliber bullets, giving our enemy a decided advantage. Many of their concussion grenades (known as "potato mashers") were duds, but those that exploded were very effective within a ten-foot radius. We found many duds lying in areas where exchanges of fire had occurred.

Finally a new rapid-fire .30-caliber automatic carbine with a thirty-round ammo magazine was shipped to Korea. We heard about them but never saw one. Like the 101 packs, these weapons could be found in the hands of the honor guard in Seoul, jeep drivers, and other rearguard personnel. They never completed their intended journey to the MLR.

•

The cooks, at a distance from the MLR, occasionally prepared hot food for us. In order to reach us, a jeep towed the food in a small trailer. On the road exposed to the Chinese, tall burlap camouflage screens hid the trail. After a series of dry days, as the jeep drove over the dirt road, it kicked up a cloud of dust, alerting the enemy despite the burlap screens. We could expect incoming fire. The cooks hurriedly distributed the food and left quickly.

When the jeep couldn't get through, or when we were on an outpost, we dined on our C-rations. An empty canister from a .30-caliber machine gun partially filled with diesel fuel was our stove for heating these meals. The franks and beans were good, and the beef stew was chewy and salty but passable; however, the ham and lima beans and corned beef hash were inedible. A handful of salt could have replaced them and would have been just as palatable. The lima beans seemed embarrassed to be associated with the ham. They gathered in a group at the bottom of the can. With a plastic spoon, we integrated the salty chunks of ham with the salty lima beans in the salty sauce. Our sympathy went out to any GI left with this awful entrée. A compassionate buddy would mix his franks and beans with the ham and beans or hash in a canteen cup and then heat the mixture over the low flame in the machine gun canister to create a semipalatable casserole.

Although I didn't have a girlfriend writing me passionate letters, Elaine did continue our friendly correspondence, and Bucky wrote regularly. His letters began with a casualty list of the men from my company who had passed through his 121st EVAC hospital. One list of the wounded ended with "And I'm anxiously awaiting your arrival." This was followed by secret info from the helicopter pilots saying that the war was coming to an end in three weeks. He sent me the news to make me feel good, but unfortunately, it was totally false.

One night we participated in a two-company raid on Hill 317, and, when we withdrew, the Chinese pursued us. As we approached the MLR, our platoon sergeant, Jeffries, called for a concentration of mortar rounds to be dropped on the Chinese. A round that fell short of the target exploded near Stan Innerfeld (from the adjacent Company I), tearing his face, mouth, and tongue, dislodging some teeth, and damaging his jaw. He was sent to the 121st EVAC, where

Bucky saw to it that everything possible was done for him. He was at Stan's side until Stan was evacuated to Tokyo Army Hospital.

•

The early heat brought an order to turn in our sweaters and field jackets. Was there a detergent powerful enough to remove the greasy filth that impregnated our jackets? Could the layers of salt from the perspiration marinating our sweaters be dissolved and neutralized by the army's laundry? A successful purging of this grime would have caused an ecological disaster in the Far East. The sewage would have percolated into the groundwater and been carried out to the Yellow Sea. Not a single fish would have been seen in the markets of the Far East.

"Pass the deodorant, MacDonald. I'm scrubbing for the Sabbath."

As the days passed, replacements became veterans. We familiarized ourselves with our weapons and the men around us.

I knew their hometowns. I knew about their families. I knew if they were married. I knew the schools they had attended. I knew the names of their girlfriends. I knew that Charley and I would be inseparable, but I still did not know or see Captain Smith.

A Few Days in May

It was unusually quiet during the last week of April. At home the men in Company L would think, "What will I wear today? T-shirt and dungarees? A blue serge suit? A gray company uniform with my name embroidered over the left shirt pocket? Will I change into something more comfortable at the end of the day?"

For us it was a selection of one. We couldn't use fashion options to express ourselves. One cotton OD herringbone twill shirt combined with a pair of matching pants was it—the ensemble known as fatigues. The marriage between them was never consummated. Invariably the pants were three or four shades lighter and thinner than the shirt from wear. But the densely sewn thread patches on them usually matched the darker shirt, which took less abuse as we went about our work.

A disappointed large bellows pocket leaned against each thigh, anticipating a cornucopia of metal widgets. We had nothing to place in these pockets, so why were we burdened with another pair on our chests? We didn't own enough personal items to fill a watch pocket. One pocket, however, had a permanent resident—a C-ration can opener about an inch and a half tall and a half inch wide. It was specific. It could only open C- ration cans. It came with each box of C-rations. A recent letter or a pocketknife sometimes kept it company in that pocket. I remember how out of place I felt when I arrived in Company L with my dark, stiff OD fatigues unscathed by a GI laundry and undamaged by the erosion to come at my new workplace.

The next day was May 1, a day observed throughout the world in honor of workers—May Day. A major attack was anticipated to celebrate the event in Korea. But the angry hisses from incoming mortar rounds, staccato belching from burp guns, and rattling canisters accompanied by bugles were strangely absent.

Our squad leader, Sergeant Jeffries, assigned Charley, Oscar, and me to man Mary Outpost (Mary OP). He warned us to be especially alert, since that evening was the onset of May Day. We met at twilight and then moved down the free lane, passed through the Smith Fence, and marched two hundred yards to Mary.

Our mission at the outpost was to watch for any enemy activity. This lone knoll at the southern end of the long, wide Chorwon Valley was manned by three soldiers who were replaced every three days. Along the front of its periphery, and up to its trench line, it was surrounded by land mines and concertina wire (coils of barbed wire about three feet in diameter), with occasional gaps for a free lane.

Charley Kauneckis on Mary OP, with the
Chinese-occupied hills behind him.

The men who had been manning Mary were happy to see us. As soon as they left, Charley began stringing trip wire (very thin wire) attached to flares across each free lane so that anyone bumping into it would activate the flares. Oscar and I, newcomers from basic training, were awed at the ease with which he handled the strange equipment. When he was through, he pointed to the trip wire. "Both of you, don't get close to it. Don't even go near it. Kick that wire and your ass will be hamburger meat."

Oscar Konnerth and Dan Wolfe frolicking on Mary OP.

We settled in small bunkers strategically positioned so that we could view the entire surrounding area. I placed extra ammo magazines, grenades, and C-rations in a corner of my bunker; then I stepped outside to explore the neighborhood.

It's not fancy, but it's home on Mary OP.

Small wizened trees with sterile branches were scattered throughout this outpost. Almost lost in the fading twilight, the same mountains and hills that stared at us from the MLR were gaping at us on Mary.

This is stupid, I thought. *What if we fall asleep during the night? Will the Chinese wake us up to tell us they've arrived?*

I reached for my BAR and crawled over to Charley's bunker. He wasn't there. Maybe Oscar knew if we had a schedule. I went through the connecting trench to Oscar's bunker.

"Hey, Oscar, what are we doing for guard duty tonight? We can't sleep through the night. Someone will have to stand guard."

"Charley was here before; he knows."

Oscar was dining on C-rations alfresco. He was actually enjoying his can of beef stew. With his appetite, I think he would have eaten the can if he'd had a saltshaker. We spoke of home, the fun we'd had in high school, and his girlfriend, Mary Ann, whom he'd married before he left for Korea.

"Do you feel you did the right thing by marrying Mary Ann before you left for Korea?"

"She wanted to get married, and so did I. What's wrong with that?"

"Nothing in normal times, but there's a good chance we won't come back. Then Mary Ann will be slightly damaged goods."

"Don't talk like that. She's my wife."

I told him I was sorry. I didn't mean to upset him.

Oscar rinsed his mouth and grimaced with puckered lips. "They must put a gallon of iodine into this water." He wiped his lips on his wrinkled sleeve and said, "Okay, let's ask Charley about guarding this hill. He was here a few minutes ago."

"I'll go to his bunker," I replied. "Maybe he's returned."

I found Charley near the base of the hill, still fiddling with the flares. A half hour later, our security literally blew apart. I thought I heard a strange noise and left my bunker in the darkness to crawl down the free lane, but my BAR tripped a wire, and a small parachute shot about a hundred feet into the air. It opened and slowly descended, suspending a bright blue-white flare that illuminated the entire area.

What's holding that damn thing up there? I wondered. I lay frozen. *Will it ever come down?*

Charley stormed through the trench line toward me. He was livid. But I knew his anger was only momentary when he told me to get into my bunker because the flare might attract incoming shells. By the time he cooled down, a few shells had landed in the valley, telling us that the Chinese had seen the flare.

Charley was now ready to discuss the plan for guarding Mary through the night. He said that the last time he'd been there, each man took a two-hour watch. Oscar was to take the eleven-to-one shift, Charley would take the one-to-three shift, and I was to be on from three to five.

Bird chirps and insect communications—sounds that I had ignored on the MLR—now had me fearfully staring in their direction. I imagined footsteps were moving near the outpost. I thought each sound had the shoe of the enemy connected to it. There was no way I was going to nod out. In spite of my fright, the night went smoothly, with no probes by the Chinese.

In the morning, Charley made his rounds. He field-stripped his cigarette as if he were on a garrison parade ground and greeted me with "Hi, Reilly. Ha, ha! Trip any wires lately?"

No comment. For the moment, in spite of my embarrassment, I was happy I was able to provide him with a laugh.

Our three days on Mary were uneventful except for the parachute and the few rounds it had elicited into the valley.

Upon returning to the MLR, Charley began a survey on the dinner chow line to determine how many men in Company L had seen the flare that Reilly had tripped.

"These New York guys need a freaking fairy queen to lead them through the darkness," roared Lancaster.

Thanks a lot, Charley.

Two days later, the comfort of the MLR was interrupted when battalion reported that the Chinese troops were being reinforced in the 317 area. We were assigned to patrol deeper than usual into the valley—to the base of Hill 317.

At dusk, Charley, our self-assigned point man (the soldier who goes ahead of the squad on a patrol or raid), arrived at the assembly area. By the time the rest of the squad had gathered, he and our armorer had completed connecting a sniperscope's screen to his carbine. The heavy wet-cell battery pack that powered the scope was harnessed onto his back. With this device, he was able to see green negative images of the enemy at a distance of about fifty yards. The heat generated by their bodies would attract the infrared rays emitted by the scope. The rays would return to form an image on a seven-inch screen connected to Charley's carbine.

We followed Charley through the free lane, passed the barbed-wire Smith Fence, and continued into the night. Sergeant Jeffries pointed to a hill on our left, which was to be an assembly area should anyone get lost.

"Roll down your sleeves. Those reeds have razor-sharp edges and can cut like razors," warned Sergeant Jeffries.

Before we reached the wide valley, two men cleared the knolls to our left and to our right. The moon, hidden behind gathering black clouds, provided very little light. We marched single file at a ten-foot interval through the darkness. The only sounds came from our fatigues brushing against the tall reeds. After passing Mary OP, we took a circuitous route, checking the low rises in the valley. Charley was our seeing-eye dog leading us toward the base of Hill 317.

Every receptor in my body was ready to be tested. I would have overreacted to any stimulus. Creeping along at a determined but deliberate pace, I stumbled over a soft mass. *Damn!* What the hell was this?

It was Charley. He should have been at least twenty-five feet ahead of us, but he was bent over like a fetus.

"What is it, Charley?"

"Shit, hold it, hold it. My back is burning and itching!"

He removed the battery backpack and his wet fatigue shirt. We checked the battery. There were no caps over the wells. He had forgotten to screw them down when he checked the height of the acid in the battery. Bouncing over the irregular path had caused the sulfuric acid in the wells to spill onto his back. An armored vest, which he never wore, might have prevented the burns.

"Guys, pour your canteen water over his back," whispered Jeffries.

After he was relieved, Charley tied his shirtsleeves around his waist, gave the battery pack to Sergeant Jeffries, and continued the patrol bare-chested. That ended the use of the sniperscope for the night.

We reached the end point of our patrol without contact. From the middle of our column, Sergeant Jeffries gave the word to return. We left a narrow scar in the field behind us as we trampled down the reeds in the valley. A pheasant's nest was hidden at the base of the dense reeds. Charley passed it by, but Ken Brockett stepped directly onto it. The screeches, the flapping of the wings, and the sound of the bird sweeping by in the darkness froze us in our tracks. When the adrenaline stopped flowing and our heartbeats returned close to normal, we made our way safely back to the Smith Fence, up the free lane, and home.

It was a good night—a very good night.

We Came, We Fought, We Became Entangled

An occasional leaf sprouted from a scarred branch, but basically the wounded trees were naked. Some of their limbs had been violently amputated. Those that had survived the assault looked down on islands of scattered hummocks surrounded by a sea of sandy soil. This was our Korean MLR–the damaged panorama of a once pristine landscape.

Wright and I survey a barren and sad landscape.

We were intruders. We were not environmentalists. We came with ordnance to fight a war in a remote nation that was outlined on a map but never imprinted on our minds. Among the many pieces of soldiering equipment that quartermaster sent us were large spools of commo (communications) wire. Its insulation was black. Its diameter was about one-sixteenth inch. It had braided copper wire running through it. It would have remained coiled around the wooden spool had reliable walkie-talkies been reliable. Instead, a large spool of wire was suspended by canvas straps from the shoulders of our commo-man, John Mendel. After it served its purpose, the wire was cut and abandoned along the path we had taken through the hills and valleys. Many raids and many patrols left miles of wire blanketing the wounded terrain. It settled onto the soil, waiting to snake around the heel or toe box of a GI boot. Had it been green, it might have been mistaken for an annoying weed. Henry Gole, a retired special forces colonel, said at a seminar on the Korean War, "We walked out on patrols along paths lined with commo wire as thick as a man's arm, spinning yet another strand."

What to do with this forsaken nuisance? Send a sample home to educate our parents on the method of communicating to our company commander? Use it as a shoelace? Braid a key ring? Remove the insulation and make a copper ball? I don't think so.

Creative minds gathered the wire to express their ingenuity. Sergeant Blackwell wound it horizontally and vertically around a large rectangular wooden frame. He set it on six number-ten cans in his bunker. Now he had a bedspring for his sleeping bag. It wasn't exactly a Beautyrest, but it kept his sleeping bag six inches off the slick, cold, damp ground. Where did he get the wood for the frame? I never saw surplus wood in this country. I never saw anything surplus except commo wire. I guess rank had its privileges.

Some GIs used the wire to tie two or three belt loops together to narrow the waistline of the oversize pants they had received at the shower point. Others used it to replace broken dog tag chains. For me, trying to connect two insulated wires was like trying to make a knot with two strings of spaghetti. A gentle pull on my knot, and the wires came apart.

"It's easy. Just make a square knot," Charley Kauneckis told me.

Knowing what Charley thought of New Yorkers, there was no way I was going to ask him what a square knot was. To me, commo wire was meant to carry an electrical message, period. Knotting it was trial and error; for me it was mostly error.

Mention commo wire to any GI who was on the MLR during the Korean War, and he will sit you down and share a few stories about his experience with this abandoned black filament.

The Lister Bag

About fifty yards down the reverse slope of the MLR, alongside a footpath, stood a prototype of austere military architecture designed for hydrating the troops. It resembled a diagram from my high school plane geometry textbook. It left the onlooker with the impression that a child's swing was going to dangle from it, or something ominous like scaffolding from the Inquisition. Four seven-foot wooden two-by-fours joined to form a peak. Suspended from that peak was a chain, and dangling from the chain was the infamous Lister bag.

The bag resembled an inflated five-foot OD duffel. At the bottom, extending from its sides, were four black plastic spigots. Within the canvas walls of this bag was our elixir of life, our drinking water; our halazoned elixir.

The pathogenic critters that made their homes in the waters of Korea could have filled a textbook on parasitology. To make our water potable, the army engineers added halazone, a member of the chemical family of halogens—a family whose genealogy should have been diagrammed in my biology textbook along with the dysfunctional Jukes and Kallikaks.

As soon as the water entered my mouth, it coated my tongue, preventing any embryonic taste bud from blossoming to maturity. If the buds did survive, it took two days of nonstimulation to recover from the halazone assault. Exhaling through the nose while imbibing the drink assured the victim that he was swallowing a bottle of iodine.

In order to hide the symptoms of malaria, we were issued a chloroquine tablet every Friday. This caustic visitor was a perfect complement to the Lister bag water that washed it down. I suspect that some of our casualties could have been attributed to dehydration caused by the refusal to drink the water.

Twice a week, a water truck came to fill the bag. The driver would lift the lid from the bag, insert a hose, press a button, and let the bile flow. I surmised from the Mona Lisa smirk on his face that he had a private supply of real drinking water squirreled away somewhere in his tent.

Pancake Revenge

In June 1952, a strange order came from Sergeant Jeffries. Moving quickly through the trench line, he told us to leave ten grenades and five bandoliers of ammo in our bunkers and to dump any surplus in a collecting area at the base of the reverse slope.

"What if we need the grenades and ammo?"

"There are no patrols and no raids scheduled," said Jeffries.

"What's going on?" I asked.

"Just do as I say."

Sitting on top of two rectangular pine boxes in my bunker were a clump of grenades and bands of bandoliers that I had accumulated over the weeks. Inside the boxes, resting like eggs in a carton were British grenades nestled in thin wood shavings. Potentially, these grenades could be very effective. Unlike our US grenades, their ends could be screwed into one another, causing a devastating blast with twice as many fragments. But they were old and unreliable, legacies from a previous British company, and definitely candidates for the collecting area.

It was an extremely hot day. While I was struggling with the excess bandoliers and US grenades on the slope, I tried to find a better way of hauling the two heavy boxes of British grenades waiting in my bunker. Upon my return, I tied their rope handles to one another with commo wire. Then I attached some wire to the front rope handle and began pulling the boxes down the slope to the collecting area. Midway down the hill, Sergeant Jeffries spotted me and the boxes. He ran over and whacked me across my forearm.

"What the hell are you doing? Do you want to blow us apart?"

"It's unlikely," I replied. "The pins are bent."

"I'll bend your head! Anything can happen with grenades. I ought to write you up for a court-martial!"

I untied the boxes and carried each one down the hill to the collecting area, where they joined mortar rounds stacked on wooden skids and an arsenal of rounds for recoilless rifles.

After breakfast, Sergeant Jeffries gathered the platoon to tell us that we were going to the rear for rest, training, and replacements. As a treat, George Whitefeather invited the boys to see his sapling before he straightened and dismantled it.

"Go near that bunker and you might not return," I advised Charley.

"What's that crazy Indian up to?"

"Don't go near that tree. There's a crateful of grenades hanging from the branches."

"What? I have to see it. I don't believe it. He ought to be sent back to the reservation."

As Mr. Tolerance delivered that remark, a jeep arrived with our hot meal. Since we didn't have hanging over us the pall of raids, patrols, and blasts of incoming mortars, the plastic slices of ham became a savory entrée. Coffee had a stateside aroma, but not quite the taste. Our impending move to the rear put an end to Charley's daily scheme of going on a "one-man patrol" in the evening. This was my opportunity to learn what drove Charley.

"You're an RA [Regular Army], I was drafted," I began. "Why didn't you wait to be drafted?"

"If you were living in my house, you would have enlisted before your bar mitzvah, and you would have taken your rabbi along to keep an eye on you."

"What's going on here?"

Lancaster, who had returned with his squad from an early patrol, joined us.

"We were hit last night," he reported. "We couldn't find our way back. We were lost. Those suckers in battalion think there's a highway in that valley."

"Were there wounded?"

"Only a few scratches."

"Shut up, Lancaster. Charley was telling me about his life before the army."

Lancaster asked, "Where did you live, Charley?"

Charley was getting annoyed.

"You don't know where it is. You probably failed geography in your cracker, one-room schoolhouse. I lived in Newark, New Jersey, okay?"

"New Jersey? That's not living; that's dying."

"Get the hell out of here, Lancaster."

Of course Lancaster was not about to leave.

Charley went on. "My father hardly worked. He was a drunk who beat my mother. When my older brothers tried to stop him, she told them to get away and mind their own business. Both my brothers joined the navy as soon as they were eighteen. After they left, I dropped out of high school and joined the army."

"How old were you?"

"I was six-foot-two and sixteen and a half years old."

"Don't hand me that crap, Charley. The army took you at sixteen and a half?"

"I did a lousy job of changing my age on my birth certificate. The recruiting officer spotted it and sent me home. Then I went back when another recruiter was on duty. He didn't give a shit. I was in the army."

"Do you have a girlfriend?" I asked.

"Yeah. At every camp I've been to. Ask me their names. I was so drunk they could have been my mother."

At last the stars and moon appeared. The sound of men crawling up the reverse slope of our hill alerted me to the arrival of the Forty-Fifth Regimental Combat Team. In complete darkness, there was a somber exchange of positions with their men. It was an unfair exchange: a month of relaxation for a month of tension. Faceless silhouettes passed each other without uttering a word. We had no idea where we were going, but happily, we were going. Company L marched south for three miles. We couldn't move fast enough away from the MLR. Like gymnasts, we climbed into waiting two-and-a-half-ton trucks. Our silly chatter made a sharp contrast to the melancholy silence when we had passed our replacements.

When the trucks came to a halt, they became our guardians, and our backpacks became our pillows. We opened our sleeping bags, zipped up, and mummified ourselves. The stars shone brightly, twinkling as if to share the moment of pleasure we experienced knowing that our enemy was about five miles to the north.

A shrill whistle in the morning had us unzipped and eager to go—eager to go anywhere but north. Company L hopped onto the trucks, which would bring us to Shangri-la.

Some of the men of Company L in reserve.

In the morning, the smells and sounds of cooks preparing breakfast had us rushing toward a water hose for a "whore's bath" in our helmets. To celebrate our first day in reserve, Mess Sergeant Goff tried to add to our enjoyment by cooking stacks of pancakes.

I was never a fan of pancakes, so I had no idea how to gauge a good one. A cook dropped two into the center of my tray and then drenched them with syrup. With my canteen, I scooped up coffee from a large pot, and I then joined Andy Concha for the feast. Biting into the pancakes was like biting into the heel of a combat boot.

"Reilly," said Andy, "Sergeant Goff probably melted a jeep tire to make these pancakes."

"He should have melted the recipe," I replied.

When I left for the garbage drums with my two-bite pancakes, Sergeant Flaherty approached Sergeant Goff. He dropped a pancake at his feet, placed his boot over it, removed his bayonet from its scabbard, and proceeded to cut the pancake around the sole of his boot.

"We're off the line, Goff. It's time to resole our boots."

Andy Concha and I laughed hard and loud. Sergeant Goff glared at us in silence.

After breakfast, our platoon lined up on the company street. Details came rattling from Sergeant Jeffries. Most of the men were assigned to setting up squad tents. When the tents were up, cots were brought in to support our grateful bodies. Our sleeping bags, which formerly pressed against thin ponchos spread on damp ground, were to rest on dry canvas cots. Not exactly an innerspring, but there would be space between the cold, wet ground and us. Shallow drainage ditches were scooped out around each tent to catch rainwater.

Clearing the area for our camp in reserve.

On a rise above the far end of the company street, George Whitefeather and three other men dug a deep rectangular pit over which they unfolded a portable three-man wooden crapper. On the front line, our crapper was simply a groove scoured out by an entrenching tool. Toilet tissue was a choice of a few sheets of the latest *Stars and Stripes*, an out-of-date newspaper, or the last letter delivered by the mail clerk. Magazine pages were useless. They smeared, they skidded, they did not absorb, and they fought the cover-up soil. Here in reserve, sitting over a hole, we communicated with the bottom of the pit; there was no need for reading material. We had toilet tissue. The open-door—more accurately, the no-door—policy gave us a clear view of what had sent us here in the first place—Mess Sergeant Goff's steel-plate specials. Near this crapper, a Lister bag was suspended from a tripod—a fitting juxtaposition.

When the rest of our platoon left for their details, Sergeant Jeffries sent Andy and me for assignment to Sergeant Goff. What did he have in mind? Why us?

"Go to quartermaster and get a couple of shovels," said Goff. "I need a six-by-four-by-four-foot pit dug at the end of the company street. It's going to be my refrigerator until we return to the line."

I could see that pancake sole glaring from Goff's eyes. Okay, it was payback for laughing at his pancakes.

Sergeant Goff will have his state-of-the-art refrigerator.
Andy Concha presents me with the Distinguished Piss Tube Award.

The sun joined us in gouging out a rectangle in the dry soil. Our T-shirts were soaked and salted by the time we were finished. When the last shovel of dirt was scooped, we reported to Sergeant Goff. He smiled. He decided there was no need for a refrigerator.

"Now go fill the hole with the pile of nearby gravel."

We partially filled the hole with gravel; then we stuck a 155 mm shell casing, open at both ends, into it and protruding from the soil. Then we added more gravel. Now Company L had a urinal at the end of the street just like a Paris pissoir.

Don't Play with Him

Creative minds came up with creative assignments to keep the troops busy. Charley Kauneckis and I were selected to a detail pounding metal fence posts at fifteen-foot intervals around the periphery of our company area. At home I had difficulty hammering a nail into wood. How could I possibly pound metal fence posts into the ground? When it came to handling equipment of any kind, Charley was always there to bail me out.

After lunch, Sergeant Jeffries had the platoon line up on the street. I was assigned to read an order stating that any man found outside the metal posts (that we had just hammered) without authorization would be subject to a court-martial. The boys weren't very happy about being restricted to the company area, and they glared at me as if I'd made the rules.

When we returned to work, I improved my performance with the posts after Charley told me not to concentrate on the head of the post but just to look in its general direction.

I turned to Charley.

"Maybe the army is grooming me for a civilian occupation?"

"Naw, Reilly, a Jew doesn't work with his hands."

He had every ethnic group detailed and categorized. We finished the assignment late in the afternoon and then stretched out on our cots.

No soliciting! Charley Kauneckis guards our tent.

After a leisurely rest, Charley asked me to join him outside the tent. Pointing to a group of thatched Korean huts about a quarter of a mile from where we were standing, he whispered, "I know there are some *Mooses* in that village who want to see us." (*Moose* was GI slang for a young Korean girl, adapted from the Japanese word "*moosemay*.")

"Charley, we pounded posts around the company area all day today. It's a flat path to that village. We'll be court-martialed if they catch us."

"Follow me when it gets dark. The most obvious way is the least suspected. We won't get caught," he assured me.

The sun went down. At nightfall, we took off, Charley with a can of beer in his hand and a good deal more in his blood. Whatever possessed me to go with him? My mother would have said, "Beer? Danny. Beer? Don't play with him."

We were no more than two city blocks past the metal posts when I saw the silhouettes of three men approaching. I fell facedown on the ground. Through the corner of my eye I could see Charley sitting, sipping from his can and singing, "Arriang, Arriang, Ah-Ah Ree Oh." This was part of a Korean folk song popular with the GIs.

"Shut up and get down, Charley!" I whispered.

It was too late. The officer of the day and two corporals were standing over us.

"You know that if you're found outside the fence posts, you can be court-martialed. Walk back to the camp!"

After a few yards, I stopped.

"Sir, would you take into account that we were on the line for two months and—"

"Don't beg! Don't beg, Reilly! If there's one thing I can't stand, it's a beggar," growled Charley.

"Keep on moving to the camp," the officer said.

We moved on. Charley, unhappy to leave things as they were, threw his beer can up in the air and behind him.

"Look out, a grenade!" he shouted.

The officer and two corporals dropped to the ground.

Charley, saturated with beer, pointed to them and laughed. The embarrassed officer stood up, brushed himself off, and said, "I was going to let you guys go, but you've gone too far. We're going to your company commander!"

He marched us to our command post. Captain Smith wasn't there, but the officer who had brought us in identified us by checking our dog tags and left a note explaining what had taken place.

Within a week, Charley and I were told to report to the battalion commander's tent for a court-martial. We reported and waited. There was no sign of the commander. Finally I went to the sergeant to ask if the colonel knew we were there.

"Oh, yes, he knows. He'll be a while. He's wasted from a case of the Whistling GIs ["GIs" being the army term for diarrhea]."

"Whistling GIs? What's that?" I asked.

"Son, did you ever shit so fast your asshole whistled? That's the Whistling GIs."

When I get home I will look this up in the Merck Manual.

Finally the drained colonel joined us. He read the particulars of our crime and asked if we denied the charge. How could we?

For punishment, one month's salary was garnished, we would not be put in for promotion, and we couldn't change our allotment. We were felons.

He was not a candidate for the Good Conduct Medal, but Charley eased the stress in our lives with his outrageous, irreverent behavior and fearless heroics—on and off the line.

Unlisted Casualties

Sergeant Jeffries, our platoon sergeant, accumulated his forty points and went stateside. Sergeant Flaherty was assigned to his position.

To the shrieking whistle of Sergeant Flaherty's auburn walrus moustache, dawn gradually separated itself from darkness. A no-nonsense paratrooper, he demanded and received undivided attention. Aching bodies groaned and arose from snug canvas cots to hear the mission for the day.

"Get ready men! We have a new company commander—Lt. "Sid" Sidney. Good-bye to Captain Smith. Wash, shave, and carry your ass to breakfast. Sid said military business is why we're here."

"I don't like this," shouted George Whitefeather. "He sounds like chickenshit to me."

"Hey, Whitefeather, that's just what's on the menu for breakfast."

"What menu?" shouted Whitefeather. "Goff's greasy trays taste better than the crap he slaps on them."

Although he was an enlisted man and performed with valor, Whitefeather could not tolerate strict military business.

After breakfast, the company fell out on the street, and Lieutenant Sidney introduced himself as our new company commander. Tall, trim, twenty-five, and handsome, a World War II vet who had distinguished himself in combat, he was a paratrooper, like many men in our company.

An official photo of Lt. "Sid" Sidney.

"This is not summer camp," he said. "As soon as we get our replacements, we will train day and night so that when we return to the line, we'll be a crack infantry unit."

"I like that 'we,'" said Charley. "He's a paratrooper, not like that wimp, CP Smith. Now we have a company commander!"

With the prodding of Lieutenant Sidney, Goff made a serious effort in the kitchen to satisfy the men. Whitefeather said that there should be a can of beer with breakfast, lunch, and supper. Lancaster followed with "We need some real food. Where are the grits?"

"What are grits?" I asked.

"Grits?" asked Lancaster. "Grits could make SOS taste better than bacon and eggs."

The unmarked border surrounding the Bronx ghetto in which I was born and bred had limited my social and ethnic experience. A Long Island or Queens accent seemed alien but was easily understood. Enter Truman Bastin from Kentucky. He shared a bunker with Ken Brockett from Joliet, Illinois. Ken brought some accent baggage with him, but I had no difficulty with the translation. Truman spoke slowly, as if each word were a fragile gem that had to be polished before it was displayed. For John Hollier, a handsome, six-foot Cajun from Lafayette, Louisiana, I needed an interpreter. Words tumbled off his tongue through a gentle smile while I struggled to gather and piece them together. George Whitefeather came from an Indian reservation in Oklahoma. He spoke sharply and distinctly. Benny Hoover, from the hills of Appalachia in West Virginia, had a heavy southern accent highly spiced with local color. All of them, fun-loving GIs who either were drafted or had enlisted in the army, brought their colloquialisms with them. If I couldn't figure out their idioms, I smiled. We were an amalgam of various ethnicities, educations, social classes, and accents blended together into a rifle platoon seven thousand miles from home. Living in a tent together rather than in separate bunkers spread out on the MLR gave us an opportunity to discover our singularity.

Benny Hoover and Philip Dickson.

C-rations weren't exactly haute cuisine, but they produced very little garbage on the MLR. With Mess Sergeant Goff now cooking for about seventy men and following the exciting daily menu designated by the army manual, augmented with a few original steel-plate specials of his own, mounds of tested and rejected meals now waited to be carted off to the garbage dump.

Goff's creations generated three, sometimes four, overflowing gasoline drums of garbage daily. Their contents were to be disposed of by a two-man detail. The second week in reserve, Charley and I drew the assignment.

With the July heat as a catalyst, fumes of rot overwhelmed the mess area. Each open drum was covered by a "lid" of flies. We lifted the drums onto a small trailer hitched to a jeep. The driver moved along slowly so that our treasure wouldn't topple. An open pit about a mile from camp was our destination.

One would think that the stench of decay would have discouraged anyone with a sense of smell from approaching the jeep. No, I heard jabbering to our rear and turned to find a group of gaunt, shabby villagers following us, holding a variety of empty cans.

A dusty, narrow trail cutting through a wood led the Koreans and us to the garbage dump. It looked as if a bomb had gouged out a thirty-foot crater. Chattering birds competed with the monotone buzz of swarming, multicolored insects hovering, darting, and courting over the putrid garbage. Like a garnish on a dessert, beer cans impaled into a thick yellow custard reflected the sun's rays in every direction. This would have been an entomologist's collecting heaven, had such a scientist been able to forge through the quagmire of decay.

The driver backed the load to the edge of the crater. Charley and I jumped out. We lowered the door of the trailer, inverted the drums, and let our delivery bounce and flow to the bottom of the pit, where our flies joined their kin performing acrobatics over the muck. I couldn't wait to leave the filth and nauseating odor.

While we were unloading, the Koreans quietly formed around the crater's parapet. No sooner had we lifted the empty drums onto the trailer than these ragged, shoeless villagers scrambled down into the pit, running over open cans and broken bottles to gather Company L's fresh leavings. It was a painful, tragic scene. We left quickly.

Charley and I were hosing down the trailer and garbage drums near the mess tent when Sergeant Goff came by.

"Do you know those starving villagers are eating our garbage?" Charley asked. "Those poor *Gooks* ran over broken glass with bare feet to scoop it up."

The horrific sight had obviously registered with Charley, who I assumed would be the last man in our company to be sympathetic to a famished Korean. An enlisted man, a paratrooper-ranger, he was a warrior who rarely spoke about his feelings. I suspect, in his mind, using the word *"Gook"* tempered his uncomfortable evidence of compassion.

"Yeah, I heard it from Gillis," said Goff. "I told Lieutenant Sidney about it. He said he'll see what could be done."

The following day, Charley and I returned to the garbage detail. Just as on the preceding day, we were accompanied by the odor and the Koreans—not *Gooks*, but real people. Real people wearing real skin tightly covering their scrawny bones, wrapped in rags, waiting, with their toes curled over the rim of the crater, to scoot down and scoop up our garbage.

After we emptied the drums, our jeep driver took a five-gallon gasoline can from the jeep and walked around the parapet, drenching the garbage with gasoline. He backed us up, lit a match, and threw it into the pit. We stepped back as a roaring flame encircled the garbage. When the garbage reached its kindling point, a low flame covered the entire dump. With their arms limp, empty cans dangling from them, the Koreans glared at us as if we had snatched the food from their mouths. How could we explain this action to these pathetic, innocent victims of a barbaric war? I returned to the mess tent shaken by the experience.

Sergeant Goff asked if the garbage had been burned. Charley said yes and added that the Koreans were stunned by what we had done to their food.

"Last night Lieutenant Sidney told us that a number of Koreans were coming to our aid station with serious digestive problems. The Medical Corps ordered him to burn the garbage."

"Can't quartermaster send food?" I asked. "There aren't many of them."

"I have nothing to do with that," Goff replied.

I was a naive twenty-two-year-old. Giving them food seemed to me a simple remedy for this shocking tragedy. But military business continued in reserve under the old army adage: There's a right way, a wrong way, and the army way. We tried the right way. We disposed of our garbage in a dump. It turned out to be the wrong way. The Koreans ate it. The solution was the army way: Burn the garbage and offer no food assistance, the Koreans be damned.

Replacements

Where were the promised replacements? We needed men, we needed medics, and we needed officers. How could we return to the front line without them? While we were waiting for our assignments on the company street, three two-and-a-half-ton trucks pulled up to the command post. Bewildered GIs came tumbling out draped in stiff new OD fatigues. Typical of replacements, they huddled together waiting for someone to tell them where to go or what to do. No doubt I had been just as confused when I came to the company. But now I was a veteran.

Otis Curry, a huge man, was assigned to Sergeant Staszewski's machine gun team. Earl Davis and Ed Koster went to the weapons platoon; William Sappington, sent to our third squad, was immediately given a BAR; and CP Jones became a rifleman in our first squad. (We called him CP because when the men ribbed him, he always threatened to go to the command post to report them.) We needed a medic.

He blocked the sunlight, leaving a dark silhouette at the entrance to our squad tent. His compact medic bag was slung over his right shoulder. It was to become the hallmark of our new buddy. "Hi, I'm Wayne Caton." With a broad smile, he added, "I'm your medic."

"The red hair and freckles tell me you might be from the miserable coal mines of West Virginia—my country," said Benny Hoover.

"No, I'm from the miserable nothing of Frackville, Pennsylvania," replied Wayne.

Wayne said there was no future for a high school graduate in Frackville. With neither academic nor vocational skills, he'd dropped out of high school in the eleventh grade. When he turned eighteen, he enlisted in the army. After basic training, he was trained as a medic. Now here he was, the army's gift to the Second Platoon.

I don't know what generated our friendship. The only thing we had in common was our height—or rather our lack of it. He was Catholic; I was Jewish. He'd dropped out of high school; I was considering college. He came from a small town in Pennsylvania; I was born and bred in New York City. We eventually became inseparable.

How many of us would admit to our fear, our apprehension, about moving up to the MLR? Wayne was not anxious about his own safety, but could he do his job under the pressure of combat? That was his concern.

"What if I'm so scared I freeze and can't treat the wounded? What if the men need me and I run away when the shit starts coming at us? What if—"

Staszewski ended the discussion. "All of us are scared—even Charley, our point man. But we do what we have to do, and we get it done."

Wayne had a wonderful sense of humor. His pretense of deep concern upon opening his medic bag to find his morphine syrettes "missing" was an Oscar-worthy performance. He accused our entire platoon of stealing them.

"If the morphine isn't returned in two minutes, there will be general court-martials around here," he warned.

He waited without a response. We were onto his prank. When he turned to "leave the tent to report us to Lieutenant Sidney," we jumped him and scattered the contents of his medic bag. There were the syrettes, neatly stacked among his medic gear.

On a quiet Sunday morning, after breakfast, Wayne, with a bayonet in his hand, "attacked" George Whitefeather on his cot. George, a burly paratrooper, fell prone onto his cot, pretending that Wayne had successfully mugged him. He whimpered like a child, calling for Lieutenant Sidney. No one could have guessed that a war was going on about ten miles to the north.

Wayne Caton mugs George Whitefeather.

Wayne often spoke about his girlfriend, Carol, a high school cheerleader. Her photo revealed a very pretty and perky teenager.

"Do you think she'll wait until I return?" he asked.

I, Mr. Experience, replied, "I don't know, but if you're asking, maybe you think there's a problem. When did she last write to you?"

"About a month ago, when I was stateside."

"Let's knock her out of her saddle shoes with a letter," I said.

To get her close to Wayne's family, we pleaded with her to visit his mother regularly.

"When I shave in the morning," we wrote, "I see your face in the mirror." He assured her that he used sharp blades so "I won't cut you. If I did, I'm a medic. I'll take care of you."

The football season was approaching, and Wayne remembered how beautiful Carol looked in her cheerleader outfit.

"Please send a photo," we wrote. "Please remember me."

The letter didn't score any points. In a few weeks, he received a "Dear John" telling him she had begun dating a classmate after Wayne had left for the army. That was the end of our cheerleader.

Bent Pots, Bent Lids

Back in March, aboard the *General Simon Buckner*, we were shown the movie *Romance on the High Seas*. Although it was difficult to concentrate while hearing the waves pounding the sides of the ship, I remembered a fragment of that movie: it was Doris Day singing "It's Magic."

Months later, during the long, vacant hours between patrols and raids on the MLR, we wrote letters to family and friends. During one lull in the action, the segment of Doris Day singing "It's Magic" persisted in my mind. The place and the time were ripe to contact her. Facetiously, I wrote, "Maybe the sounds of war have distorted my sense of values. But I beg of you on bended knee, flecked with blackheads and scarred from barbed wire, please send me a photo of yourself." I addressed the letter to Paramount Pictures, Hollywood, California, and forgot about it soon after our mail clerk left in his jeep.

Three weeks later, a large manila envelope containing an eight-by-ten-inch photo of Doris Day arrived. Written in the lower right-hand corner was "Dear Danny" followed by a short apology for the delay in shipment. I kept the photo in my canvas backpack until our company was sent into reserve.

At the reserve camp, squad tents were set up alongside one another. Two wooden poles inside supported each tent. As soon as I was settled, I removed Doris Day's photo from the envelope and tacked it to the tent pole near my cot.

"Charley, what do you think of this interior decorating?"

Revealing the artistic sense I had expected, he replied, "I don't know, but I'd like to decorate her interior."

Why did I ask him?

Charley probably passed the word around that Doris Day was in our tent. Men from other platoons came in, touched the photo, and then kissed their hands. Others taped their girlfriends' photos below Doris's. It became a shrine.

A military camp is incomplete without an inspection. Saturday, after we'd had two weeks of training, Colonel Middlebrook, the regimental commander, arrived in a helicopter. He was trailed by the usual suspects, along with a chaplain and Lieutenant Sidney. The colonel started with the First Platoon's tent. He was apparently satisfied.

We stood at attention as the entourage entered our Second Platoon tent. Within seconds, the colonel came tearing out in an apoplectic fit, madly waving Doris Day's photo. In a frenzy, he shouted, "Where's the platoon sergeant?"

Sergeant Flaherty stepped forward.

"Who's Danny?" asked the officer

"Which Danny, sir? We have two of them."

"The Danny on this photo!"

"Reilly, step forward," snapped Flaherty.

The officer shook the photo in my face. "Does this belong in a tent?"

"No, sir," I replied.

After tearing the photo in half, he turned to Sergeant Flaherty and said, "Put this man on duty for a week."

"Yes, sir."

Upon completing the inspection, Colonel Middlebrook and his coterie left. Calm returned to Company L. The following day was Sunday. Usually attendance at services was not mandatory. However, this time Lieutenant Sidney ordered the entire company to attend. We marched to bleachers, where the chaplain greeted us. He apologized for intruding upon those who did not want to be there, but he felt he had a very important message for everyone.

"Yesterday," he said, "I accompanied Colonel Middlebrook in his inspection of your company. Everything was fine until we saw a photo of a movie star tacked to a tent pole. It should not have been there. It should not have been there because this is a military base. It should not have been there because you are setting a distorted standard for the woman you would want as your wife."

He paused.

"As I look over your company, I see many bent pots. And waiting for you when you get home, there are many bent lids that fit perfectly onto the bent pots. A perfect lid for you is a fantasy. It will not fit!"

The "bent pots" of the Second Platoon, second squad:
left to right, John Hollier, Dan Wolfe, Ken Brockett,
Wayne Caton, Truman Bastin, and Oscar Konnerth.

Glancing at one another, some men snickered, some sat quietly, and others restrained themselves from bursting out with laughter.

"God bless all of you. I will pray that you get home safely."

"For us bent pots?" whispered Wayne.

As Sid led the company back to camp, men were muttering about "bent pots" and where the indentations were on the lids.

Charley said he had never gone to services before, and after that one he never would go again.

Whitefeather was bent—bent over with laughter.

"You palefaces have powerful medicine men," he roared.

It's good to be friends with George Whitefeather.

It was a short and dusty march back to the company street. Before we were dismissed, Sid stood tall and silent before us. His pressed fatigues closely followed the contours of his athletic build. *Why can't I look as sharp as Sid?* I asked myself. *Is it my baggy fatigues? I'm not six foot two—maybe that's why. I don't have a handsome chiseled face—maybe that's why.*

Now it was Sid's turn to deliver his sermon.

"Men, my men, I am ashamed of you. You worship a picture of Doris Day fully dressed? The least you could do, not to embarrass me during inspection, is to have a naked broad nailed to your tent post. Company dismissed!"

He was new to the company. We didn't know much about him, but this was great for starters.

Sergeant Flaherty celebrated the inspection by ignoring the order to put me on duty for a week.

A Bale of Hay

One Saturday, after lunch, we had organized athletics, commonly called organized grabass, the cardiovascular and aerobic activities for the day. Some men just hung around, and others sparred with huge boxing gloves. There was a contest for throwing dummy grenades into an oil drum from a distance of twenty-five feet.

Two heavyweights put on gloves. Both were agile and dancing at a distance where neither could land a blow. The shuffling continued into the second round, accompanied by very angry glares. Earl Davis leaned over to me and said, "Look at that. One is scared, and the other is glad."

The match ended as it began. Not a blow was landed.

A softball game was organized. Yes, softball! Back home, Sunday mornings were softball mornings. I ran to get a lefty glove from quartermaster. But when I saw the opposing pitcher warm up, I realized I should have left the glove with quartermaster. He was a tall, muscular black man with a screaming fastball.

In the second inning, it was my turn to bat.

"Strike one!" shouted the black ump when the ball streaked across the middle of home plate.

Next pitch.

"Ball one," called the ump as the ball whistled through the same path as the first.

The pitcher stepped off the mound, trotted menacingly toward the ump and asked,

"What did you call that?"

With booming authority, the ump shouted,
"Strike two!"

"I thought I heard you call ball one."

"Oh, no," quavered the ump. "I … I just speak with an accent."

The game continued with bursts of laughter woven into each inning. I don't recall anyone on my team getting even a foul tip off that impossible-to-hit fastball. As the game was drawing to a close, a speeding jeep enveloped in a cloud of dust screeched to a halt near home plate. An officer was at the wheel, and two MPs were in the rear. Emerging from between them was Sgt. Benny Hoover from our platoon. His fatigues looked as if they'd been dragged through a rice paddy and rejected at a shower point. His eyes, redder than tracer bullets, competed with the lipstick smeared over his nose, lips, and jaw.

"Where's your CO [commanding officer]?" asked the officer.

"Try the command post," replied Sergeant Staszewski.

Pointing to Benny Hoover, who was frozen in an alcoholic daze, the officer said, "Put him under a shower and hose him down with sulfuric acid before I write him up for a court-martial."

"Why a court-martial? What did he do?" asked Staszewski.

"First of all, he was out of uniform. Then—"

Benny recovered enough to interrupt. "I'm sorry, sir. I forgot to steam and iron my corduroy spats!"

The officer and the MPs had had enough. They drove off. Benny managed to stagger toward us. Fumes of whiskey accompanied each exhale. Just standing upright was a major balancing act; reaching us was a monumental achievement.

"What did you do?" asked Truman.

"Aw, nothing. All I did was nicely ask a *Moose* (a Korean girl) to leave some lipstick on my dick as I held a broken beer bottle to her neck, and the low-down bitch called the MPs."

That being said, he belched and then cut loose with an earsplitting fart that could have fertilized all the rice paddy fields in the surrounding area.

"Now, now, Jungles," said Hoover, "don't go sniffing it all up. There's enough to go around for everyone!"

I deposited this line securely into my memory bank. What was there to say after this tasty tidbit? We returned to the end of the softball game.

I dressed down for a visit from Bucky Praver.

"I told you to take a *little* off the top, Benny."

In the evening formation, Lieutenant Sidney announced that beer, which had accumulated while we were on the MLR, would be available at dinner. The company responded with a roar.

Before I came to company L, beer rations were allocated on a limited basis. Men who didn't drink gave their cans to the men who drank beer. A sergeant who emptied a number of cans led an evening patrol. In his attempt to return to the MLR, he led his men north instead of south. They ran into a Chinese patrol, and one man was killed. After this alcoholic blunder, beer rations came to a halt.

The cans of beer were consumed before their tabs hit the ground. A festive energy in the air brought out the best and worst of Company L. Gillis, our wimpy company clerk, became drunk and aggressive. Sergeant Lancaster was trying to support, as well as restrain, him.

"Reilly, give me a hand," he shouted.

I ran over to take Gillis's free arm. Before I could grab it, his fist rocketed up from the ground and came crashing onto the side of my jaw. It was as if my skeleton had dissolved. There was no pain; I just dropped to the ground like a deflated balloon.

From my sandy repose, I hazily focused on a pair of dusty boots moving toward me. The bottoms of his grimy fatigues formed a ragged veil around them. Above the fatigue shirt was a disheveled awning of wavy white hair shading beet-red skin splotches reserved for people with wavy white hair. If there was a casting call for a wizened combat infantry veteran who disregarded his own safety in order to protect his men, Sergeant Hoover's heroics defined him. The squint in the eyes had a look of disbelief, no matter what he was being told. This was Sgt. Benny Hoover.

Hoover offered me his hand. On the line, we had met during dry runs for raids, or occasionally on patrol. His bunker was off to the far right. Now, in our squad tent, his cot was within whispering distance from mine.

"Hi, I'm Dan Wolfe. Charley Kauneckis calls me Reilly. I'm in the second squad. I guess you didn't see too much of me on the MLR."

"Yeah, I saw your ass around," he replied.

Not too friendly, I concluded. But I continued. "Whenever I see you, Jungles from the Third Platoon is attached to you like a barnacle."

"That Jungles. I can't get rid of that snaggletoothed scalawag. I tried everything—even the insecticide we were issued last week."

"He told me you're the funniest guy he ever met."

"Did you ever hear him laugh? God damn it, every time he laughs, he makes my asshole pucker. How can we ship that bucket of lard back to Wisconsin?"

"Where are you from, Benny?"

"Hinton—Hinton, West Virginia. Did you ever hear of it?"

"No."

"I didn't expect you would. It's so small it has a bale of hay for a train station. When a passenger wants to get off at Hinton, the train slows down, the passenger squats, the conductor kicks him in the ass, and he lands on the bale of hay; then the train moves on."

Jungles spotted us and ran over to report the latest news. "Lieutenant Wilhoit told me we're moving up next Friday," he said.

"Jungles," said Benny, pointing to his fly, "get on your kneepads and hit this thing a lick or two."

I realized why Jungles followed Benny. Gales of laughter always swirled around him. As the days in reserve passed, I became as friendly as one could with Benny Hoover. He was a private person who kept a space between him and the rest of us.

The beery sounds of celebration were everywhere. I wandered toward the beginning of our company street where the officer's tent was staked. Sitting on a cot, Lieutenant Sidney; our new platoon sergeant, Sergeant Flaherty; and Sergeant Massengale were reminiscing about their paratrooper school days.

Do I dare listen? I wondered. *Why not? Flaherty and I are buddies. I frequently speak to Sergeant Massengale. He feels his paratrooper training can get him through any mission. We'll depend upon one another when we return to the MLR. Sid wouldn't mind having me hear them.*

How did Sergeant Flaherty inflate those pants?

Ignoring me, they lined up behind one another, reliving the shuffle paratroopers do as they approach the open door of the airplane. Under the influence of alcohol, the choreography was not pretty. For their finale, they plopped onto a cot for another brew.

Sid asked, "Which jump frightened you most, Flaherty?"

Without hesitating, Flaherty said, "All of them."

Although I was an eavesdropper, I worked up the courage to ask, "What about the first jump? That must have been a fright."

"No," said Flaherty. "You don't know what to expect. After that, we knew what to expect, and we kept a tight asshole."

Massengale turned to me and said, "Don't listen to him, Reilly. I just about shit in my pants on my first jump."

All of them nodded in unison.

I noticed a flickering candle at the far end of the company street. What was going on there? Like a moth, I made for the light. The candle was pushed into the depression of a pup tent pole segment that had been pierced into the ground. Alongside the flame, Whitefeather was in the process of draining the beer from a twenty-four-can carton. Encouraged by alcohol, he was singing what sounded like an Indian chant to the accompaniment of two colliding crushed beer cans. I was not about to interrupt, so I left.

The following morning, on the breakfast chow line, I was describing Whitefeather's solo to Andy Concha. Whitefeather was a few places in front of me. His vacant stare was lost in a face that appeared to be inflated by a gas station air hose. I asked him what song he'd been singing the night before. He did not reply. It appeared to me that the alcohol was still in his veins. Stupidly, I repeated the question.

He spun around, glared, and asked, "What are you, a wise guy?" His eyes narrowed. "I just want to know one thing; are you a wise guy?"

I did not answer. For a few days, I made sure our paths did not cross. The hangover wore off, the incident wore off, and we were buddies again.

In the Line of Duty

Now we had a medic and a platoon sergeant. All we needed was a platoon leader. Lt. James Boatner was assigned to us after graduating from West Point. He was correct, and he kept a distance between himself and the men. When preparing for a trial raid or patrol, he offered a thorough explanation of each man's role—a product of his West Point training. He was the son of Gen. Haydon Boatner, who had put down a bloody Chinese Communist uprising at the prison island of Koje-Do two months before Lieutenant Boatner came to us.

Our new platoon leader noticed that Wayne always made a special effort in our exercises to be at the center of the platoon, where he could be seen and be quickly available to the wounded. One morning when we were lined up in formation, Lieutenant Boatner said, "I saw you in our training exercises, Caton. The men know where you are. They can count on you."

"Yeah, but the bullets and shrapnel weren't coming at me, sir."

Lieutenant Boatner was startled. "The men know they can count on you, Caton," he repeated.

After breakfast, on a rainy morning, the company gathered under two connected squad tents. Lieutenant Sidney stood at a chalkboard, diagramming our training exercise—an attack on a fortified position. The rhythmic tapping of raindrops played a sluggish lullaby on the stretched roofs above us. Some men were half asleep, while others were fighting it. Seated on his helmet, about fifteen feet to my left, one of our drowsing replacements was making a serious effort to stay awake. To avoid falling forward, he supported himself by clutching onto the trigger housing of his BAR. A magazine was in the chamber, his finger was on the trigger; the safety was not engaged. He nodded and then leaned forward. Suddenly a short burst of bullets fractured the air inside the tent. Everyone dropped to the ground. *Should I look up? Who fired? Are we in danger? What happened?* I wasn't about to find out, so I lay there. Sid had our platoon sergeants quickly move the men out of the tents and into rain. Bohrer, a friend of Benny Hoover, had been shot in the head. He had been due to rotate in a month. Bohrer had been sitting next to Enrique, a recent replacement who was given a BAR as his weapon. Medics arrived and removed the body.

Benny angrily snapped, "He hasn't seen the last of this."

In a combat zone, accidental deaths occur; but in reserve, we did not expect it. Our elation at being pulled off the line was tempered by this horrible accident.

"What will the army tell his parents?" asked Wayne.

"A chaplain comes and says he was killed in the line of duty," replied Charley.

"That's a lie!" Wayne exclaimed.

Charley couldn't put up with this. "Do you want the chaplain to tell them he was killed by a man sitting next to him while in reserve?"

Wayne was left without a response.

With Lieutenant Sidney at the front, Company L marched to the training area. We gathered around Lieutenant Boatner to review our role in the capture of the fortified position. In spite of having a new company commander, the men went listlessly through a dry run, with Bohrer weighing heavily on their minds. Then we repeated the exercise halfheartedly, capturing the "enemy's" fortified position using live ammo.

Before we were dismissed, Lieutenant Sidney addressed the men.

"What happened today was an accident. Accidents should not happen. Accidents will not happen in my company in the future. Rounds or no rounds in your weapon, your weapon will always be locked. We will not lose a man again because of an accident. Company dismissed."

The Naked Maja

Upon returning to camp from capturing the fortified position in the training exercise, a refreshing fine drizzle awakened our platoon of dejected riflemen. Slick brown patches of mud at the bottoms of evaporating puddles pocked the company street. Sid decided that these pools of muck could be leveled and dried by mounding them with sand. So, after lunch, there was a call to volunteers for a sand detail. Company L's biggest goof-offs and eight-balls eagerly volunteered. Because eight-balls and volunteers are immiscible categories, I suspected it was more than sand they were after.

"I don't know," said one GI when I asked, "but if Hoover's going, I'm going."

I thought this was a wise observation, so I hopped into a trailer with the rest of the volunteers.

The road had more grooves in it than my preteen corduroy knickers. Potholes? These were cauldron holes, and the jeep driver didn't miss any of them.

"Damn! This ride is mashing my hemorrhoids to a blood pudding," wailed Benny. "It's rougher than a cruise on a Higgins boat."

"What's a Higgins boat, Benny?

"You saw them in the World War II newsreels. They were the boats that carried the infantry to shore on D-day. Twenty of us were heading toward Utah Beach when the Germans zeroed in on our boat with a heavy machine gun. The sound of the bullets bouncing off the front ramp was like a snare drum. When the ramp was lowered, seven men in front of me dropped—they were hit."

This might have contributed to the rapid tic in Benny's jowls.

"Speaking of hit," he fumed, "that son-of-a-bitch who killed Bohrer hasn't yet heard from me."

I wasn't about to ask him what he had in mind, but within a few minutes, we arrived at a village. Its primitive huts were arranged in a semicircle. They appeared to be composed of dried mud supported by occasional stripped tree trunks embedded into their walls. The roofs were dense with straw. All the villagers probably had the same architect; their huts were tan clones of one another. The sun's rays focused on a nearby community privy. I suppose it wasn't a violation of the zoning code, but in this heat and recent rain, the escaping fumes broadcast an aroma through the area that could have stunted the growth of a newborn.

Our men hopped off the trailers. With haste in their legs and determination in their eyes, they rushed to the right.

Where are they going? I wondered. *The sand pile is on the left. Well, why not follow them?*

A queue had already formed in front of a hut, as if Canadian Club or weed was being sold within at discount prices. This notion was soon dispelled when I saw a GI emerge not with a bottle or a joint, but buttoning his fly.

I got in line behind Benny. He came out quickly, shaking his head.

"I've seen a better ass on my neighbor's sow back in Hinton," he said.

It was my turn. I crossed the threshold into a dark, dreary dampness. *Mamasan* was off in the far corner, ironing a white cotton garment with an iron whose base was filled with embers of glowing charcoal. A dejected *Papasan* was squatting in another corner, puffing on a long, narrow pipe and staring off into space. What was he smoking?

Suspended from a rope connected to opposite walls was a rag of a curtain. I pushed it aside. Lying on her side, stretched out like the subject of Goya's *Naked Maja,* wearing baggy, once buff-colored GI-issue long johns, was the magnet that drew the volunteers. Her feet and ankles and the cuffs of her baggy underwear suggested that she had scampered through a recently fertilized rice paddy. Deep brown faded to tan as the eye traveled north. Dirt stains tinted the elastic waistband and its surrounding areas from the active fingers that had raised and lowered the garment. As I approached her, she went through her sensual calisthenics. Smiling demurely, she wiggled, lowering her long johns. Irregular globules of flesh skidded toward whichever direction she leaned, forming a puddle of cellulite on her straw mat. Through no fault of her own, her mouth was a candidate for a medical textbook on dental pathology. The three or four teeth taking temporary residence in her lower gums were color-coordinated with the stained waistband of her long johns.

When she began a circular seductive rub of the mounds of dimpled flesh that had migrated toward her side, I pivoted and ran toward the door. Andy was not far off. He was one of the few men actually shoveling sand.

"Hey, Andy, did you see that mess?"

"Which mess? The girl or the house?"

"Both," I said.

"So what? Do you have anything better?"

"Yeah. Nothing."

What a day! Death and living death.

When the casualty lists for the Korean War were finalized, under which category did this tragic soul fall?

Paradise Lost

Lieutenant Boatner had been with us only two weeks when we received orders to move up to a blocking position behind an untested South Korean company on the MLR. That afternoon, a helicopter landed at the edge of our camp. A short, bulky officer stepped out. It was Gen. Haydon Boatner. After the general had a brief chat with our officers, Lieutenant Boatner, our platoon leader, stepped into the helicopter with his father. The helicopter rose and turned south. That was the last we saw of our platoon leader.

I turned to Charley and Joe Trippi from the Third Platoon. "It's nice to have a papa in the business."

"That's all you Jews think about—business," replied Charley.

Joe came from a small town near Buffalo, New York. We'd spent evenings reminiscing about our pre-army lives with Wayne and Charlie. One evening Joe turned to me and asked, "Were you a delinquent?"

"A delinquent?" I asked. "What are you, nuts?"

"You stole potatoes from the market and broomsticks from the fire escapes, didn't you?"

Sweet Joe insisted this was stealing. Charley chimed in.

"Reilly's gang were a bunch of pussycats. We had criminal records."

"I'd better get out of here," said Wayne. "I'm surrounded by a bunch of gangsters."

In response to my remark about Boatner and his papa, Joe asked, "Where do you think Boatner has gone to?"

"Not where we're going," I replied.

"Not we—you," said Joe. "I'm sorry; I'm rotating in a week."

"Sorry?"

"I hate leaving the company when you're moving up."

This was Joe. He wasn't playing the hero game. He truly meant what he said.

"The men will probably look at me the way you looked at Boatner heading south."

"Joe, I wish I was in your boots."

Three days later, we boarded trucks heading toward the blocking position. Joe was there to see us off.

Left to right, Joe Trippi, Sergeant Fostine Rutledge, and John Mendel.

Lieutenant Theiss, a redhead from Washington Heights in Manhattan, replaced Lieutenant Boatner as our platoon leader. Our platoon was designated the advance party for our move to the blocking position. We broke down our tents, gathered our gear, and picked up all the marbles; the game was over. Our playground was gone. Our paradise was lost.

Note

During the uprising at Koje-Do, the Chinese prisoners captured General Dodd, a negotiator for the army, and then forced General Colson, the commander of the island to sign a document admitting to the maltreatment of prisoners. This was an extreme embarrassment to the United States. General Boatner was called in because of his toughness and familiarity with Chinese culture. He issued an ultimatum to the prisoners in Compound 76, telling them to halt the uprising lest live ammo be used to stop it. On June 12, after six tanks and paratroopers marched in to end the revolt, the prisoners surrendered. Forty-five Chinese and one paratrooper had been killed.

When Lieutenant Boatner took off in a helicopter heading south just before we moved up to the blocking position, the men in our platoon thought he was being transferred to a safer area. Forty-five years later, at a reunion of my company, he told me that he was transferred to the regiment and line company in which his father had served when the general was a platoon leader.

Lieutenant Boatner distinguished himself as an officer and heroic leader. He retired from the army as a lieutenant general.

Let Me Entertain You

Who knew where we were going? I didn't. What was a blocking position? Was it like the MLR, with bunkers, barbed wire, and trenches? At this point, it was just another new word in my expanding military vocabulary.

In the morning formation, Lieutenant Theiss introduced himself as our new platoon leader. He had recently graduated from Officer Candidate School, he said, and was ready to learn whatever we could offer. Accompanied by Lieutenant Sidney, he walked through the ranks, learning the names of his men.

At breakfast, Lieutenant Theiss joined Charley and me as we were declumping the powdered scrambled eggs that were bouncing on our trays.

"Wolfe, you sound like a New Yorker, from my part of the world."

"Call him Reilly," said Charley. "Yeah, he's one of your guys, a New York Irishman."

Lieutenant Theiss looked me over, "New York, yes. Irishman, I don't think so."

We needed a leader with a sense of humor. Lieutenant Theiss was our man.

"Lieutenant Sidney said you two work well together."

"Did he figure that out from our court-martial?" asked Charley.

Theiss laughed. Then he asked if I would be the runner for the platoon.

What's a runner? I wondered. We didn't have one when we were on line previously. I asked Charley what was involved.

"Take it. We'll work together."

I quickly replied, "Yes."

To Gus Chobot's chagrin, Lieutenant Theiss appointed him to take my BAR, joining Truman Bastin as the second BAR man for our squad. I handed the heavy weapon and cartridge belt to Gus with relief and ran to Massey, our armorer, for a lightweight carbine.

"To your health!" Gus Chobot in our blocking position.
Truman Bastin at the ready.

Our platoon was to be the advance party at the blocking site. After breakfast, we gathered our gear and boarded a waiting truck. We searched for comfortable niches between tent stakes, poles, two heavy folded canvas squad tents, and a load of other military paraphernalia. I squeezed in with my backpack, my carbine, and the image in my head of the pitiful Koreans in tattered clothes gathered around the edge of our garbage dump. Their startled gaze as the flames consumed their food still haunted me.

With the truck moving steadily north, CP Jones burst out with a melancholy Negro spiritual. It was like a scene from a 1940s Hollywood movie. When his song ended, applause from the men brought a wide grin from Jones, brightening the dismal canvas-covered rear of the truck.

When we finally came to a halt, there was no sign that humans had ever been in the area. Healthy trees dense with leaves told me we were not close to the MLR. We dragged the tents and supplies from the rear of the truck. I could easily do that. I was also able to hold a pole that supported our tent, and I could help clear the bushes, but I deferred to Charley Kauneckis and Ed Heister for pounding in stakes. Once the tent was standing, the branches overhead with their lush blanket of leaves had us well hidden. Our beloved canvas cots became the highlight of the tent's interior decor.

Ed Heister in the blocking position.

After three days, our creativity with C-rations had grown as stale as the dull, dry crackers inside the tins. Hoover was poking at his ham and lima beans.

"By God, I was so hungry I could eat the asshole out of a skunk. But this crap is manure even in Hinton."

While our men were daring their digestive systems to break down and absorb these rations, Wayne pulled out and lit a "Cuban cigar" and puffed away in cadence to our gasping. His red hair and freckled face were completely lost in smoke. He hacked, he coughed. With tears in his eyes, he wheezed, "It's the perfect treat after a dinner such as this." Then he flicked the ashes into his empty C-ration can.

Wayne Caton puffs on his stogie as he and John Hollier prune Otis Curry, with CP Jones in the background as an audience.

"Whitefeather, where did he get that cigar?" I asked.

"From the way it stinks, he probably rolled up some sheets of slightly used toilet paper."

Wayne, flushing the smoke from his mouth, replied, "You guys got to learn what a good Cuban cigar smells like."

"What a good Cuban cigar smells like?" asked Benny Hoover. "It smells like an outhouse for a family wasted by an overdose of chitlins."

"Chitlins? What's chitlins?" I asked.

"Don't make me tell you. My boots will be caked with vomit just thinking about them."

On the fourth day, the rest of the company arrived, along with Mess Sergeant Goff. Certain that he had no refrigerator-digging plans, I was overjoyed to see him and his men. Real infantry food! We gladly helped unload his supplies and equipment.

It was the practice of the Chinese to hit a South Korean unit with an all-out assault whenever they were assigned to the MLR. Evidently the South Korean company for whom we were blocking was giving a good account of itself. There was no call for backup.

The stars and moon provided our evening light. At nightfall, I saw the shadow of Benny Hoover returning from what he called "hoeing the garden" (digging a slit trench with his entrenching tool and emptying his bowels into it). He began the evening's forum by cursing out the moose who had called the MPs on him when we were in reserve. This initiated a dialogue by the more experienced men about their sexual conquests. John Hollier, Oscar Konnerth, Truman Bastin, and Ed Heister listened uncomfortably. Whitefeather said it was nobody's business. Charley Kauneckis's wild story began when he was a fifteen-year-old, with his neighbor in Newark, and ended in Japan, with sneaking out of the Camp Drake reception center through a large sewer pipe leading to a cab outside, which took him to a cathouse in Yokohama.

Wayne said, "I pass."

I told my story about the terror that consumed me at the age of sixteen when my friend Peter took me to a whorehouse in Montreal.

CP Jones, our black baritone, was a recent replacement. Perhaps he thought that telling his story would further ingratiate him with the boys. He was a devout black Southern Baptist, he said, and he had committed no sins that he knew of, but one day while he was in the field with his friend, they picked a ripe watermelon. His friend reamed out a hole in the sun-baked fruit and proceeded to insert his penis into the watermelon while fantasizing that he had a woman. CP said that his friend then bored another hole for him.

Lancaster, our tolerant representative from South Carolina, found this hilarious. "Why didn't you put some grits in that hole after your nasty carousing? They would have cooked in all that sizzle, and you would have had a meal."

After this bizarre tale, we went to sleep. In fifteen minutes, I heard some shuffling followed by silence. I could see Lancaster's silhouette near CP Jones's cot. Lancaster had attached his luminescent watch to a thin twig. After jostling Jones's cot, he circled the watch over Jones' head. Jones awoke with a start and saw the spiraling glow. In a daze, he pleaded, "Please, Lord, I didn't do anything. I didn't violate any woman."

By this time, everyone was up. Although some men were half asleep, others were overcome with laughter.

•

On Saturday, to complete our defensive positions, Lieutenant Theiss selected areas that had good fields of fire. This, of course, meant digging. It was midday. The July sun was merciless. Hands, arms, and fatigues were caked with tracks of mud.

After a while, Lieutenant Theiss emerged from the bushes to tell us to stop digging and clean up. "Take your weapons. Trucks are waiting to bring us to a USO show a couple of miles to the rear."

There was very little water for cleaning, so we sponged off from a helmet full of quickly muddying water.

Trucks brought us to a clearing where a hill gently sloped toward a stage. Once we were settled on the hill, the star of the show was waiting to be introduced. She was an attractive young lady with long black hair. Our debonair fashion connoisseurs enthusiastically appreciated her very tight, shimmering blue satin gown. As the sophisticates of Company L eagerly awaited her performance, an emcee stepped onto the stage to announce, "Straight from the concert halls stateside, I give you Rima Rudina!"

"I'll take her! I'll take her!" replied a suave GI from the First Platoon.

"Hey! I'd like to ream her!" shouted Charley.

The pieces she played on her violin were unfamiliar, but it didn't matter. The boys were following her every move as if she were a stripper, not a violinist.

A pathetic comedian in oversize fatigues followed. He tried to entertain, but his act was embarrassing. Probably the free meals had induced him to come to this unhappy part of the world.

Closing the show was the pièce de résistance. She went by the name of Olga—a faded, aging accordionist with intense jet-black hair and fleshy upper arms that vibrated to the tune she squeezed out of her instrument. Her giant black eyelashes resembled the bristles of a shoe brush I had at home. She looked as if she'd been hit in the eyes by two blue-green paintballs. She wore a world-weary, low-cut, red strapless gown. The gown could have been cut down to her ankles without revealing a thing or two. Her aging skin resembled the undulating topography of Korea. She had come to entertain the boys, and she had a captive audience.

Olga ended her performance by playing and singing, "A Guy Is a Guy," gyrating like an aging diner waitress in cadence to the discordant notes escaping from her mouth and her accordion. When her recital was over, an officer stepped up to the mike and said, "Let's hear it for Olga! Wasn't she great?"

This brought whistles and applause from the appreciative GIs of Company L.

"Where are you from, Olga?" asked the officer.

"I'm from the Bronx, New York."

"Is anyone out there from the Bronx?" he asked.

A few of us shouted, "Yes!"

"Well, come on down to have a group photo taken with Olga."

We rushed down to the stage and bunched together. The *Stars and Stripes* photographer asked us to make a tighter group. I thought I had washed my arms, but I guess I missed a few spots. I placed my forearm over Olga's shoulder and upper arm, thinking she'd be delighted to have a twenty-two-year-old press down her wrinkles. But she looked at the sweat and muddy tracks I'd left on her shoulder and said,

"Oh, no! Get him ahvay. He's impussible!"

Playing to the boys from the Bronx, I replied, "Oh, I'm quite pussible; try me."

"Soldier, is this how you treat an artist who traveled to this dangerous area in order to entertain you?"

"I'm sorry, sir. I thought I was being clever."

I escaped without punishment.

Although these weren't outstanding performers who came to entertain us, it didn't matter. The sight and sound of a civilian trying to divert us was very much appreciated. Despite the publicity they received, stars from Hollywood came no closer than Seoul.

•

At the end of the second week, Company L received orders to move up to the MLR. By now Lieutenant Theiss and the platoon were a cohesive unit of grown-up Depression babies. Without a higher education, without connections, we formed the nucleus of the front line infantry as similar units had in World War I and World War II. Here were twenty-two-year-olds, with blue collars under our armored vests, fighting a war seven thousand miles from home because of a domino theory proposed by striped-pants old men in Washington.

We left for the western flank of the Iron Triangle in the Chorwon Valley, near our old position. I was the platoon runner. My BAR was history. Runner sounded like a much better assignment. I had no idea what was in store for me.

A Room with a View

Our week and a half in the blocking position gave us a brief life of leisure. Blocking position was a temporary assignment a few ridgelines behind a unit that was expected to receive heavy attention from the Chinese; however, we were behind a South Korean unit whose performance on the line was excellent, so our support services weren't required. Now it was our turn to move up and practice our trade.

We bid our treasured canvas cots bye-bye, loaded our equipment onto trailers pulled by jeeps, climbed into trucks, and headed north. Company L was going back to the MLR.

A company's location is usually identified by the outposts it controls. The Imjin River snaked between our position and our outposts: Little Nori, Big Nori, and the Bubble. In order to reach them, we used a four-man jon boat (a small, flat-bottomed metal boat). One man in the boat pulled us across, using an overhead rope anchored to a pole on each side of the river. Frequently, the Chinese would detonate variable time (VT) mortar rounds above the rope. Their goal was to sever the rope and kill or injure the men in the boat. Occasionally they succeeded. This brought a call to battalion for engineers to replace the rope.

Wayne Caton and I shared a bunker overlooking the Imjin. Massey, our armorer, had a surprise for the troops. He distributed rubberized gray air mattresses so that the damp soil wouldn't penetrate our sleeping bags. We inflated the mattresses with our mouths and then tucked in the stoppers. Now we were sleeping about two inches above the ground. After three days, Wayne and I descended to earth on two flat rubber sheets. Sharp pebbles, unhappy with our comfort, had penetrated our luxury beds and added another layer to our poncho carpeting.

Our bunker was a rectangular hole in the ground. Interior decorating was limited to bandoliers and magazines of ammo in wooden grenade boxes, two limp sleeping bags, and our backpack.

In the morning, we tried in vain to fluff our damp fart sacks (sleeping bags), which were compacted at the points where our bodies made contact with the deflated air mattresses. To acquaint the bags with fresh air, we spread them, unzipped, on the roof, where they blended in with the existing camouflage of sturdy logs interspersed with tree branches to protect us from incoming mortar rounds. At the front of our bunker, facing the river, was a rectangular firing hole. With our outposts on the other side, and the river in front of us, an assault on our position was unlikely.

Our little shack would not have been on the real estate market very long, in spite of its hazardous location. The rental fee, with the option to buy, was reasonable. The immediate neighbors were friendly. Dress for dinner was informal. The central location gave the resident easy foot access to points of interest. It had a wonderful view of the Imjin River flowing gently by. The peaks and arcs of endless mountains across the horizon created a dramatic sylvan panorama. An enticing ad for this prime piece of real estate would have been a photo captioned "A Room with a View!" The negative— no utilities—could be readily dismissed: reasonably priced candles were purchased by any soldier going on R & R to Japan. Clean drinking water was always available from a nearby Lister bag, if one enjoyed the taste of iodine. Running rapidly in place generated no-cost heat. For toilet relief, we grabbed an entrenching tool, dug a slit in the ground, and were in business. Supermarket? Ridiculous. Mouthwatering varieties of well-balanced, nutritious meals were delivered cost-free in easily opened C-ration cans, which came with their own can opener. This was a must-not-miss deal.

While in reserve and at the blocking position, we had forgotten the rules of the game.

"Spread it out! Spread it out! One Ping-Pong ball will get you all!" was the cry from Lieutenant Theiss when we lined up too tightly for our first hot meal on the chow line.

The summer heat and humidity were relentless. Within a week, a white T-shirt became a camouflaged garment. After three weeks of pickling our fatigues in sweat and dirt, we were taken, in groups of three, to a shower point in the rear. With plastic gloves, a corporal at the strip area fingered our peeled-off fatigues and added them to a growing pile on a tarpaulin.

The showers were in a squad tent hidden in a grove of trees. Sprinkles of water dampened us from overhead pipes. It was not easy parting with the layers of perspiration we had accumulated from a scorching two weeks in blocking position and three weeks on the line. While washing one other's backs, we leveled a multitude of pimples and blackheads with a block of GI soap. Soap! Water! Towels! For brief moments after our exposure to these, we were no longer burrowing animals. With the baptism of dribbling water, we became human beings!

Dried and naked, I left the shower tent. A corporal handed me a T-shirt, socks, and underwear, plus a fatigue shirt and pants. Usually this last couple had a marriage that was barely consummated in color and size. The tops of the shirt's chest pockets began slightly above my waist and ended somewhere near my knees. I wore shirt size thirty-six; size forty-four had been thrown at me. Lost in the shirt, I returned to the corporal to ask, "Where are the pegs for this tent?"

He did not appreciate this.

"How would you like the fatigues you just turned in?" he asked.

I left. For the next two months, I would struggle and sweat with my upper body lost in yards of olive drab cotton above and below my beltline. I probably resembled a dwarf. But in the society I was moving in, no one noticed.

A jeep brought the three showered GIs back to the business of soldiering. Clean and refreshed, we were home in time for dinner. Diesel fuel burning in a machine gun canister was waiting to heat our C-rations. I removed my can opener from my bellows pocket and began rocking it around the can. Then I mixed my corned beef hash with Charley's prized can of frankfurters and beans. Yes, we were back in the soldier business. Our company had yet to explore the new neighborhood.

Dulce et Decorum Est

On Tuesday, August 5, 1952, the Second and Third Platoons were awaiting a briefing from Lieutenant Sidney.

"This Friday we're going to raid Hill 117. The Third Platoon will provide the base of fire, and the Second Platoon will attack. Save some ammo for when we withdraw, and try to grab a prisoner. Before we leave, test fire your weapons. Pick up your bandoliers, grenades, and canisters from Massey. Any questions?"

"Where are we going?"

"We're going to move along the ridgeline on the other side of the Imjin, opposite our positions, and on to Hill 117."

Charley interrupted. "I didn't know the *Gooks* were there."

If there was a word to stigmatize an individual or a group, we could depend on Charley to dig it out from his vast inventory.

"There doesn't appear to be much activity in the area. But battalion has info that a platoon of Chinese moved up to that hill a few days ago," replied Sid.

"Why do we need two platoons just to to see if the Chinks are there?" continued Charley.

"Because battalion said so; that's why."

"It's flat ground with some bushes. Charley will lead the way."

The usual bitching was followed by Lancaster's keen observation, "Even a death row jailbird gets a meal of his choosing before he sits and fries. Where are my grits?"

Hoover chimed in. "Damn your grits, Lancaster. Will we get a hot meal for supper, or will we dig out the crap in a C-ration can? With the shit in those cans, we should get toilet paper as napkins."

That drew the usual laughs that followed Hoover wherever he went.

As the days passed, with the impending raid on my mind, a bubble containing the usual apprehensions began to inflate in my psyche.

Unless one has experienced it, the dread of walking into darkness toward a waiting enemy is beyond comprehension. The fright fuses with every molecule of the air we breathe. It forms a composite that controls every cell of our personae. It lurks behind every thought. Oh no, I didn't curl up in my bunker and wait for the dreaded night. I made small talk with my buddies. But the night of Friday, August 8 lurked behind every syllable.

Wayne and I returned to our bunker. The stagnant air was polluted by our fart sacks, which had been airing out on the roof. A couple of shakes and they were ready to do their feeble job of protecting us from the bunker's miserable dampness.

Within an hour, the cooks had brought hot meals and coffee. Lieutenant Sidney had insisted that the cooks move closer to the MLR, and from then on our C-ration can openers went into semiretirement.

By the time the cooks had collected the empty trays and scurried to their jeep, it was twilight. We returned to our bunkers. It was Wayne's turn to stand guard. Rarely did I nap the allotted two hours. I stepped out, I stretched, I scratched, and I joined my buddy.

"Anything happening?"

"There's nothing happening here, and there's nothing happening in Frackville, Pennsylvania. When I return, it'll be as if I never left. Shit, I'm going to re-up, maybe make a career of the army. I'll have three meals a day and a bed. Three hots and a flop, as Charley says."

"Yeah, now we have three hots and a thin fart sack as a flop. Wait until we return from the patrol. You'll change your mind."

Two days followed. Two days of waiting: waiting for food, waiting for mail, and waiting to cross the Imjin.

A day had passed. It was Thursday. Why did I want Friday night to be tonight? Twenty-four more hours to grind out. The anxiety unnerved me. *Let's get done with it and wait for our next outing.*

Oh! A perfumed letter from Elaine. The same old bullshit: "Take care of yourself. I miss you. It's been hot for a few days."

Crap, I didn't miss her. *If she thinks it's hot there, she should try wearing month-old underwear in this heat, and using an entrenching tool for her toilet.*

August 8, 1952 is a night I wish I could erase from my memory. Like a nightmare that compulsively clings and just won't let go, the night of August 8, 1952, still lingers after sixty-four years.

On that night, a full moon was conducting a chorus of stars to illuminate the clobbered Korean landscape. Two platoons were to move along the heights of the Imjin River opposite our position. In reviewing the operation at battalion headquarters, Lieutenant Sidney had requested artillery fire to soften Hill 117 before the attack. He circled the arillery impact zone on a map. Battalion disapproved. It would compromise the secrecy of the operation, they said. But in deference to his caution, they agreed to provide artillery concentrations once we made contact with the enemy.

At dusk we gathered on the reverse slope near the supply bunker of our armorer, Massey. He distributed bandoliers and grenades to the riflemen and canisters for the machine gun team.

How did Massey get this job? I asked myself. *What a great deal—he gives us our ammo and then sends us off with a "good luck!"*

We waited for Sid. He led us to a dense grove of trees near the Imjin.

He reviewed the order of attack.

"Make sure your weapons are locked. Any questions?"

"How far are we going?"

"We're going to Hill 117 if we don't meet opposition before that hill."

Then the chaplain stepped in. We gathered around him in a cluster as he recited the twenty-third psalm: "Yea, though we walk through the valley of the shadow of death, we will fear no evil, for Thou art with me." If he feared "no evil" why didn't he join us? We needed replacements for our casualties. *"Thou"? "Thou"? Where is "Thou"? I haven't seen Him.* Was the psalm intended to motivate me as a killer? Why would a man of God preach that "Thou" was with me as I hunted for a human to kill?

How many times had we gone through this? How many times had I glanced at my buddies and wondered which of them would be on the chow line with me tomorrow? Of course I thought I was going to be there.

It was the usual smoldering, humid, summer Korean evening. With a lid formed by the canopy of trees, the humidity just sat, mingling with the odor of decaying vegetation to form a hot and putrid gas. Wrapped in those damned plastic laminated OD armored vests, our torsos resembled the grainy shells of horseshoe crabs. The vests ensured that sweat would flow but not evaporate. My clammy discomfort made me wish I could, like the crab, molt the vest and free my ribs from its grip.

At approximately 10:00 p.m. the Second and Third Platoons of Company L reached the bank of the Imjin River. Like empty sardine cans littering my backyard tenement in the Bronx, four-man jon boats lay scattered along the shore. John Hollier stepped into a jon boat and grasped the overhead rope to steady the boat. Whitefeather, Wayne, and I followed. Hand over hand, John started to pull us across. Wayne, alongside of me, began singing, "I'd like to get you on a slow boat to China." Whitefeather said his voice stunk and told him to shut up.

The moon's glow reflecting off our armored vests brought them clearly into view, leaving our blackened faces and torsos in the background.

At the opposite shore of the Imjin, we assembled near our unmanned outpost, the Bubble. When everyone was accounted for, Lieutenant Sidney ordered our platoon to move out. It was a given that Charley was to point the way. As the runner, I was to be the contact between Lieutenant Sidney and Charley. The trek toward our target led us past the soldiers manning our outposts—Little Nori and Big Nori. The usual well-meaning "Give 'em hell!" and "See you on the way back" brought me as much comfort as the twenty-third psalm.

Soon we were on the cliff overlooking the Imjin River to our right. Our hidden positions on the opposite side of the river served as a backdrop to the moonlight shimmering on the river. Single file, we trampled over brush and into the blackness of no-man's-land. Although a grenade in each pocket kept bouncing off each thigh, I patted them occasionally to assure myself they were there. Any unusual sound raised the hairs on the back of my neck. I wanted to get closer to the GI in front of me, but I remembered Lieutenant Theiss's "One Ping-Pong ball will get you all." So I restrained myself and maintained the ten-foot interval.

Where in the hell are we going? What am I doing here? Wait 'til the boys back in the candy store hear about this one.

We moved through the underlying brush uneventfully. As we approached Hill 117, Lieutenant Sidney sent me forward to contact Charley. I found him lying behind a bush. He whispered that he had just passed a listening post. I looked around. All I could see were the outlines of trees and bushes.

"How do you know that?" I whispered.

"Take a deep breath. Don't you smell garlic? It's kimchi (pickled cabbage, a Korean favorite dish). It's the *Gooks*! They're breathing heavy. They're shitting like we are."

Was I scared? No. They'd have to invent a new word.

I ran back to relay Charley's message to Lieutenant Sidney.

"Tell him to move up about ten yards, and we'll catch up to him."

I became one with the earth as I crawled toward Charley. The Chinese might have been able to hear my heart pounding, but they weren't going to see me. Charley was keyed up and anxious when I reached him.

"What did Sid say? What did he say?"

This was not the Charley I knew. I had never seen him so intense. He had volunteered for this lonely and dangerous assignment. Of all the men in the platoon, he was usually the most composed.

"Sid said to move forward ten yards and then stop. We'll catch up to you."

I crawled back to Lieutenant Sidney. He signaled for the platoon to move out. As soon as we reached Charley, a Chinese arsenal erupted. Cackling burp gun fire ripped the air, and exploding concussion grenades pierced our ears. The output of our M1s was no match for the relentless buzz of the Chinese burp guns.

When the enemy decides where and when an action will take place, they have the upper hand. They know the terrain. They know the ideal fields of fire. They can replace casualties quickly, and they have unlimited ammunition. They are in control.

They were no more than twenty yards to our left. The arc of blue flashes from their weapons told us we were caught within a crescent. We were surrounded, trapped in an ambush. I hadn't as yet fired my carbine or thrown a grenade. I was frozen, terrified, impotent. My hands were glued to my carbine, but I wondered, *Will my carbine's flash reveal my position? If I fire now, will I have enough ammo when we withdraw?* I threw my two grenades at the burp gun flashes and then dropped to the ground. *Why didn't I bring more grenades?* A burst from a concussion grenade lifted me off the ground. The force of the blast and its sour taste rushed down my throat. I belched, bringing up acid. The bubble burst, the tension broke, and all the angst flowed out onto the field of fire.

Creeping up to me, Wayne showed me the handle of his pistol. "Look at this. Look what those sons of bitches did."

It had been ripped apart in his holster by a piece of shrapnel. He left crawling, searching for the wounded

On my far right, above the tumult of the bursts and blasts, I heard shouting. "We're coming at you, you bastards!"

I could see a silhouette formed by the moonlight and exploding rounds. It was Sid, our company commander, shouting at the Chinese, moving among us while calling us by name, directing the automatic weapons, and giving us words of encouragement. Sid's aggressive behavior was infectious. My trigger finger relaxed.

"Fire in bursts! Fire in bursts!" shouted Sid.

The staccato from the weapons nearby told me the word was spreading. We responded to the zip of the burp guns. Although we were handicapped by the lack of firepower from our semiautomatic M1s and carbines, Ken's and Truman's BARs and Staszewski's machine gun team responded with a deadly spray.

Sid called back to artillery for the prearranged concentrations. He waited. A short round plopped into the river behind us; another flew over our heads and burst somewhere behind the Chinese. That was it. Fortunately there were no additional "supporting rounds," which might have hit us instead of the enemy.

We were running low on ammo. Casualties had to be evacuated. Sid determined that the safest return to the MLR would be to move down the cliff to our rear and wade back through the Imjin for about a mile to the Bubble. This quick decision put a stop to the casualties we were taking.

Some men from the Third Platoon, unable to hear Sid, were led by their squad leaders back on the same path that had brought them there. Unfortunately this choice increased the casualties as they ran past the Chinese position that had first hit us.

Sid stood by with Sgt. Benny Hoover as the men began their descent from the cliff above the river. Men ran, slid, and tumbled the eighty feet to the water. As I moved toward the slope, Poodles, a rifleman from the Third Platoon, crept toward me, picking up two abandoned rifles. Pointing to an area about ten yards to our forward right, he said Sergeant Massengale was lying there.

"He ain't moving! I didn't see him move!"

"Drop those goddamn rifles and help me get him!"

Poodles took off shouting, "*Supply Economy!*" This was the title of a basic training movie emphasizing the care and protection of equipment.

The Chinese, apparently unaware of our withdrawal, continued spraying the area with their burp guns and concussion grenades. Lieutenant Sidney and Benny Hoover covered me as I crawled over the brush to Massengale. I managed to reach him without getting hit. He was lying facedown, motionless. I grasped the back of his collar and dragged him to the edge of heights above the river. Lieutenant Sidney returned to the men who were wading toward our jon boats. He left Benny to cover me as I brought Massengale back.

The cliff was eighty feet of vertical rock carpeted by dense bushes. I shouldered my carbine to free my hands as we moved down the vertical slope. With Massengale in my arms, it was a difficult descent. Halfway down, I stopped. *Is he wounded or is he gone?* I grabbed a bush for support and then pinched his cheek. It was like pinching a padded canvas canteen cover. He was gone.

I heard Benny Hoover cursing the Chinese as he came down the cliff and slid past me.

With my carbine sliding toward my head whenever I bent over, it was difficult to drag Massengale. I removed my belt and buckled it around his legs, and then I pulled him by the belt with my left hand, leaving my right hand free to grab a bush if I slipped. But the teeth of the belt buckle didn't hold; he slipped out. I grabbed

Massengale by his legs and continued down the slope. Massengale was responding like a rag doll, bouncing off bushes and outcrops. After a few steps, I couldn't control the weight, and we rolled together to the bottom.

The descent down the cliff was a tumbling nightmare. The density of the bushes prevented me from seeing Benny Hoover below me. As I neared the river, I heard a report from an M1. In the river, Benny eliminated a Chinese soldier who tried to ambush him. The lifeless soldier floated by us.

Walking backward in the stream, I floated Massengale close to the cliff to avoid the burp gun bullets from the top. Like raindrops, they pockmarked the surface of the river. Fortunately we were moving with its flow. Its buoyancy relieved me of the cumbersome weight, and the current helped me quickly cover the mile and a half back to our jon boats near the Bubble. I had a strange feeling that this was not me floating Massengale down the river; it was a robot floating a log. I was totally without feeling, an automaton, benumbed by this hellish experience. By some miracle, we were not hit. I wondered whether the twenty-third psalm had reached its target.

At last we reached the Bubble. Truman, who saw us coming, held a jon boat. Benny and I placed Massengale into the boat, and then we crossed the river. We left him on shore, hoping the medics could perform a miracle. A medic told us to move on. Graves Registration attended to the body.

Our trucks, about a quarter of a mile to the rear, brought soaked and stunned platoons to battalion headquarters.

During our debriefing, we learned that Camacho, Moen, and Massengale had been killed. One of the jon boats had overturned, and Brown, weighed down by his armored vest and equipment, had fallen out of a jon boat and drowned. Lieutenant Edmunds had suffered critical abdominal wounds that eventually led to his demise. Sergeant Smith, who had been through paratrooper school with Massengale, was extremely agitated by news of his death and was sent to the rear. Charley Nunns had been machine-gunned in his arm and left shoulder. Ralph Gerecke had taken some bullets to his bowels and kidneys. Ingrham had received shrapnel to his back. Seventeen-year-old Philip Dickson, who had been sent to a summary court-martial that afternoon for insubordination, had returned in time to snap on his armored vest and accompany his machine gun squad on the patrol. It was a case of very bad timing. Mortar shrapnel tore his chest, eventually leading to death. Francis Mette had received a critical wound to the abdomen, which hospitalized him for a year and a half.

Airborne training had produced in Massengale the same type of valiant leadership we had seen from our company commander, Sid Sidney. The loss of Massengale, with his aggressiveness in combat, his walrus mustache, the helmet that seemed to engulf his head, his glasses, and his sense of humor, left Company L without our own comic strip caricature of Pete the Tramp.

Our heads were swarming with the evening's experience. When we returned, Wayne and I sat silently outside our bunker overlooking the tranquil Imjin until dawn.

After breakfast the following morning, our forward observer from artillery spotted Jesus Camacho's body through his BC scope (the scope used by artillery observers to zero in on targets). The Chinese were known to set traps by exposing the body of one killed in action (KIA), assured that our troops would attempt to retrieve him. To recover Camacho, Lieutenant Sidney recruited Sgt. Ray Flaherty and Ed Heister to accompany him. They crossed the river. As they passed through the platoon of Company I that was manning the Nori outposts, Flaherty exchanged his M1 for a BAR. The others were carrying M1s. They traveled along the ridgeline to the point of the ambush. Sid told the men to cover him as he climbed over the lip of the ridge and found Camacho. After a brief firefight, Sid returned with the body. The men quickly withdrew, scaled down the cliff, waded down the Imjin River, and then entered the jon boats.

While on their retrieval mission, Sid's party had also found a bloated Chinese soldier's body below the area where Benny Hoover had silenced the burp gun the previous day.

On August 8, 1952, Company L gathered at twilight. Massey, our armorer, distributed bandoliers for the M1 rifles and cartridges for my carbine. The chaplain was waiting under a grove of trees. He launched us off to our jon boats with the twenty-third psalm. Hill 117 was waiting.

Korean locations significant to Company L. (Photo taken circa 2000 by

Major Charles Knighten with a telephoto lens
from the Demilitarized Zone.)

The attack on Hill 117 had left me traumatized.

Should I write a letter about this? What is there to say? How can I describe this nightmare? Why should I describe this nightmare? What are we doing here? Was this fight worth the lives of Moen, Brown, Massengale, Camacho, and the others? Can Nunns, Ingrham, Gerecke, Dickson, Mette, and Lieutenant Edmunds say they were wounded in defense of their country? Was it worth this bloodshed merely to make contact with the enemy while the peace talk beacons from Panmunjom were mocking us no more than twenty miles from the ambush?

For my action on the night of August 8, Lieutenant Sidney cited me for the Silver Star. My behavior was neither premeditated nor courageous. It was as involuntary as blinking an eye—instinctive, reflexive, unthinking. Three days after the ambush, two jeeps, one carrying the paperwork for my award, were demolished by Chinese mortar rounds. Forty-five years later, at the first reunion of Company L, Lieutenant Sidney—by then Colonel Sidney (retired)—discovered that I had not been awarded the medal. He cited me again for the Silver Star, and on August 1, 1998, I received the Bronze Star with a *V* for valor in a ceremony at the University of North Carolina.

I have tried to convey the horror of combat, but Wilfred Owen (1893–1918), a young poet killed in World War I, masterfully depicted the madness in his poem *"Dulce et Decorum Est"* (It Is Sweet and Honorable). He vividly describes the tragedy he experienced in war. The poem ends thus:

> If you could hear, at every jolt, the blood
> Come gargling from the froth-corrupted lungs
> Obscene as cancer, bitter as the cud
> Of vile, incurable sores on innocent tongues,
> My friend, you would not tell with such high zest
> To children ardent for some desperate glory,
> The old Lie: *Dulce et decorum est*
> *Pro patria mori.*

Pasted on the rear bumper of my car is a sticker reading, "I Remember Korea." Does anyone remember? Does anyone care?

Where's Wayne?

And He allowed me to go to the top of the mountain.
And I've looked it over. And I've seen the Promised
Land.

—Martin Luther King Jr.

Company L had been at the base of a mountain. And we had looked it over. And we had seen hell.

In 1952 it was a battle for hills. There was no shortage of them in Korea. Hill 121, occupied by the Chinese, was a pimple in the center of Chorwon Valley. Battalion decided that Company L, with support from heavy weapons, would conduct a raid on that hill in order to inflict casualties and try to capture enemy soldiers.

As usual, my bunker buddy, Wayne, and I were trying to make sense of this or any raid. We were agonizing over our losses from the August 8 ambush three days prior when orders came to prepare for a raid on August 12. Lieutenant Theiss stopped by to tell me that for this raid we were going to pass through a flat, wide valley, so he didn't need a runner.

"You're going to launch a flare. Get an M1 from Massey, then see Flaherty."

What is this launch? What is this flare? A flare? My only experience with a flare was the night the sky lit up on Outpost Mary when I accidentally kicked a trip wire over a month ago.

An M1? A carbine was my weapon. What had I gotten into as a runner?

Flaherty was waiting near his bunker with what appeared to be a short pipe (the launcher) in one hand and something else I'd never seen (the flare) in the other.

We went to a clearing. He connected the launcher to the end of the rifle barrel and set the flare in it.

Flaherty had me put a strange round into the M1 rifle. He told me to wedge the stock of the rifle firmly into the ground.

"Hold the rifle firmly, and close your eyes when you pull the trigger, because a bright flash will burst from trigger housing."

It was a simple procedure, and it went well.

"What's with this grenade launcher, Flaherty?"

"Just before our platoon goes into the attack, the flare will signal the support weapons to cease fire. Then we will wait for Lieutenant Theiss to signal for the attack."

Who had planned this operation? We were exhausted from the August 8 nightmare. Men had been killed and wounded. But orders are orders. John Wayne, in *She Wore a Yellow Ribbon,* said that the only freedom a soldier has is the freedom to follow orders. Like good soldiers, we began exercising our freedom.

A skeletal crew remained in the bunkers while the men involved in the raid scrambled down the reverse slope toward a clearing for an orientation. Whitefeather steadied himself by grabbing bushes to support his slide down the hill. *How did he ever become a paratrooper?* I wondered.

Sweating, C-rations, and no mail for a week had left Lancaster in a foul mood. "Hey, Oscar, where the hell is this 121? I think I'm not going."

The heat was setting everyone on edge. Benny Hoover was in no mood for humor. He stripped his cigarette and spit the remaining bits from his lip; then, narrowing his beady eyes, he glared at Lancaster.

"Lancaster, you'd better bring your ass and your machine gun crew or I'll recommend your miserable ass for a general court-martial."

Oscar, trying to snap the tension, quickly cut in.

"From our bunkers, the Noris are blocking the view of Hill 121. It's on the other side of Nori, about a mile away, at the end of a wide valley. There's a knocked-out US tank there."

Charley, also anticipating a clash, took the edge off the bickering with "Hey, Oscar, when you're discharged, you could return here as a tour guide."

Sweaty, somber faces stretched into smiles. The Second Platoon was restored.

Lieutenant Theiss led us to an open area surrounded by the omnipresent hills. Gathered around a tilted sand table were our regimental commander, Colonel Middlebrook; our battalion commander, Colonel Welch; our company commander, Lieutenant Sidney; and the two platoon leaders involved in the raid, Lieutenants Theiss and Wilhoit. On the table, wet sand was molded into a mock-up of the approach, the surrounding terrain, and our target—Hill 121. To me, the lumps in the diorama resembled a combination of dog turds, cow flops, and horse dung. How was I to recognize these hills and valleys in the darkness? I'd just follow my platoon leader, Sergeant Flaherty. But sitting alongside me now, he was as bewildered as I was.

We were briefed on the order of approach—which platoon would form the base of fire and which platoon would attack. The base-of-fire platoon would be the first to leave. Its mission was to clear the area, set up a defensive position, and prevent an assault on the attacking platoon passing through them. The attacking platoon would then close in on Hill 121.

Briefing for the raid on Hill 121: *left to right,*
Lieutenants Theiss, Sidney, and Wilhoit.

Supporting the assault were the cannon and heavy machine guns of a British Centurion tank, 105 mm howitzers from artillery, 81 mm mortars from a heavy weapons company, and our Fourth Platoon's recoilless rifle team. This was a major operation. My platoon was selected for the assault; the Third Platoon for the base of fire.

At the end of the briefing, Theiss asked if there were any questions. Coy Jaegers, who had never brought home a grade higher than an F, raised his hand.

"Why can't we have that big ole tank come with us instead of it staying back safe in the woods?"

"Jaegers, what's between that tank and Hill 121?"

"Trees?"

A roar of laughter exploded from heads swiveling in disbelief. Theiss removed his helmet, wiped his brow to contain his laughter, and then shouted with a grin, "There's the Imjin River, you idiot!

I'll see you guys tomorrow morning for the dry run. Meanwhile, Jaegers, when we return, take a trot through the minefield."

The following morning, we familiarized ourselves with the operation. We went through a couple of dry runs (no live ammo) in the rear. On the return to our bunkers, John Hollier's hands broke the tension. No sooner had I removed my helmet than his familiar hand, like a baseball glove, formed a viselike grip around my scalp. He loved my glistening pate beneath the thinning hairs of my shaved head. Lancaster kept goosing CP Jones with the barrel of his carbine in an attempt to get him to move faster. Little Gus Chobot walked in a circuitous path, seeming to follow his twenty-pound BAR wherever it wanted to go. Was this silly horseplay a method of maintaining our sanity, or were we simply a platoon of immature twenty-two-year-olds?

Wayne Caton, our medic, was like the doting grandfather. He enjoyed the foolery around him but didn't join in with the little ones.

Charley Kauneckis said he had a plan to sneak out into the valley later in the evening. He'd scout the area we were to pass through.

"Bullshit. You're not going anywhere," said Whitefeather.

Charley smiled. "If I'm not back by 2:00 a.m., mail me what happened on the raid to a POW camp somewhere in North Korea."

In the evening, we repeated the exercise. We could have been in Jalalabad or Timbuktu. We were confused. Men were wandering about looking for their squads, and platoon leaders were trying to locate their missing men. Almost everyone was disoriented. Chaos turned to order when we were sobered by the sound of live ammunition on the next run. Everyone knew his role. The bases of fire were in position. We passed through them and reached our target. Lieutenant Theiss signaled to fire the flare. I anchored my stock into the ground, squeezed the trigger, and closed my eyes. When I opened them, a beautiful pale blue luminous streak arched through the darkness. We moved up the hill. The throb of the machine guns, the crackle of rifle fire, and the smell of gunpowder awakened us to the reality of our mission. Quietly we returned to our bunkers.

At twilight on August 12, 1952, a silence enveloped the breakfast chow line, punctuated by monosyllables. The raid weighed heavily on our psyches. Digestive systems were completely out of sync. Coffee was the appetizer, entrée, and dessert. Wayne and I promised we would stay in sight of one another. What else was there to say?

In the afternoon, we cleaned our weapons. Wayne checked his medic bag. I made sure the grenade launcher was secured to my M1. But how many times could I check my ammo, secure the launcher, and clean my equipment? How many times could Wayne inventory his morphine syrettes, dried plasma tubes, sterile water, and bandages?

Massengale's death was raw on my mind. Unbearable tension crept in. The shock of the ambush in the last raid hadn't worn off. It had taken place only four days ago.

"Who do you think is going to be your first patient?"

"That's not funny. It might be you," replied Wayne.

"You're right," I said, wondering if it might be me.

Finally dusk crept in.

Why so quickly? Couldn't it have been delayed for an hour or two? Maybe till tomorrow? Next week? Never?

From his supply bunker on the reverse slope, Massey distributed bandoliers of ammo, grenades, machine gun canisters, and rounds for the recoilless rifle team. He handed me the flare and the round to propel it. On to the assembly area.

The chaplain was waiting. We got on our knees as he recited the twenty-third psalm. "The Lord is my shepherd, I shall not want. He maketh me to lie down in green pastures. He anointeth my …"

Are these words supposed to give me confidence? Did they protect me in the ambush? Will I write a letter to my parents tomorrow? Who will I see in the chow line in the morning? Will I be there? Too much time to think. Let's get on with it.

Dusk darkened to nightfall. I glanced at the men around me, envying those who derived solace from the psalm. Then I recalled the same chaplain in the same grove, standing among the same men while reciting the same psalm, which had had the same irreverent effect upon me four nights earlier before the ambush. Hadn't I returned safely? But this was logical thinking. When fear grips your muscles and your mind, logic is also trapped in its grasp. Isn't it strange that we could feel invulnerable before one operation and become paralyzed with fear before another?

The only comfort I could garner was from Lieutenant Sidney, our company commander. He strode confidently among us, carrying his M1 rifle like a toy in his right hand, saying a few words while ostensibly checking and adjusting our equipment. In spite of his detached and correct military bearing, he knew our need for contact with him.

What is Frye doing here? I wondered. *I thought he was stateside, trying to resolve a serious marital problem.* We'd wished him good luck a few weeks before when he left. Now here he was, wrapped in an armored vest, his grimy, stubbly beard glistening in the moonlight, his distant reddened eyes focused on nothing as he stood clutching the strap of his BAR.

Lieutenant Theiss ordered us to move out. The path was hidden by a grove of trees interlaced with dense vines. This trail had never seen the sun. Most of the vegetation beneath our boots had lost its battle with the bacteria of decay, producing a pungent, obnoxious odor—so perfect a setting for all our missions. We groped our way through the darkness to the jon boats scattered on the shore of the Imjin.

The dependable four-man jon boats were always there, waiting to carry us to a new adventure. Wayne, Charley, Truman, and I bunched up for our turn to enter the boat. My anxiety was working overtime.

Can a Chinese FO [forward observer] *see us? Will he transmit the info to his buddies to launch the horrible mortars with their VT fuses, sending a shower of shrapnel onto us?*

We stepped into the boat. Charley grasped the heavy rope anchored to metal stakes at opposite sides of the river to pull us across. Wayne, Truman, and I, trying to neutralize our fear, clustered close to Charley, forming a four-man clump. I wanted to say something clever, but my tank was dry. Wayne smiled; Truman returned it. Maybe that loosened the knots in their intestines. Charley continued to pull the boat while I was trying to chase the demons that had harassed me since the night we were ambushed. Once ashore, our platoon assembled at the base of our outpost, the Bubble. Sergeant Flaherty gathered us to review the mission.

"Do you have enough ammo for your BAR, Truman?"

"My pouches are full."

"I didn't ask you that. I asked you if you have enough ammo."

The strain was changing friends into foes. Flaherty was interrupted by earsplitting booms from the cannon of a Centurion tank across the river behind us. Its shells joined the 105 mm howitzers and 81 mm mortars to rip apart Hill 121. Accompanying the thunder was the crackling staccato of the tank's heavy machine guns joining the prelude to our attack.

The First Platoon moved out. I was on one side of Lieutenant Theiss with my grenade launcher, and Mendel, our commo man, was on the other with his reel of commo wire connecting Theiss's phone to the tank. On Theiss's signal, our platoon moved out.

My thoughts ran wild. *Surely Hill 121 will be flattened by the time we reach it.* We moved on. There was only one approach to Hill 121, and the Chinese knew it. Theiss continued to direct the tank's cannon and machine guns.

The base-of-fire platoon moved out to clear an area. Lancaster and Staszewski set up their machine gun crews at opposite ends of a long knoll where they had a good field of fire. Riflemen fanned out to protect our flanks and rear. Our recoilless team scrambled up to a ridge to our right, opposite Hill 121. The riflemen waited. So far, it was a textbook operation.

The shelling increased. The whistles and the sizzling hisses of the tank's shells penetrating the air above us followed by the thunder of shell bursts were earsplitting and numbing. With each blast of ordnance, the vibrations pressed tightly agaist my pants and my thighs. They ricocheted off my vest, causing a tremble in my cheeks. For a moment I stood petrified. Suddenly all the tension, all the fear, and all the apprehension rushed out. It was exhilarating standing in the middle of all this chaos. Later I read poet Wilfred Owen's description of this phenomenon in World War I: *"When we heard the guns ... it was a sound not without a certain sublimity."*

Pinstriped tracers pointed the way to Hill 121 as we awaited the signal to proceed. I thought back to the day I had been assigned to Company L, when I asked myself, "How does one go to war?" The question had been firmly answered four days ago, on August 8, the night of the ambush. It was reinforced tonight as we prepared to attack Hill 121.

We passed through the base of fire and moved toward our objective. There was still no response from the Chinese. About fifty feet from the hill, Lieutenant Theiss signaled to halt. He tapped me on the shoulder. I fired the flare. I did exactly what I'd done the night before, but curiosity got the better of me, and I kept my eyes open. A blinding flash burst from my rifle chamber. The supporting tank, which served as an artillery piece; the howitzers; the heavy machine guns; and the mortars ceased fire. Then there was silence—that awful silence.

Lieutenant Theiss raised and then lowered his arm, shouting, "Let's go!" Our platoon went into the attack. Burp gun fire buzzed overhead like a swarm of bees. *What's this?* A searchlight company bounced its beams off low-hanging clouds. Hill 121 was lit up like a wedding cake. *Are we going to be the blown-out candles?*

Suddenly I thought, *Why didn't I ask whether I could fire this rifle with the grenade launcher attached to the barrel?* I'd forgotten to take a few bandoliers of ammo. Except for my two grenades, I was useless.

As I climbed Hill 121, whenever I blinked, a flashbulb went off in my eyes. Between flashes I caught sight of Sergeant Flaherty with his men moving forward. Wayne was alongside him to his left. I gave them a thumbs-up.

A series of deep concentric trenches ringed the hill. Why hadn't we been told that? The Chinese lay at the bottom of these trenches, which reduced the effect of our artillery. Subsequently they climbed to firing steps to defend their positions. If necessary, they could withdraw to the trench line behind them.

I crouched as I went up the hill. I threw a grenade and then stepped into space. I'd fallen into an abandoned trench, hitting my forehead against its rear edge. My helmet toppled off and rolled somewhere. It was a very deep trench, but I soon found the firing step. Standing on it, I threw my rifle over the lip of the trench, and then grasped the top to pull myself up and out. This candle was still lit!

Burp guns were belching, and concussion grenades added to the confusion. I reached my squad. But where was Wayne? I dropped when a blast from a Chinese concussion grenade blurred my vision.

Where was Wayne? He had been to my left with Flaherty when we charged up the hill. I crawled forward, with my armored vest plowing the ground. The exchange of fire amplified by grenade blasts was earsplitting. I couldn't crawl any lower. I crept toward Gus, who was lower to the ground than I. He was replacing a magazine in his BAR.

"Hey, Gus, have you seen Wayne?"

"He's probably behind us with the wounded."

We were distracted for a moment by piercing shrieks echoing in the valley to our rear. On a ridge of the hill behind us, our recoilless rifle team had spotted a squad of Chinese attempting to encircle us. Three incendiary rounds from our riflemen carbonized them. How had Sid known to place the recoiless team there?

Lieutenant Theiss shouted to withdraw. I crawled to the area where I thought Wayne might be. There was nothing–no one. He'd been alongside Flaherty the last time I'd seen him. *I'll check with Flaherty as soon as I see him*, I thought.

KATUSAs, our Korean litter bearers.

Like sprinters, our men crouched and dashed through our supporting platoon. Every cell in my body seemed to be producing an amphetamine. I wanted to leave my skin because it wasn't moving as fast as my heartbeat. I caught sight of Flaherty. He was draped on a litter, being evacuated by the KATUSAs. A concussion grenade had pulverized his jaw; it lay like a wet sock, bleeding on his chest. Ed Heister was running frantically with a wounded man on his shoulders.

Where was Wayne?

At the shore of the Imjin, I joined three shaken men. A jon boat brought us across the river. A battalion truck was waiting a half mile to the rear. We folded down the slatted benches in the back of the truck and then collapsed onto them in drained silence.

Spent and numb from the operation, Frye, sitting on the bench opposite me, had a glassy, vacant gaze on his sweaty face. He was in a hypnotic trance with his BAR between his knees. Once we were underway, he raised the BAR to his lap and then pointed it upward. He stuck his finger into the trigger housing and squeezed, emptying his magazine. Everyone fell to the floor. We didn't rise until the truck with its shredded canvas cover arrived at battalion headquarters. Frye was sitting in the same spot, gazing, motionless. The medics evacuated him.

At battalion headquarters, the same questions came at us during the debriefing: "How many did you kill?" "Did you see anything unusual?" "What could we do better next time?"

The honest answer was "I don't know." How could we absorb what was happening in this mayhem?

Lieutenants Sidney, Theiss, and Wilhoit remained at the battalion tent to await further news. Ten yards from the tent, I joined Charley Kauneckis, George Whitefeather, and Oscar Konnerth. We sat in benumbed silence, lost in a state of shock.

From the side of a doughnut truck, we rose to get coffee and partially cooked greasy doughnuts. They slid down my throat in raw lumps. The minutes dragged. Without a word, Charley, Whitefeather, Oscar, and I made for a clearing to the left of the battalion tents. No one was going to intrude on our trauma. Hunched over on the ground, we sat silently awaiting another truck. A motor hummed in the distance. The truck pulled up near the tents.

"Hey, Gus! Where's Wayne? Don, did you see Wayne Caton?"

"Maybe he's on the next truck."

There was no next truck.

Chorwon Valley

Wiorek's Helmet

Where could Wayne be? Who said no news is good news? How long should I wait for good news? I couldn't think of bad news, but as the hours passed, every possibility of good news began to end with bad news. Without Wayne, our six-foot-by-eight-foot bunker became as desolate as a desert.

My appetite was on hold. The powdered eggs tasted like a marathon sock, the coffee like rice paddy water. I dropped down next to Massey, who was sitting with some men on the trunk of a felled tree. He was enjoying the army signature breakfast–SOS. How could he forage through that gray clot with those ground-up pieces of pig floating in it? Ugh! He dedicated himself to keeping us supplied with ammo and gladly replaced our tools and clothing when they were lost or malfunctioned.

"Where's your helmet, Reilly?" he asked.

"I lost it when I fell into a trench on Hill 121 last night."

"Come on over after breakfast; I'll find you one."

I nodded, but a helmet was not on my list of priorities. First I needed sleep, and then I had to rearrange the scrambled events of the previous night. I crept into my bunker and collapsed onto my sleeping bag. I awoke with my face pressing against its slick, black, greasy area where my head had rested for a few months. It was colder and oilier than the rest of the bag, but it was my bag. I slipped it open, crawled out of the bunker, and went to Massey for a helmet.

Unlike ours, Massey's bunker and the reinforced supply bunker were at the base of the reverse slope, just behind our forward position. Inside, Ed Heister was standing in a blood-streaked T-shirt and jockey shorts.

"What happened last night? asked Massey. "Was anyone killed? Who was wounded?"

Slipping into a clean uniform and T-shirt, Ed replied, "Truman Bastin was a mess. I don't think he'll make it."

Ed was a man of very few, but graphic, words. He didn't say what I found out later: that the blood on his shirt was that of the hemorrhaging Truman, whom Ed had carried over a mile to the medics.

Massey pulled out a helmet liner from a tangle of liners, backpacks, and cartridge belts, threw it to me, and then asked, "Are you sure we lost Caton?" The possibility unnerved him. Wayne was a buddy to everyone. "Take the liner," he said. "I'll find you a pot [helmet] later."

With the liner on my head, I joined Ed in the climb back to our bunkers. I needed sleep, but Charley, Gus, Oscar, and Whitefeather were waiting to continue the previous night's vigil. We agreed that it was a stroke of genius for Sid to place the recoilless rifle team on the hill behind us. Although we did not take any prisoners, the raid was considered a success. Artillery and tank fire had cratered the hill, causing heavy casualties. We'd lost Wayne and had seven men wounded, which was considered low by army standards. In spite of the "success," we were left with unanswered questions. Flaherty had been evacuated. What was the extent of his wounds? What had happened to Caton? Where was Bastin? Who else had been hit?

Frustrated by the lack of answers, Charley could be depended upon to distract us.

"Hey, Reilly, where did you get that helmet liner—in a surplus army-navy store? You guys are always looking for bargains."

"Why? Massey just gave it to me."

When I removed the rigid fiber helmet liner, I saw a meandering hairline crack starting at the top and running down its side. I turned it over to adjust the straps. I was shocked. The interior and some of the suspending straps were stained with blood. Stenciled in block letters on the greasy headband was "L. WIOREK."

Massey was quite upset. "I never saw a name inside a helmet liner before." He gave me a steel pot and another liner. Wiorek, he said, had been evacuated from Big Nori after the mortar bombardment a few nights before.

I tucked the new liner into my steel pot. Now I was back in uniform. But who, in a Chinese uniform on the other side of the Imjin, had my oily, shock-absorbing helmet liner's straps resting on his head?

Baptism and Resurrection

When Sgt. Fostine Rutledge climbed above the trench line, a sniper had ended his young life with a bullet passing through his wafer-thin helmet.

It was now August 1952. Most of the men were wearing their armored vests and helmets by this point, whether they were on patrol or going to the Lister bag to fill their canteens. We had nothing to do to occupy our time. There was something strange about this rare "nothing to do." What did I do with it? When a raid or patrol was scheduled, I focused on playing out chilling scenarios of the impending action. Sometimes we went through a dry run; sometimes we used live ammo. Sometimes I vented my anger at the reckless stupidity of those planning a raid; sometimes we just had fun. Without anything to fill my day now, I waited for news from home and wrote letters to all the return addresses I had torn off the envelopes.

I thought that blending in with my environment was an exercise in futility, but after Fostine Douglas was killed, my attempt at concealment became serious.

While sitting on my helmet in the trench outside my bunker, I rocked back to the comfortable, cold, damp wall and mulled over some moments of my life.

> Did you ever see a lassie?
> A lassie? A lassie?
> Did you ever see a lassie
> Go this way and that?

My first-grade teacher was singing this ditty in PS 61's schoolyard while we formed a circle around a classmate who was merrily gyrating in the center. In third grade, I graduated to a dip-in inkwell in my desk and a dip-in pen with a yellow chamois pen wiper. With all the multiplication tables mastered in fourth grade, I went on to division. Math story problems in fifth grade were a bit of a challenge. Finally, in sixth grade, after the Japanese bombed Pearl Harbor, my classmate Donny and I were given permission return to school late in the afternoon. We went to collect newspapers and magazines for the war effort. What role collecting them played in the war effort was a mystery, but it freed us from school for part of the afternoon.

Hermann Ridder Junior High School was full of mischievous fun. At James Monroe High School, in the Bronx, in spite of being a 126-pound mesomorph, my maximum academic effort was getting in shape for the varsity football team.

As the hours passed in the trench, I saw the rest of my life filtering through a gauzelike haze. I had been a busboy in the Catskills, a billing clerk in the Garment District, and a switchtender/brakeman at the New York Central Railroad. Now now I was a private in the military.

At twenty-two, there weren't many notable highlights in my life. My girlfriend, Elaine, wrote regularly and sent pictures, but there was a seat in the last row at the back of the room for her, and a seat farther back for my maturity.

I knew there was a right way, a wrong way, and the army way. Lieutenant Theiss said Intelligence believed the sniper that killed Rutledge was using a camouflaged bunker at the base of a cliff near Hill 117 where our platoon had been ambushed. They suspected he was sniping during the day and sleeping there at night. Company L had been ordered to kill the sniper and destroy his bunker. His bunker, they claimed, was at the bottom of a cliff overlooking the Imjin River. I was certain the army way was the wrong way. From our side of the river, we could have blasted the bunker with a recoilless rifle or a .50-caliber machine gun, but the army way was to carry out this risky mission with a bunker bomb.

The "nothing to do" didn't last long. We settled around Lieutenant Theiss soon after the cooks took off in their jeep. A week of boredom came to an end.

"Put your ass on the ground, Lancaster. I can't see Lieutenant Theiss."

"You must have been smoking Whitefeather's weed. I'm squatting, Hoover."

I could see the tic in Benny Hoover's jaw working overtime. "You'll be eating dirt if you don't sit on it."

Lieutenant Theiss saw an impending problem and muffled their words quickly and loudly. "The second squad, pointed by Charley, is going to get rid of that bunker with a bunker bomb. If he survives, two men will capture him."

"Since we've been up here," said Whitefeather, "the company hasn't captured anyone on a raid or a patrol. Why do they keep telling us to get prisoners?"

"We might be lucky this time," replied Theiss.

Capturing prisoners was always part of a patrol. Eliminating a bunker with a bunker bomb had never been part of any previous patrol. A dry run was scheduled for the next day. The attack was to be carried out in two days.

A bunker bomb? What was that? I knew that anything that exploded excited Charley.

"Hey Charley, what's a bunker bomb?"

"What's the difference, Reilly? Theiss will show it to us, and then we'll know."

Charley was a dedicated RA (an enlisted man). He didn't ask questions. He followed orders.

In reviewing the patrol, Lieutenant Theiss showed us an empty .30-caliber machine gun canister attached to a four-foot pole. The canister, he said, would be partially filled with napalm. A white phosphorus grenade would be connected to the side of the canister, and when it was activated, it would ignite the napalm, causing a fiery blast. The four-foot pole allowed the carrier to maneuver the bomb into the bunker before it exploded. This was the bunker bomb. Theiss said that other companies on the line had used it successfully.

He went on to describe the plan. Our squad was to enter the Imjin River where the jon boats sat. Our men, Company I, and the Greeks on our right overlooking the Imjin would be informed of the day and time of our mission. We were to wade a mile up on our side of the river to a sandbar where the river bent, cross the sandbar, and then make a short climb up a slope to the bunker. To locate it, the squad was to lay down a field of fire to draw a response from the bunker. This would pinpoint it. As the man carrying the bomb approached the bunker, the fire would be lifted. He would pull the pin on the white phosphorus grenade and quickly push the canister into the bunker, while the rest of the squad covered his withdrawal. Two men would then move up to search for the prisoner. The squad would quickly return, crossing the sandbar and wading back to the point where we entered the river.

This was another mission where contact between our platoon leader and Charley was not a problem. As a runner, I would be unemployed. I was consumed with unanswered questions. I sat frozen, like a stamp on an envelope.

What would Theiss have me do on this raid? Why can't we demolish the position from our side with a heavy machine gun or a recoilless rifle? Is the capture or killing of one prisoner worth placing so many lives on the line? Did Lieutenant Theiss ask himself this question? Who is to carry the bunker bomb? Who will search for prisoners? Maybe Gus? No, with Truman Bastin gone, Gus is our only BAR man. Whitefeather is heavy, not agile. Can we depend on our new men?

I suspected who would carry the bomb, but I acted as though by repeating the question of, Who will carry the bunker bomb? could conjure some reason to scrap the mission. Our platoon was under strength. We had lost Caton. Konnerth, Bastin, Flaherty, Gerecke, Dickson, and Nunns were in a MASH, were at the Tokyo Army Hospital, or had been sent stateside. Brockett had been sent to a school on standards (whatever that was).

It came as no surprise when Theiss told me I was to carry the bomb.

The mission had all the ingredients of a disaster. Shaken by the news, I went off to try to make sense of what I had just heard.

Why can't they demolish the position from our side? The thought persisted throughout the day. *What do our men think? Is the risk worth the mission? Where is Charley? What does he think?*

He was no comfort. Charley was always eager for a new adventure. This certainly would be one. A bunker bomb—an explosion! He was ecstatic.

"Charley, what do you think our chances are of destroying that bunker?"

"I don't give a shit about chances," he said. "I'm here to take them."

God, why did I ask him?

I recalled how happy I had been in reserve when Lieutenant Theiss had designated me the platoon runner. He'd told me to pass my BAR to Gus and requisition a lightweight carbine. How was I to know I would be the utility man when I was not a runner? At that, I was a utility man who was called off the bench to help carry out a mission with utter disregard for my safety. I was now convinced I was a dead man. I pictured my mother falling apart upon receiving the telegram, my gentle father so distressed that he could be no comfort to her.

In the morning, our reverse slope was occupied by strangers with hot meals—our cooks. Heartburn from C-rations has a place all of its own in the annals of hyperacidity. With three days before our raid, my digstive system plastered anything I ate with hydrochloric acid. Even the Lister bag water generated acid reflux.

The only redemption I had was the realization that I was not alone. I had complete confidence in Charley Kauneckis, Gus Chobot, and George Whitefeather. The replacements had performed beyond our expectations on patrols, although they had not as yet confronted the enemy.

Next came the practice run with live ammo. We kept reminding each other not to throw grenades because the bunker was on a steep slope and they would roll back to explode on us. Our men raked the improvised bunker with their M1s and a BAR as I crawled up with the bomb. They were warned to listen for the order to cease fire as I crawled close to the bunker with the bomb. I pulled the pin on the grenade, pushed the bomb into the bunker, and then ran like hell in spite of my combat boots. A gigantic blast was followed by a huge orange ball of fire that incinerated the bunker. Had I been a bit closer, the heat from the blast would have melted my vest. Two of our men moved up to check for prisoners. Everyone knew his role and did it properly.

I spent a sleepless night alone. Wayne was gone. I'm sure the rest of my squad wasn't refreshed when they woke up the following morning. There wasn't much to do. Write a letter? How long does that take? What could I say when I was so focused on the coming night? I killed some time by filling my canteens at the Lister bag, where I met Ed and Whitefeather. Ed was holding a couple of C-ration cans. Whitefeather bent over to rinse out a number-ten can. They asked me to join them at Gus Chobot's bunker.

"Bring two C-ration cans you like," said Ed.

That was easy. I didn't like any of them.

Later in the evening, when I reached Gus's bunker, Charley was pouring diesel fuel into a .30-caliber machine gun canister.

What is going on?

Charley appointed himself chef. "Open your C-rations, guys."

He mixed the contents of all the C-rations into the number-ten can. A low flame was burning in the canister containing the diesel fuel. He rested the can holding the C- rations over the flame and stirred it with his spoon, wisecracking, "If those *Gooks* get us tonight, they won't have to worry about feeding us for a week, but they'll hear us farting like their burp guns."

A slightly widened part of the tenchline was our *mess hall.* It was a memorable feast—tonight's patrol chomping together before our mission. Perhaps this banquet represented a spirit of camaraderie to Charley, who, surprisingly, had had the sensitivity to arrange it.

Charley dug his spoon into the mixture and came up with a spoonful of ham and lima beans.

"Phew! This tastes and smells like pig shit."

Gus laughed and then asked, "How do you know what pig shit smells and tastes like?"

"I smelled your breath this morning, and if that isn't pig shit, then pigs don't shit," replied Charley.

This was the gourmet dessert for our olive drab meal.

Why do the hands on the clock freeze when I am anxious? I wondered. I had reached that familiar point in the day when I was eager for nightfall to arrive. No, it was not a death wish; rather it was "Let's get over with it so I might be able to see tomorrow."

After an anxious night, D-day arrived. Silence became the conversation for the afternoon. Finally daylight crept to dusk. Massey at the supply bunker distributed ammo to our men and then handed me the bunker bomb. The sight of that thing erased everything and anything that had ever happened in my life. I could focus only on that canister with the white phosphorus grenade and the pole attached to it.

We gathered around Lieutenant Theiss.

"Remember what we said about grenades? They will roll back. Any questions?"

Everyone was on edge.

"What if there is no bunker? What if there's no one in the bunker?" asked Gus.

"Just assume that someone is in the bunker, and do what we practiced."

Before we left, the chaplain was there to ease our anxiety. He read the twenty-third psalm to my bunker bomb.

Lieutenant Theiss reviewed the plan at the shore of the Imjin.

"There will be no conversation. It carries at night."

"On stage, everybody; it's opening night!"

Charley stepped into the river to point the way into ankle-deep water. The rest of our squad followed, twenty feet behind him. I was alongside Lieutenant Theiss at the center of the column. We dragged through knee-high water for about two hundred yards. Moving against the current while wearing our fatigues and struggling against the tide added another burden to this madness. Anyway, I'm sure that the tepid water dissolved some flakes in my month-old underwear.

I'm carrying a bomb to blow up a hole in the ground with a person in it. Would the boys back home in the candy store believe this one?

A gradual drop in the riverbed brought the water close to my elbows. The water continued to rise slowly. We reached a water level where I had to raise the bunker bomb above my head. Gus, who was my height, had his BAR suspended on two vertical arms. Charley was six feet two; I was five seven. If this drop continued, I wouldn't be able to go on. Didn't Intelligence know the depth of the river near the shore? What's the difference. I guess the mission looked good on paper.

We continued slowly, walking against the flow of the river, and eventually the water level stabilized. My arms ached. I lowered the bomb to my shoulders.

"Plunge the damn bomb into the river, turn around, and wade back to shore," whispered common sense.

About twenty yards before the sandbar, a couple of bursts drew our attention.

"Get close to the cliff!" shouted Theiss.

We hugged the cliff and waited. Charley, in a panic, came plowing toward us.

"The dummies up there [the Greeks at the top of the cliff] threw a couple of grenades at me! It'll pass on up the river. The *Gooks* will be alerted now. We'll never get through!"

Without hesitation, Lieutenant Theiss ordered us to return to the assembly area. Chest-high in water, without any shame, I could have kissed him on his lips. I felt as if I had been baptized in the Imjin, had suffered a living death for the past three days, and had been resurrected by Lieutenant Theiss. *Alive! Yes, alive!* I spun around. The current was with me. I was first to reach shore.

With water-soaked boots, fatigues clinging wherever they could reach the skin, and our helmets for seats, we waited for a truck to carry us to battalion for a critique. Each man selected a private spot to release the anxiety that had been built up for days and carried into the river. Saturated from the chest down, with insects buzzing at my ears, I quietly soaked in the wealth of my good fortune.

The silence was soon broken. It began with a slow chuckle by Lieutenant Theiss. He was sitting on his helmet, staring fixedly off into space. Then the chuckle became loud, rapid, pathological. The conflict he must have felt between his duty to accomplish the mission and his duty to safeguard his men must have been overwhelming—beyond endurance. At this moment, he was not the first-rate leader we had trained with and respected in reserve—not the man who had led us on patrols and the raid on Hill 121. Numbed by the experience we had just been through, we just sat there, unmoved by our officer's breakdown. Finally a truck arrived. In our debriefing at battalion headquarters, Lieutenant Theiss was not present.

The squad returned to their holes in the ground. *The hell with guarding my bunker.* Like a stringless marionette, I collapsed onto my sleeping bag and slept through the night.

Breakfast? The cooks came with their grill and eggs.

"Have you seen Theiss yet?"

I told Charley I hadn't, but it was early. I didn't see any other members of the platoon. I guess each one chose to celebrate or chase the demons in his own way.

Later that morning, Massey came to my bunker. He wanted to know how well the bunker bomb had worked. A few men from other squads joined to hear the news. By the time I had retraced the previous evening's events and the comments that followed, it was time for lunch and mail call.

•

The little treasures of letters came to us in spurts. We stood in the chow line, waiting to hear our names. We would go two to three days with no mail, and then there would be a cluster. When a man heard his name, like a dog with a meaty bone, he took off to a secluded spot to savor his fix for the day.

It was only an envelope with my name on it. It was only a few pieces of folded paper inside, sometimes perfumed. It was only script on the folded paper. But it was like an addictive drug; I wanted more.

Whether they arrived on the company street during basic training or were delivered by the mail clerk to the MLR, letters recharged me for another day. A photograph? Oh, yes, a photograph! There is nothing like a photo to stimulate the creative fantasies. With my mental airbrush, I deleted any warts on the subject. A letter from Elaine soaked in perfume accompanied by a photo of her in a bathing suit set the airbrush in motion. This casual acquaintance became Miss America. The terror of the previous night faded.

The next day, a short, heavy, bald older officer came to see me. The intellects in our platoon deduced he was a Jewish chaplain. They reasoned that an elderly, short, fat, bald officer visiting the only Jewish soldier in the platoon must be a rabbi. Actually, he was an officer from the Chemical Corps who had come to learn the effect of the bunker bomb. Apparently no one had told him that the operation had been scrubbed.

Will this hellish nightmare appear anywhere but on these pages? Will Lieutenant Theiss and my buddies remember this night, or will it be dissolved by the passing years? I recall it as if it happened yesterday.

What value is placed on the life of a GI? He's merely a serial number. But this serial number translates to a son, a husband, a father, a brother, a lover, or a friend. A poorly planned operation such as the bunker bomb mission confirmed it. Who cares except the unknowing parents, wives, children, and friends at home?

Assignment: Big Nori

The Imjin River snaked lazily through the caverns it had been sculpting since its birth. The valleys leading to it, the hills, and the pale blue sky in the background suggested a landscape by a painter from the Hudson River school.

Did the Imjin River behind us, the hills, the sky, or the valleys know that a war was going on? Did they know what war was? Among the figures of speech that Ms. Rothstein, our ninth-grade English teacher, had taught and encouraged us to use was personification—that is, giving life to an inanimate object. A river knows? Hills and valleys know? Caverns know? The sky knows? If, with a pen, we breathe life into it, then does the river ask why a grown man, fully clothed, is floating a dead body downstream, or why armed men, one carrying a bunker bomb, are wading upstream? Do the hills and valleys ask why they are being scarred by bunkers; why healthy young men are being crippled, killed, or lost; or why the living landscape is littered with dying trees, spent shells, commo wire, and craters? Does the blue sky ask why it is darkened by the ashes of bodies cremated by napalm? Do the river, the caverns, the hills, or the sky ask those questions? There are no answers. Forget about personification. Will it protect me? I have to defend the life that was breathed into me.

Our outposts, Big Nori and Little Nori, two contiguous hills opposite the MLR, stood about 150 feet above the river. West of the Noris, a blister of an outpost called the Bubble sat at the entrance to the wide Chorwon Valley. To reach these outposts, we pulled a jon boat across the Imjin River.

From my bunker, Hill 121 was obstructed by the Noris. The absence of Wayne was a constant reminder of the events that had occurred on that hill. In my young life, I had never experienced a trauma such as the loss of Wayne. Perhaps a letter to Frackville might connect a thread between the Caton family and myself. What could I tell them? What hope could I give them? Completely unaware of what had happened to Wayne, I rehearsed a few lines and then scribbled an account of that evening and mailed it to Wayne's mother.

It was the Second Platoon's turn to man Big Nori for five days. At nightfall we assembled on the shore of the Imjin. The river was so calm that it required very little effort for Charley to pull the four of us across. From the Bubble, it was a short march to Big Nori.

The relief on the faces of the men defending the outpost contrasted sharply with the anxiety on ours. The last of the outgoing tenants passed us by with a nod; then there was silence.

Which one of these men bayoneted and captured the Chinese infiltrator two days ago? I wondered. I knew it had been one of our recent replacements. He had been rewarded with R & R. *Could I plunge a bayonet into another human?*

A permanent trenchline was dug along the forward slope of Nori, our home for the next five days. Sergeant Flaherty came by to see that everyone was settled and to arrange for guard duty through the night. Since Charley and I had already found a position, Oscar decided to occupy a spot farther down, closer to Little Nori on our left.

Our *Zenith Transoceanic* (a wet-cell-battery radio) was turned off as the sun began to sink behind the mountains of the Chorwon Valley. Remnants of sunlight faded the stars, but soon they'd begin to twinkle in the blackened sky, and insects would perform their nocturnal symphony.

Charley's boot brushed away some loose earth at the bottom of the trench, and then we sat down.

"How do you like the new neighborhood?" I asked.

"I saw it before. I didn't like it then. I don't like it now."

Except for the soft crackle of gunfire far off in the valley, the night was so quiet that both of us nearly fell asleep. Suddenly, from out of the blackness, hellish whistles screamed, horns blared, and metal canisters rattled somewhere below us. My heart nearly burst out of my fatigues. Where were they? Were they coming at us? They were masters in the art of harassment and attack. The Chinese had been at war since the 1930s, when I was in elementary school.

I looked at Charley, and then we both searched the darkness for the men making the noise near our position. Psychologically, their harmless toys were as effective on the mind as shrapnel was on the body. Charley and I responded with grenades. Grenades would not pinpoint our position. Where the hell were they? Would the grenades piss them off and make them come at us with weapons? I decided I wasn't going to sleep for a while.

Making no attempt to overrun us, the Chinese left their calling card and then withdrew. It was my turn at guard. Charley joined me. He couldn't sleep. We collapsed against the earthen wall of the trench, listening to our hearts pound. Later I fell asleep. Charley woke me to see the dawn gently creeping over the horizon. The hills, valleys and mountains were staring directly at us, and the Imjin was soothingly streaming its waters to our rear. Some of our men were sleeping, some were stretching, and others were opening their C-rations as if nothing had happened the previous night. What was Charley staring at? Two GIs in the distance were stealthily moving through the brush carrying what appeared to be a long OD canvas tube.

"Hey, Charley! What are they doing?"

"They're going to open up signal panels for a spotter plane."

Soon a narrow rectangular panel of iridescent orange-pink appeared. A single-engine plane came flying slowly by and then dropped canisters of surging colored smoke near the panels. There were pops from Chinese rifles attempting to shoot down the plane. A sortie of three of jets zoomed overhead. How I envied those pilots. After rising from dry cots, they probably showered, shaved, and slipped into clean uniforms. Hot breakfast followed while they caught up on the latest news. Then, seated on clean leather seats in clean cockpits, they left the ground, knowing there was a remote chance that Chinese rifle fire would bring them down. They returned to their base, prepared for a good, clean dinner and an evening with their *Moosemay*.

The planes flew a distance beyond the red smoke signal, turned toward us, and dropped napalm. Large orange globs with black veins streaked and then billowed upward and sideways, forming a rolling curtain of fire. It was bloodcurdling. Who knew who or what was charred in that fireball. Lieutenant Sidney had told us that the jets always flew beyond their target and turned back to drop their bombs. Should a pilot be shot down, he hoped to parachute into friendly territory. Following a napalm attack, our large black radio always transmitted a female voice saying, "Once again, countless women and children were cremated by Yankee napalm."

Soon after twilight, men of the First Platoon passed by on a patrol. I spent some time debating who had the better deal—we, confined to a trench line, or they, tramping into the darkness. We had no roofs for protection against incoming fire. We communed totally with nature. Not more than five minutes after their passage, a barrage of mortar rounds hit us. All we could do was become intimate with the walls of our trenches.

Late at night, after the incoming fire relented, Charlie took it upon himself to check whether we had any casualties. He returned to tell me that Oscar Konnerth was missing. What had happened to him? Sergeant Flaherty, our temporary platoon leader, did not know.

On the third day, the rains came—a record rainfall. It was as if fire hoses were trained on our position. Water in the trenches rose to our knees. Our boots, socks, and fatigues were soaked. Aside from my sweat, my socks, fatigues, and underwear felt water for the first time since we had been brought to a shower point a month before. No matter how I tried to shift my poncho, water would find a space to drench my fatigues. As the surrounding earth absorbed the rain, shelves we had dug into the trench walls to hold our ammo, C-rations, and radio collapsed. Our boots, rubbery and slick, released bubbles when we walked above the trench line. It was summer and very hot. Mosquitoes zeroed in on us. Oh, how good it felt to crush those little bastards against my skin.

The wet clothing was annoying but manageable; the mud had us immobilized. We must have looked stupid standing in the downpour. But where were we to go? The Imjin swirled and rushed to wherever it was going. The jon boats, which the men pulled farther away from the shoreline to keep them from being swept away, could never cross this turbulence.

When were we going to return to the MLR? In two days, it would be our fifth day, the time to go home. The rain was relentless. We couldn't return in two days even if the rains let up. White suds of foam swirling and rolling in the waves told us that the river would not be navigable.

Sergeant Flaherty radioed Lieutenant Sidney that we were going to be short of food. Within an hour, a single-engine plane flew overhead. We could hear crackling from the Chinese rifles. The plane descended. From an open door, a GI pushed out two cardboard boxes of C-rations. The plane circled and repeated its delivery four times. One of our KATUSAs was so intrigued by the operation that he climbed out of his trench to get a better view. A carton hit him on the hip, breaking it. He was writhing on the ground until a morphine shot relieved him of the pain, but the rushing river prevented his evacuation.

On the seventh day, the rain finally let up. Three days later, the river returned to its normal flow. After ten days on Nori, we had replacements at last!

A Chinese FO probably saw us preparing to evacuate. At dusk, before the exchange took place, we were hit by incoming mortar rounds. Hollier received shapnel to his back. Two KATUSAs were ordered by Sgt. Benny Hoover to place him on a litter and take him across the river immediately. The mortars continued. They placed

Hollier on a litter, but one of the KATUSAs was so terrified that his hands clenched. His arms froze and were pressed against his chest. He stood trembling "like a dog shitting peach pits" (Benny's words). Benny had been seething ever since his buddy Bohrer had been accidentally killed by a replacement. He waved his pistol, motioning to the Korean to assist in the evacuation. The Korean remained fixed. Benny raised his .45 and shot him in the hip. The KATUSA rose, spun, and fell to the ground. Behind the gushing blood, his exposed hipbone resembled the gray wax of a Sabbath candle. Arthur Salinger, our new medic, tended to him and safely crossed the river with the KATUSA and Hollier. After the rest of the company crossed, we went on to battalion headquarters for debriefing.

As a reward for our extended period on Nori, battalion allowed us to sleep overnight on cots in their squad tents and gave us a festive late breakfast: two pork chops and mashed potatoes. Pork was verboten in my kosher home. Now, in front of me, smothered in a red sauce, sitting in a metal tray, it looked as appealing as a pork chop could be in a red sauce resting in a metal tray. *Why not?* I thought. *I'm sure I would be forgiven, considering.* I cut off a piece and bit into it. There was no resistance; my teeth clashed together. Hidden beneath the sauce was a white chunk of fat—no meat. This put an end to my temptation for the "forbidden fruit."

Finally our platoon settled back into the sanity of the MLR. We were home. We had a roof over our heads. When I removed my socks, I noticed a purple haze from the boot top down to my toes. It had the appearance of a thin, purple nylon sock.

What was a purple haze compared to Oscar Konnerth's lying somewhere in an EVAC hospital or John Hollier's having shrapnel picked out of his back? In spite of not being tested, our ordeal was considered a successful defense of Big Nori.

Forty years later, at our company's first reunion, Oscar Konnerth entered the reception with his wife, Mary Ann. We embraced, and then jokingly, I asked him if he had bugged out when we were guarding Nori. A medic from the Third Platoon had found him, treated his wounds, and then crossed the river with him.

He lifted his pants leg and showed me a gray plastic brace near the calf of his left leg. Another piece of shrapnel had entered his buttock. He was evacuated to Tokyo Army Hospital, treated, and then sent stateside.

Killed in Action

Our caked and wrinkled fatigues no longer clung to the knolls and depressions of our clammy bodies. With the onset of cooler weather, they were liberated from our pimply, sweltering summer skin. Did we smell? Did we stink? By now, who knew? When everyone is generating the same aroma, that fragrance becomes the norm.

Theoretically the weather was ideal for a patrol. As far as we were concerned, no weather was ideal for a patrol, and no patrol was ideal. We were thoroughly familiar with every approach to every target, and so were the Chinese. Had the Chinese moved closer? Had they moved back Hill 117? The hills were always contested pieces of nondescript scrub and trees. There was only one answer—a company patrol.

In the afternoon, we gathered around Sid. He was still fuming about the night we'd been ambushed on that hill. Determined to let the Chinese know it was Company L they were challenging for that insignificant lump, he gripped the pole of a Company L guidon (a navy-blue-and-white pennant that was carried on parades) and then announced, "In three days, we're going to claim Hill 117 for Company L. We can't remain there, but we can plant our flag. We'll just let the bastards know they don't own it. The Second and Third Platoons will clear. The First Platoon will pass through them and close in on the hill and plant the flag. Check with your platoon leaders. We'll run through it tomorrow."

"Where is this Hill 117?" asked Arthur Salinger, our new medic.

"The company was ambushed there about two weeks before you came here," I replied. "This time we're not the attacking platoon. We're backing them up."

"Crap. If I'd known I was going to be part of this, I'd have stayed back in that hospital in Seoul."

"What did you expect when you volunteered to come up to the MLR?"

"I really didn't know. I needed a change—a quick change. My wife was giving me a hard time."

Arthur had been stationed in a hemorrhagic fever ward in Seoul. Finding that his marriage was deteriorating with the exchange of each letter, he had volunteered for front line duty. He was sent to Company L after we lost Wayne Caton on Hill 121.

The dry run the next afternoon went smoothly. On our return to the bunkers, Arthur gave us his unsolicited biography. His father was part owner of a chain of fleabag Lyons Hotels that catered to the alcoholics on New York's Bowery.

"Hey, Arthur, tell your father to save a suite for Benny after this is over," shouted Lancaster.

"You son of a bitch, you'll never get out of here alive. You'll rot in your fart sack if I have anything to do with it," said Hoover.

After the laughter died down, Arthur continued. During his formative years, his family lived in an upscale community on Long Island, New York, and drove a Chrysler sedan—quite a contrast to the Depression backgrounds of the rest of our platoon. When he announced his intention to get married, his parents advised him to wait until he returned from the service, but he ignored their wishes. The sex that had sparked the shaky marriage was quickly extinguished by distance. Now he was our medic in Company L.

The setting sun was a signal to gather for a run-through of the attack on Hill 117 with live ammo. Aside from the guidon, the plan followed the same tactic as it had on the night of the ambush, but with many new players. The new men hadn't passed through our period in reserve, or our short period in the blocking position, or the bunker bomb sortie, or the attack on Hill 121. This was to be their introduction to live fire.

"Do you guys expect anyone to be killed?"

"Will they trap the company the way they did before?" another asked.

"Can we stay together tomorrow night?"

The questions came, but there were no answers. Hadn't I been a frightened greenhorn some months ago? Wasn't I a frightened veteran now? I knew what was going through their minds. These were legitimate questions for replacements going on their first patrol—legitimate questions for a vet going on any patrol. The clowning around, real or pretended, accompanying our return to the bunkers in the past was absent. The stupidity of planting a guidon just to show we had been there boggled my mind. Our failure to capture a prisoner was a given by now.

It was a bright, brisk morning the day of the patrol. Everyone was moving with a purpose. The purpose was breakfast. I climbed over and down the reverse slope toward the cook's grill, which was hidden among a few crippled trees.

All I thought was, *How does that cook crack the eggs in one hand and drop them onto the grill without breaking the yolks? I wish I could do that.*

There was very little conversation between our men and the cooks. It was almost as if they thought we were trying to evict them from their hidden enclave a few ridgelines to the rear of the MLR.

From the chow line, I nodded to Benny and Charley, who were already eating their breakfast. Both were RAs, and I was sure that a career of mess hall chow, C-rations, and oceans of liquor had by now desensitized their taste buds.

Charley was disappointed that we weren't the attacking platoon. "I want to get at those *Gook* bastards. They're probably the ones who ambushed us."

Benny paid no attention to him. He paid no attention to anyone. In spite of his humor, he was a very private person. Did he have a wife? Did he have children? I guess the answers were dissolved in the alcohol he consumed. Eventually they might be liberated, as the tales of his hometown and his participation in World War II had been.

It then came time to sit and wait for twilight. I had three issues of the *New York Journal American* in my bunker. Of all the New York City newspapers, it covered the Korean War with greatest detail. Copies came in clusters. There would be one, two, three days, and sometimes a week of no papers, and then three or four would come in a day.

Let's take a look, I decided. *Is there anything about this battalion's role in Korea? No. The marines are taking a beating on the west coast of Korea. Forget it; what place are the Yankees in? Who cares. Let's see what the civilians are wearing this year.*

To me, the ads, which I had ignored as a civilian, were now the most interesting part of the newspaper. They showed what people were wearing instead of our filthy fatigues. They showed young men in suits, dressed for an evening out, alongside beautiful women. Not my thing, but that's what classy folks were doing. *Hey*, I thought, looking at a young man modeling a suit, *why isn't he in the army?*

It was then on to Massey for ammo and grenades, and then on to the assembly area. Lieutenant Crowe, who had replaced Lieutenant Theiss as our platoon leader, reviewed our mission. *There's that chaplain again. There are the jon boats again. There's the overhead rope again. Crap, there's that guidon again.*

We pulled ourselves across a river silver-plated with moonlight. The platoons lined up at the Bubble in the order of attack, just as we had practiced the previous day. That damn guidon at the rear of us bothered me. It just didn't belong. This wasn't a parade.

The Third Platoon stepped out, and our platoon moved behind them. We advanced through the Noris and out onto the trail we had beaten down the night of the ambush. Although we weren't the attacking platoon, Charley volunteered to point the way and insisted that I be the runner. So far, we had received no opposition. We approached Hill 117 unopposed. Our platoon and the Third Platoon fanned out to clear the area and secure the rear. No opposition. Sid and his M1 were at the center of the First Platoon, which would attack. The guidon, carried by someone behind him, passed through us. There was a lull—a silence before the storm. It was the loudest hush to penetrate the human ear. Then the hum of burp guns and blasts of concussion grenades awakened us. A chattered response by our machine guns and rifles was followed by grenade bursts. The buzz from the burp guns always made me wonder how they could possibly miss their targets.

I hoped our men were hugging the ground. When were we going to get out of here? Who was this, running by with a machine gun tripod on his back?

Sid ran after him.

"Where are you going with that tripod?" growled Sid.

"Our machine gun is jammed."

"You have a carbine. Get the hell back there! Blackwell, move your men up to the First Platoon!"

KATUSAs ran by carrying a wounded man on a litter. How many more would come by?

Finally the First Platoon began its withdrawal. They passed through us. *No guidon!* They had probably stuck it in the ground somewhere. Mission accomplished? Prisoners? No.

Next, our platoon withdrew. Passing through the Third Platoon, we moved quickly toward the Noris. The GIs on the outpost asked what had happened. Our motor was running. We had no time for a chat. The Third Platoon followed. Jon boats carried us back to the shore of the MLR.

Waiting trucks brought our men back to battalion headquarters for a briefing. As usual, the attacking platoon was subjected to most of the questions. I walked past the doughnut truck. No more greasy circles for me. We sat, waiting to get a casualty report. Two replacements in the First Platoon had received minor wounds from burp gun fire. Next came a report that we had a KIA from the Third Platoon. The death startled us. The Third Platoon was a supporting platoon. As far as we knew, it hadn't received fire. How had he been hit? Who was he? Someone said he had come to Company L when we were in reserve. That was the end of the story for that night.

Forty-five years later, at Company L's first reunion, I asked Sid if he remembered that day in reserve when one of our men had been killed by fire from a sleeping replacement's BAR. He remembered; he also remembered the guidon on Hill 117. He remembered everything. He told my wife and me that the dead GI was Bohrer, a good friend of Benny Hoover. Then he went on. "Do you remember the night we planted the guidon on Hill 117? First the attacking platoon withdrew. Then Benny Hoover's squad withdrew. Sometime later, Whitefeather completed the story of that evening. While moving back, he said, Benny saw the replacement who had accidentally killed his buddy Bohrer. The man was asleep against a bush. Benny waited until everyone had passed through; then he siezed the opportunity to pull a pin on a fragmentary grenade. He placed the grenade on the replacement's lap and then caught up with his platoon."

My wife, Sheila, was stunned. She asked Sid, "Then what happened?"

"His parents probably received a 'killed in action' telegram," he replied.

Frozen in Chosin

It was mid-September. *Sayonara, sweltering heat.* My T-shirt was as brown as the trench outside my bunker. The buttons on my fatigue shirt were to become reaquainted with their loops, as autumn was stealthily sneaking in on us. I had heard about Korean winters from the older veterans, but I had arrived in March, when a field jacket was an adequate insulator. Now the sun was shining brightly, and the last few days had been in the midsixties—very comfortable days to dry the dampness in my bunker.

As the days passed, we added field jackets to our ensembles. They were quite comfortable and didn't interfere witn our movement. In fact, they added warmth when we zipped ourselves into our sleeping bags. Soon our field jacketets were no match for the wicked winds accompying the chill. No matter how I tried, the cold won the battle.

Hints of the Korean winter bit through our field jackets in mid-September. As the sun went down and the forbidding darkness enveloped the MLR, a chill began to nip at my fingers and toes. Oily cotton field jackets, filthy fatigues, summer underwear, and grimy, threadbare socks were no match for the raw evenings. Cold had no problem penetrating my sleeping bag, which by now was as thin as a necktie. The odor from the chemical preservative saturating the burlap sandbags pervaded our bunker's dank, stale, cold air. Was anyone else chilled by the weather? I met Lancaster at the Lister bag.

"Lancaster, I don't know why I've been so cold the last few days. Has the weather gotten to you?"

"My sleeping bag is a rag. Last night I couldn't get warm. I was colder than a well digger's asshole. Let's go to Lieutenant Crowe."

Lieutenant Crowe spoke to Lieutenant Sidney about the unexpected change in the weather. In two days, a jeep arrived with a bundle of button-in field jacket vests. They were probably a trial run—an experiment. On one side was a looped fiberglass fabric resembling a bright white terry cloth towel. On the reverse side shimmered a thin, silky OD fabric. These vests were as useless as the nearly vacant 101 packs sent to us from the rear.

As Lieutenant Crowe distributed these vests, he said with a grin, "Battalion wants you to keep these vests clean when they're returned."

There we were, sleeping on filthy, deflated air mattresses laid over patches of damp earth, rubbing along the dirt walls of the trenches and bunkers, lying prone on the ground on patrols, and we were being asked to keep the liners clean? Their insulating property might have been excellent for copper wire, but as far as insulating our bodies from the Korean cold, they were a total failure. As the days grew colder, so did the liners, and they quickly transferred their chill to our bodies. The welcome mat in Korea had long ago become a tattered rag.

With the wind making icicles from the drips of our noses, and the tips of our fingers numb behind the nails, the flavor of coffee improved. Although the powdered eggs quickly surrendered their warmth to the chilled metal trays, they were far superior to anything waiting to be scooped up from the inside of a cold C-ration can.

A warm-up tent was pitched among the survivors of a once-dense grove of trees. I guess it could have been called Company L's social club. Here a rotating number of men got a chance to eat, talk, and improve the temperature of their underwear. Charley Kauneckis, who had become our squad leader, came over to Gus and me.

"Did you guys hear the freaking noise from the Noris the past few nights? The Chinks got a bug up their ass. They're blowing more horns and rattling more ammo canisters and screaming like banshees. Lieutenant Crowe said battalion wants to know where they're coming from, so I volunteered our squad to find out."

"You *what?*" shouted Gus.

"Yeah. In two days, we'll see if they're coming from Hill 121. I'm going to tell the rest of the squad to be ready."

Gus turned to me. "What's he trying to do? Get a battlefield commission? I'm sick of his shit."

Although he knew I hadn't planned it, Gus had not been a happy warrior since Lieutenant Theiss asked him to take over my BAR. His conversation was limited, so it was difficult to learn how he felt. But he smiled a lot. Gus was an enlistee, a paratrooper, from Long Island, New York, and like the rest of the paratroopers in the company, he was there when we needed him. Maybe it was the change in the weather, or maybe it was the impending patrol; whatever it was, this wasn't the Gus we knew. To bring back that Gus, I asked him if he had a photo of his girlfriend. He told me he didn't have a girlfriend. "Neither do I," I said, although Elaine's photo was getting damp somewhere in my bunker. She was just a friend, but she did look good in that bathing suit. Take enough photos and in one you'll look like a movie star.

Our squad gathered at Massey's bunker to prepare for the patrol. I stuffed two extra magazines for my carbine into my field jacket and a grenade in each of my pants pockets. Massey wished us good luck, and then we stomped down the trail toward the jon boats.

Ever since the deluge some weeks earlier, the speed of the Imjin River had picked up considerably. To prevent our boat from getting swept away by the current, Charley held tightly to the overhead rope as Gus, Whitefeather, and I hopped in. A splash over the side was not as welcome as it would have been a few weeks before, when the nights were warm. My cold, wet pants leg clung to me like the blackheads on my knees. No matter how I tried to shake it loose, that damp cloth kept finding my legs.

We assembled at the Bubble. Charley ignored his sergeant stripes when it came to a patrol or a raid. "Point man" was tattooed onto his brain. He led us through the same tank trail we had used the night we'd raided Hill 121. When he reached the base of Big Nori, Charley made a right. He was about to lead us up its side. I ran up to him.

"Charley, do you remember what happened in the river when we went to take out that bunker below 117? Some of our own men heard you and lobbed grenades at you that night, mistaking you for a Chink."

"It's okay. I checked with Crowe. He said our men up in the trenches expect us."

We climbed halfway up Nori and then set up shop along a ledge hidden by trees and bushes. Now we were between our men above us on Nori and the tank trail in the valley below.

Sitting about ten feet apart, we waited and we waited. The temperature began to drop outside, along with the field jacket liners inside. I curled my toes, and then I removed my mittens. I rubbed my thumb over my fingers and made a fist. James, one of our recent replacements, passed a hand warmer to Ed.

"After you warm up, pass it on. It really works."

"Shut up, you two," whispered Charley. "Sound travels a long way out here, you dummies."

We sat late into the night. It was getting colder. No activity. Charley finally decided to return to the MLR.

As if they had been shaken out from the open rings of a loose-leaf binder, white sheets of paper were scattered along the path back to the jon boats. Cold and tired, I just wanted to get across the Imjin and crawl into my sleeping bag. I picked up a paper, folded it, and placed it in my pocket. My sleeping bag was waiting.

•

Like a dog waking from his nap, I stretched out the stiffness from a damp night's sleep—my first major event in the morning. Finally, when my blood began circulating and my joints were once again elastic, I remembered the paper I had placed in my pocket.

The Chinese, masters at propaganda, had evidently sent some men to scatter the leaflets along the path while we were sitting and waiting. The sheet showed a bright color photo of a smiling entrepreneur with a lit cigar, sunglasses shielding his eyes. He was dressed in a bathing suit and leaning over two beautiful ladies who were also in bathing suits. The caption read, "Mr. Moneybags is in Florida this Christmas."

Below, in black-and-white, a dismal group of GIs were marching in the snow. That caption read, "Where are you? ... In Korea. You risk your life. Big Business rakes in the dough."

Coordinated with the cold weather, I would grade the leaflet an A+. When Lieutenant Sidney saw it, he sent some men to police the area. I mailed the leaflet to my brother, but the censor saw it, and that was the end of its journey.

Soon there was a break in the weather. We returned the field jacket liners along with all the brown Korean earth we had accumulated on them. I guess the army agreed with us. Those "towels" were never reissued.

Good-bye, Company L

It was mid-October. A directive came to Lieutenant Sidney offering senior members of our company the choice of remaining in Korea, where in two or three months' time they would have accumulated the thirty-six points required to rotate home, or being integrated into the inexperienced infantry battalions in Japan. If I chose to stay in Korea, in three more months I would rotate home. If I opted for Japan, I would complete my remaining ten months there and then rotate home.

Three more months of line duty, I thought. Flaherty's jaw was pulp. Where was Wayne? Where was Konnerth? Burp gun bullets had pierced Nunns's shoulder and left arm. Bastin's head wounds were so bad we thought he probably hadn't made it through the night. Shrapnel had left Mette with severe abdominal wounds. Shrapnel had gone through Gerecke's abdomen and pierced his intestines. A helicopter had evacuated an unconscious, hemorrhaging Lt. William Edmunds. The thin plastic layers of young Phil Dickson's vest had been shredded by shrapnel. Massingale, Camacho, and Moen had been killed on a raid. A sniper had killed Rutledge. *Should I chance the three months or go to Japan for ten months?*

I asked Lieutenant Crowe, "If your son were here, what would you advise him to do?"

Without hesitation he replied, "You'll never know when a piece of shrapnel or a bullet has your name on it. If you were my son, I'd advise you to go to Japan."

How do you say good-bye to the men who have shared the nightmare with you? I recalled Sergeant Springer walking down the reverse slope a week after I came to Company L. He was carrying his backpack in his hand, his rifle slung over his right shoulder. I asked him where he was going. He said he was going home.

"Don't you say good-bye?" I asked.

He didn't believe in making friends, he said, and he added, "I don't believe in good-byes."

Should I follow this World War II veteran's path? Walk away, hop into a truck, and leave all this history behind me? No, I couldn't do that. But how could I look directly at the men and say good-bye when I was leaving them for the sake of my security? I was determined to leave.

I said good-bye to my gentle, decent, anything-but-militant friends and recent replacements. Charley Kauneckis, now Sergeant Kauneckis, my closest buddy, was stunned. He was our squad leader and self-appointed point man. I was the runner.

"What are you doing? I could go too, but I'm staying. We're a team. You can't leave us!"

"Charley, you know I earned my way out of here. Even Lieutenant Crowe told me to leave."

"Yeah, him. Since we lost Theiss, I've never trusted him."

I wasn't happy about his attitude, because remorse at "abandoning the platoon" was churning inside me. On the other hand, I was a draftee in a war that made no sense to me. Back when we were in reserve, a reporter for the *Stars and Stripes* had asked me what my mission was in Korea. I told him, "To get thirty-six points and get the hell out of here."

Charley had enlisted; he was a career man. His mission was to follow orders.

Will I see him after I'm discharged? I wondered. I asked him for his home address.

"The army is my home. You can write me, but don't expect answers. I don't write."

I wondered whether I would ever see him again.

He offered me a limp hand; then I left. The book on Charley was closed, I thought.

"Oh, yes, we'll exchange letters" was repeated with every good-bye to the other men. I had written letters for them to their girlfriends, but were they going to write to me?

Benny Hoover was adjusting the sandbags on the trench outside his bunker. He knew I was leaving. Hesitantly, I said, "Benny, I'm leaving Company L. I'm going to Japan."

I was shocked when he replied, "I might be going too. I'm thinking about it."

He just nodded when I thanked him for the laughs and for saving our lives on the night of the ambush. Then I left him.

My next visit was to Whitefeather. When I told him I was leaving for Japan, he shook my hand and wished me good luck. That was it. Why did I feel so bad about leaving him? Maybe because Whitefeather never spoke of home, maybe because he never spoke of friends, or maybe because what I saw of him was what I got—no more, no less. Were Indians not supposed to have a home, friends, or history? He was a friend, but the glue remained a gel—it had never set between Whitefeather and the rest of the men in the platoon. He looked so alone outside his bunker that I choked up after leaving this distant man.

Ah! There was CP Jones. I needed a lift, and he was the man to give me one. He, too, knew I was leaving. With his impish smile, he said, "Take me along. I'll carry your duffel."

I thanked him for his songs and laughs. There was no handshake; we grabbed each other's arms.

I left the trenches and went to the command post. Saying good-bye to Lieutenant Sidney was going to be difficult. I was sure he would try to sell me on remaining in Korea. Fortunately he was at battalion headquarters.

I slid down the reverse slope to Massey. My helmet, canteen, carbine, and armored vest were now in his hands. Soon they would be the property of a replacement, but they could not pass on the vivid, bitter, and happy memories of my life wearing them with the men of Company L. With my backpack in my hand, I walked to the road.

My discomfort would be relieved only by the arrival of something, anything, that would take me out of there—the sooner the better. Finally a truck arrived. To my surprise, John Hollier and Herbert Niehoff appeared, ready to board with me. We hopped up, pulled down a wooden plank bench, and sat down. Niehoff, who'd been in basic training with me, was bitching about the Purple Heart he should have been awarded when some pebbles kicked up by an incoming mortar round had scratched his leg. I had thought that Hollier was already stateside with his injured back. He said he had just returned from a MASH, where they'd stitched him up. We shared the recent news of Company L and then turned to some men from Company I who were also in the truck. Frankie Scudero, a rabid Giants football fan, was hoping to get home before the season ended. Pat Dostilio couldn't wait to get to a phone to call his wife. Art Schuyler was looking forward to doing anything that was not in a trench. John Sheilds was unfocused, apathetic, unresponsive, and burnt out.

After a thirty-minute drive, we passed through Seoul. It had not changed much. There was the same scenery—the same skeleton graveyard of buildings that I'd seen on the trip to the Seder in April. The truck continued on. In twenty minutes we were at the port of Inchon, where we were billeted in a high school.

I collapsed onto the splendor of a cot, a blanket, and a pillow. I tried to fall asleep, but the enticing sound of sprinkling water lured me to a shower room. Korean soil and pungent sweat had been my bunker buddies for the last seven months. As I tried to remove my T-shirt, it clung tenaciously to its bosom buddy, my skin. I finally disengaged it and its mate, my jockey shorts. These delicates, which I had worn for at least a month, I left hanging limply on a hook. Like devoted dogs, they patiently awaited my return from the shower. I abandoned them with the hope that they would be adopted and sterilized by the Korean laundry personnel.

I think I spent a record length of time under the spray. My soap was prospecting through areas I had never explored. My rancid fatigues were waiting when I stepped out of the shower. Without underwear, they adhered to me, trusting they would not suffer the fate of my undergarments.

I thought of claiming the duffel bag I had left months ago at battalion headquarters when I arrived in Korea during the rainstorm. They had promised it would be waiting for me. Waiting where? Who cared. I was evolving into a person.

Clean fatigues and underwear were scheduled for the following morning. Shivering on the floor of the school gym, we were told to remove our old fatigues. The only heat in that gym was escaping from our naked bodies. I threw my filthy fatigues on the left side of a large pile. All that we were wearing was our skin, so the army could now be assured that we were leaving Korea with neither ammunition nor a weapon.

The spoon I would not surrender.

I kept an eye on the far edge of the pile where I had thrown my fatigues. My irreplaceable loyal spoon was in the shirt pocket. It looked as if it had been snatched from a pegboard of tools hanging in a garage. It would have undermined the elegance of a soup bowl from a diner, but it coordinated perfectly with the steel tray in the basic training mess hall. It was designed to be a half-inch wider than the maximum aperture formed by human lips. Two generous scoops with this bent piece of metal left my C- ration can nearly depleted. But the spoon was mine, all mine, and I was not ready to part with it.

The processing went quickly. As soon as I was dressed in my clean underwear and fatigues, I casually ambled to the discarded fatigue pile and found my shirt. I unbuttoned the pocket and removed my cherished relic.

That afternoon at the Inchon pier, the albatross, Korea, remained in place. I left for Japan with my trusty spoon resting securely in my clean chest pocket.

It Was Beautiful

MSTS *Sadao S. Munemori*, the same mottled, gray, rust-coated vessel that had brought me to Korea, was anchored at the port of Inchon, waiting to deliver me to Japan. Why did it look so good now? Why did I see it as a trim cruise ship waiting to leave for a Caribbean port? From all outward appearances, it was the same tub. The same irregular patches of rust still reached for one another along its bow. In fact, the corrosion had spread like a contagion to the deck. But it was beautiful.

Once I was inside the lower deck, the same moldy dampness as before assaulted my nose. But it was beautiful. I splashed along a wet floor in semidarkness until I reached a bunk. I had very little to throw on it to stake my claim—no duffel bag, no backpack just a toilet kit. What I wore was what I owned. I was certain there would be a wardrobe and soldier tools waiting for me somewhere in Japan.

The PA system announced that lunch was being served in the mess. It should have announced that mess was being served for lunch. The men who had been seized for KP seemed embarrassed to dish out the slop. Gray squares of meatloaf slid off a spatula and onto my tray. A glob of dehydrated potatoes hung from a serving spoon like a stalactite; then it detached and cemented itself alongside the meatloaf. Wrinkled green peas, clustered in a slotted spoon, added color to the dreary mural on my steel tray. I thought of Mess Sergeant Goff. Would he have allowed this to escape from his kitchen? I doubt it. But it was beautiful.

In three days, we arrived at the port of Sasebo, Japan. A sergeant came through the *Munemori* blaring, "Get your gear. Get off the boat. Give your name to the sergeant at the bottom of the gangway, and get on the train at the station!"

There was not a moment to view the landscape. I went down the gangplank and onto a train where cots were suspended by chains from the inner walls of the cars. During the day, we sat on them; in the evening, we slept on them.

I thought I had seen the last of those little OD tin cans. Had they followed me from Korea? For lunch, C-rations were distributed throughout the car. I couldn't wait to open the crackers and tin of jelly, which might work to dissolve the ham-and-lima-bean residue coating my tongue. When the fauna and flora in my mouth were finally stabilized, I decided to visit my buddy John Hollier.

"John, do you think those C-rations will follow us stateside?"

"They're not so bad. A couple of shakes of Tabasco sauce and a few chiles, and they'd be perfect."

I didn't know about Tabasco sauce, and what were chiles? All I knew was that C-rations and my taste buds were incompatible. Neither Tabasco nor any other sauce could consummate a marriage between them. I left John, who was writing a letter to his girlfriend.

As we sped north, a checkerboard of rice paddies was repeated on the flat, wet terrain. When we passed through Hiroshima, I looked for the frame of the famous building that had been damaged by the atomic bomb. Farmer shacks near the paddies were the only whole buildings on the horizon.

The next day, we detrained at Sendai, a large city in the northern part of Honshu Island, the largest island of Japan. The arrival of a covered two-and-a-half-ton truck brought back memories of the night when Frye had shredded the canvas cover of our truck with the bullets from his BAR. A one-hour ride led us to Camp Younghans at the outskirts of a small town called Jinmachi.

In sharp contrast to the Korean landscape, the terrain approaching the camp was totally flat and green. Once inside the camp, our truck passed a wide, bell-shaped 150-foot hill towering over the parade ground. Later I learned that US POWs had built this hill during World War II for the storage of bombs.

We hopped out of the truck without any possessions. A swollen duffel bag would have given me the security of knowing I owned something and therefore was someone. My toilet kit could fit in a bellows pocket I suspect that my father, arriving from his shtetl in Lithuania, had had this same empty feeling when he stood alone with his pathetic cardboard valise on the dock at Ellis Island.

Hollier, Niehoff, Scudero, Dostilio, and Schuyler were sent to other companies in the camp. A jeep brought me to my company. At quartermaster, I received my new wardrobe. My Achilles tendons cringed when I was told to turn in my two-month-old soft, worn, water-abused, user-friendly combat boots for a stiff new pair. I remembered the torture I had experienced while breaking my first boots in during basic training; the damage they'd done to my tendons had convinced me I would never walk like a human again. With my new boots loosely laced, new chinos, new fatigues, new underwear, and a new coat in my new duffel bag, I walked to my barracks looking like a new draftee.

Japanese army personnel had occupied these platoon-size barracks during World War II. They were made of a wood like balsa, so fireguard duty was required throughout the night. But it was a new home in a quiet neighborhood, and it was beautiful.

As I unfolded a mattress cover and slipped it over the mattress, I recalled the midnight outing in basic training over the Blue Mountains, when we had returned at 2:00 a.m. to remove and shake our mattress covers in front of Sergeant Roach. I topped my mattress cover with a bedsheet and tightened another sheet over it. On top of the sheet, I tucked in a coarse woolen OD blanket. A too-soft, overused pillow was lost in my pillowcase. Now I could lie down and stare at the locker holding my new wardrobe. *A pillow! A mattress! A blanket! A bed! A new wardrobe! Do I dog-paddle or do I float as I cruise through this elegance?*

The men returning from a field exercise interrupted my euphoria. My platoon sergeant, Sergeant Perez, walked me through the barracks, introducing the members of the platoon.

The lavatory was as wide and open as a large living room. Directly to the rear were six unpartitioned showers, encouraging conversation and horseplay. Now, during rush hour, activity in the room resembled an opera featuring ballet dancers twisting, jumping, and turning at stage left, the chorus in the rear, walk-ons conversing to the right, and principals preening at center stage. Our opera had men soaping in the showers at stage left, men relieving themselves into the urinals at stage right, men straining themselves on the toilet bowls to the rear, and men washing, shaving, combing their hair, and adjusting their uniforms at center stage. It was a flush of activity.

After lights out, the only sound was the occasional stroll to the bathroom by the fireguard.

•

How long had it been since I'd fallen out for reveille? I quickly shaved, slipped into my new fatigues, and followed the men to the company street. Captain Moman, the company commander, a black officer, called on me to step out of formation. While he was introducing me as a recently arrived Korean vet, a speeding jeep braked between the two of us. Escorted by an MP, a disheveled black soldier with unlaced bleached boots, a wrinkled uniform, and hair piercing the air in every direction of a compass shuffled toward us. Walking slowly around him, Captain Moman carefully examined the GI. Then, glaring at him in disgust, he said, "Robbins, you're supposed to be with the men in formation this morning. Your boots are unlaced and unpolished; your cap is so wrinkled it looks like you just pulled it out of an asshole. You smell like a honey bucket [the buckets of human feces used by farmers to fertilize their rice paddies]. Half your ass is hanging out of your chinos. Your hair looks like you just got orders to return to Korea.

The MP pulled you out of that whore's shack. I know you don't have any money to pay her. What are you doing to that mama that she's keeping you there? Show me and the boys what she taught you on her straw mattress."

The company roared with laughter, and no one howled louder than Captain Moman. *This assignment*, I thought, *is my reward for Korea.*

The smile hadn't yet left his lips when Moman shouted, "Company dismissed!"

We ran over the white gravel path to the mess hall. *A tray, a fork, a knife, a spoon, a napkin, hot grits, and scrambled eggs on a warm ceramic plate. Where do I reenlist?*

"Wolfe, come over here."

Sergeant Perez was seriously salting his grits, eggs, napkin, tray, and table. He looked up. "They want you at the Service Club. It's the building next to the movie theater."

"Who wants me? What for?"

"Be there at ten, and you'll find out."

When I reached the Service Club, twelve GIs and an aging woman (probably in her forties) were seated around a large table. I recognized Frank Scudero, Pat Dostilio, Art Schuyler, John Sheilds, John Hollier, and Herbert Niehoff. They and six other GIs were watching intently as the woman removed squares of leather and long, thin leather strips from a cardboard box.

"Have a seat," she said. "We'll be here for the rest of the week. This class will ease your return to barracks life."

The grits, flatware, and eggs have already done an excellent job of easing, I thought, *but I'll play the game.*

My handmade therapeutic wallet (made in Japan).

She distributed sheets of paper illustrating various wallets and then held up some small leatherworking tools. We were not about to argue. The room was clean and warm. Why not make a wallet?

For a week, using a flower template, a hammer, and a pointy metal tool, I tapped, squeezed, and cut on the smooth side of a precut piece of leather. By the end of the week, I was eased into my return to barracks life and had a custom-designed wallet. It was beautiful!

But what was happening to the boys of Company L?

The Clarion Call
of Testosterone

Button-in linings had not been issued when the winter winds on northern Honshu Island whistled through the cracks of our barracks. Those button-in white fiberglass linings needed some serious tutoring in the art of insulation after failing their test in Korea. So, in Japan, I settled for something I swore I would never wear: long johns. I wasn't accustomed to having a long garment so intimate with my body. While trying to warm to their embrace, I was called to the CP.

Awaiting me there was a phone call from Earl Davis, a charismatic black machine-gunner from Company L's heavy weapons platoon. He was on R & R in Japan. *How did he know I was here? How did he get my number? How did he find me?* We immediately turned to family business. Company L had been transferred to an area west of the Noris called Jackson Heights. Incoming fire was especially intense. They were taking many casualties.

When I had rotated to Japan, Murray Lichtman, who was a mortarman in the Fourth Platoon, replaced Massey as the armorer. He had fulfilled his dream of having a .45-caliber pistol hanging from his garrison belt, only to be blown apart by an incoming mortar round. Davis told me that my buddy Charley Kauneckis had returned from a patrol feeling a burning sensation in his chest. Upon removing his parka, OG shirt (a woolen flannel garment like Polartec), and fatigue shirt, he found his T-shirt stained with blood.

He patched his wound with alcohol and gauze. On the same patrol, Bill Gardner had been treated at an aid station, and Evertie Moore had been transferred to a MASH. Lt. Don Daly, who replaced Sid, was severely wounded when his patrol came under enemy fire. Davis passed on his only good news—that he was due to rotate in a month.

•

In a few days, my entire base was scheduled for a winter exercise. Trucks carried us to a woody, mountainous area at the northern end of Honshu. The snow was relentless. Upon arrival, we tamped it down around the trucks and began unloading large, square wooden boxes. Folded arched frames and long, thickly padded waterproof sheets were tightly packed inside each box. By trial and error, we notched together the empty boxes to create a floor. Then we locked the arches to the floor and suspended the thick, insulated padded sheets over them. Now a portable Quonset hut stood where there had been virgin snow.

The cooks were setting up two squad tents. One was to be the kitchen; the other, the mess. Upon completion, the tents were completely covered with snow. Snowshoes resembling old wooden tennis racquets were issued to us, with a warning that we were not to go anywhere outside the area unless we were wearing the shoes and were accompanied by at least one buddy. The snow was eight to ten feet deep in some sunken areas. Each platoon was issued two plastic sleds of Finnish design called *ahkios*. They resembled wide white canoes with wooden strips at the bottom that acted as runners. We used them to transport our heavy equipment in the snow. Like mules, we pulled them along with ropes.

Training started the following day. There were no strategic exercises. The focus of this operation seemed to be physical conditioning, and we got plenty of it. As long as we were in motion, the cold was no challenge. In fact, I loved the brisk, clean air and the snow pelting me and forming rivulets as the flakes melted on my face.

A simple metal rectangular heater no larger than twenty by twenty-five inches produced more than ample heat for the entire Quonset hut. One night I commented about the amount of heat coming from such a small device. Johnson, our mail clerk, replied, "Some junkyard Jew will be selling them soon."

I turned to him and said, "I'm a Jew. After you're discharged, you'll probably be the first to buy one from a junkyard Jew."

His apology was followed by an embarrassing silence. The air in the Quonset hut was so explosive it could have burst the padded panels off. A few attempts at conversation ended in failure. During my entire time in the army, I wasn't confronted with anti-Semitism. Charley had a knee-jerk rersponse toward any minority, but not with venom. I couldn't wait for the next day to begin.

A "business lady" generated heat in this snowbound tent in northern Japan.

The snow and cold were no impediment to one enterprising mind or to the flow of hormones. An elderly local man with a backpack appeared. He benevolently decided that the boys needed a diversion. In the evening, he stationed himself outside the empty mess tent and deployed his stock inside. The fluffy, virgin evening snow was quickly flattened to a hard surface path by the boots of men answering the clarion call of testosterone. There was Papasan, covered with snow, collecting the tariff and transferring it to his backpack as each man passed through the tent to sample his merchandise. I found that the cold weather was incompatible with the goods he was hawking.

Ten days of frolicking in the snow came to an end. A dense snowfall blanketed our tire tracks when we traveled south. As we sat in the back of the truck, our OD field jackets and fatigues were a sad contrast to the sparkling snowdrifts accumulating behind us. But we had lived in and seen enough snow. We were going home, to Camp Younghans.

Our camp hadn't been spared the snowy weather. Company streets heavy with snow and ice bore the weight of our moaning, slipping, and sliding trucks. When they finally came to a stop, we crawled out on legs that had been dangling from truck benches since early morning. Some men deposited themselves on their beds and became as fixed as the blanket below them. Others, with soap in hand, made a rush for the bathroom, leaving a trail of fatigues and underwear behind. The barracks steamed up from the heat and moisture escaping the bathroom. Yes, we were home after an uneventful military two weeks in northern Japan.

Our lax, easy training began again. This gave me a clue to the disaster our army of occupation in Japan had suffered when they were called to defend South Korea at the beginning of the Korean War. As Max Hastings describes in his book *The Korean War*, "Within hours the first men of the 24th Division were enplaning for Korea. American forces in Japan, jerked unceremoniously from the ease and, indeed, unashamed sloth of occupation life, began the painful struggle to adapt themselves to a war footing."

Fortunately, by landing US troops at Inchon, behind the enemy, General Douglas MacArthur had trapped and later was able to destroy the North Korean Army. In response, however, a Chinese "volunteer army" had crossed the Yalu River to defend North Korea. The bloody war then ground on for two more years.

The training I was experiencing in Japan now probably duplicated that of the US army of occupation when the Korean War had begun. It was about as challenging and aerobic as going down the slide in a playground.

Mail provided the fuel that energized me in the monotonous days that followed, but now that I was in a safe area, the gaps between letters widened. I tried reading and quickly lost interest in the expurgated paperback novels printed for military personnel. I discovered a new cuisine, fried shrimp, at the service club, but the accompanying country music blasting out of the jukebox confused my digestive juices. What next? Cigarettes? They were cheap. When I finished a "loosie" (a single cigarette, which had sold for a penny at the candy store in the Bronx) my tongue felt as if it were coated with hydrochloric acid. Yet most of the men in my platoon grabbed any opportunity to inject a cigarette into their faces with complete disregard for their lungs.

September, the month I was due to rotate home, seemed very far away. I needed some diversion to occupy my remaining time in Japan.

I Don't Chew

I thought I had found the diversion I was seeking in an activity that brought back memories of my childhood. A daily customer at the candy store (our hangout) was an elderly gentleman. After years of smoking, he had sullied his snow white moustache and beard with an indelible yellow stain. *If this is what nicotine did to his facial hair*, I thought, *what did it do to his teeth and lungs?* The sight of the yellow stain convinced me never to hang a cigarette from my lips.

On the candy store counter, adjacent to the cigarettes, there lay a lonely, undisturbed stack of Red Apple chewing tobacco packets. Each packet was the size of a small rectangular chocolate bar packaged in an appealing bright yellow cellophane with a picture of a red apple near the center, along with a clear window to reveal the treasure within. In all the years we held court at the candy store, I had never seen a single package pass over the counter. I didn't dare try it myself, in spite of seeing some of my baseball heroes step up to the plate with this mobile wad of nicotine in their jowls and brown drivel streaming off their chins.

If they chew and are apparently healthy athletes with excellent reflexes, why not try it? I wondered. But then I thought, *There must be a sensible reason why no one I know chews.* So I did not make a dent into the stack of Red Apple at the candy store.

These packets appeared upon my horizon again in Korea. By the time the 101 packs full of goodies had reached Company L on the MLR, shorn of most of their desirable contents by the rear-echelon heroes, little packages of Red Apple had a place with the shoe polish and aftershave lotion. Still I did not try the chew. I detested tobacco and the few addicts who tried to hide their burning cigarettes when we were on line.

Our barracks in Japan were as dry as balsa. Therefore, fireguards were posted in all barracks throughout the night. Clyde Holmes was on fireguard one night when I had difficulty falling asleep. He was vigorously chewing and spitting spent, juicy brown balls into a number-ten can. A ball caromed off his cuspids; when it arrived at the molars, they gnashed, releasing brown rivulets from it; the saliva flowed toward the corners of his lips, found a space, and then gently trickled through it, spreading a glowing tan on his chin, which was illuminated by the lightbulb above him. Using his multifunctional fatigue sleeve, he cleared his chin of the juice.

It was not a pretty sight, but it passed his enthusiasm on to me like a virulent disease. The following day, I rushed to the PX. Ten cents sent a package of Red Apple chewing tobacco over the counter.

It was Sunday. Throughout the army, Sunday dinner consisted of cold cuts. At our base, it was boiled frankfurters, sliced bologna, and sliced ham, accompanied by slices of an orange substance that tried very hard to resemble cheddar cheese. I felt that my Red Apple would be the perfect dessert for this well-balanced meal.

I dashed for the packet. The difficulty in opening it further stimulated my lust. At last! My teeth sank into the bar. The first two or three chews were as delicious as licorice. As the rapid flow of saliva joined the tobacco to form a thin, brown, viscous ooze, my head began to whirl. Some of the gunk leached into my throat. The spinning was followed by a tidal wave of nausea. The remainder of the Red Apple joined the little brown tobacco balls fired into the number-ten can by Clyde Holmes.

War Games, Ball Games

"Get the troops into the trucks!"

Two months after returning from our winter exercise in northern Honshu, we were sent to Camp Schimmelpfennig in Sendai for combined training with the rest of the Twenty-Fourth Infantry Division.

Squad tents were set up in the field. After my experience with tent pegs in Korea, I let the farm boys handle the sledgehammers.

The first exercise was to debark from a landing craft transport (LCT). Cargo nets were hanging over the side of a mock wooden transport. The last time my boots had made contact with cargo nets was at Inchon, when our ship arrived in Korea at low tide. Now we were practicing for an invasion of North Korea.

A sergeant reviewed the procedure.

"Your boots go on the horizontal ropes, your hands on the vertical ropes."

He then climbed over the rail and down the netting to demonstrate what we were to do. We went through the exercise twice in the morning and twice in the afternoon. The men who couldn't climb down the nets remained until they could do it. *What will they do when we are at sea?* I wondered.

There was always something going at the service club. This evening the local debs had been invited to a dance. My feet never coordinated well to the music on the dance floor, especially in combat boots. My partner, who was sympathetic to my choreography, joined me for a short stroll outside the club. We walked no more than ten yards before I heard a whish. I dropped to the ground, facedown. The girl zoomed out of sight, probably thinking I was a madman. The whish had come from the wind rushing through the telephone wires overhead. It sounded exactly like incoming mortar rounds slicing though the air.

I brushed myself off and returned to my tent. Everyone there was asleep. As I removed my boots, a drunken GI wandered in. He reached for and embraced one of the tent poles to avoid a collapse. Weaver woke up and recognized him. He asked where the man had gotten the fancy officer's hat that was tilted on his head.

"I just ripped it off a captain's noggin," he replied.

"Hey, Bob, if he'd caught you, you would have been in a mess of trouble."

"Now how was he going to catch me? While I'm running on dry ground, he'd be running through two inches of thin shit!"

I fell asleep with a smile that probably lasted through the night.

Training continued on the Sea of Japan. Higgins boats brought us to the side of an LCT. Two sailors held cargo nets that were draped over its side. We hooked our boots into the net to ascend from the bobbing little Higgins boats up the net and over the ship's railing. It took a while for all the men to make it to the deck, but with the help of the sailors in the boats, they completed the exercise. The interior of the LCT had very tight quarters. Most of it was a dark, hollow space holding trucks and a tank it was to unload through its front doors when it reached shore.

The remaining food from our C-rations caked the walls of the garbage pail in the hallway. Mail call was my dessert. Along with her letter, Elaine sent a powerful sachet in an embroidered satin pouch. The scent from the sachet and the engine fumes combined to make an obnoxious sweet odor.

Weaver, honing in on the fragrance, came trotting over the grated metal gangway.

"Wolfe! What are you running here—a whorehouse?"

The innocent sachet joined the C-rations at the bottom of the garbage pail.

After breakfast, Higgins boats circled our transport. We were embarking for "the invasion." As we had practiced on the mock LCT at Sendai, we lined up for the departure. The cargo nets were slapping against the hull as the ship and the Higgins boats below us rolled with the waves. We climbed over the ship's railing and down the ropes. In the bobbing Higgins boats, two sailors were waiting to grab us. I could picture those unfortunate men for whom this was no exercise but the real thing in World War II as their boats approached the French or South Pacific beaches. Once on shore, we were to attack fortified positions. When we had completed this mock invasion, we returned to the LCT for a repetition the following day.

Our invasion was a success. We established a beachhead and overwhelmed the "enemy." It was then back to Camp Younghans, back to the barracks, back to a soft bed, and back to showers. It was early spring. It was beautiful.

Within a few days, a notice appeared on the company bulletin board announcing tryouts for the camp baseball team. Why not? It seemed a great opportunity to avoid training, play on a field maintained by Japanese gardeners, and travel throughout northern Japan. After five tryouts, the coach distributed uniforms to the men who'd made the team. I was the center fielder. Practice was scheduled daily.

Members of the Third Battalion baseball team: *squatting*, Art Schuyler and Dan Wolfe; *standing*, Engle, our coach, and Pat Dostilio.

Our first game was against Kenko High School in Sendai. The high school's coach approached our coach and asked, "Do you wish to attack, or do you wish to defend first?"

It was war, not baseball. We attacked first and then conquered them.

When we returned, the entire camp was preparing to leave for a five-day field maneuver. By evening we were in a Camp Younghans with empty barracks.

The next day, after baseball practice, I found our cook—a tall, handsome, muscular black man—in the shower, soaping himself under his underwear. There were only six showers in the room without partitions. Without lifting my eyes, I warily stepped into a far shower, turned my back to him, and bathed in record time. I wasn't about to ask him, and I never found out, why the underwear.

•

The next day's practice was called off, and the team was placed on a work detail. I was given a "yo-yo," a device with a two-sided jagged blade at the end of a three-foot wooden pole, which I swung from side to side to cut the overgrown grass in the culverts. Once I got the hang of it, the yo-yo was in continuous motion. After a while, the monotony of the detail had me standing in the culvert, leaning on the pole. I noticed a sergeant with an M1 rifle escorting a prisoner to a jeep. He pointed to the jeep and told the prisoner to get into it.

"I ain't going to no motherfucking jeep," shouted the prisoner, and he started walking away from the sergeant.

"Halt!" shouted the sergeant.

"Motherfuck you!" replied the prisoner as he continued walking.

"Halt!" the sergeant shouted again, raising his M1 to his shoulder.

There was no response; the prisoner continued walking. When he was about to jump over the culvert, the sergeant shouted, "Halt!" for the third time.

Having received no response, the sergeant aimed and fired. He hit the prisoner in the thigh as he jumped across the culvert. He spun in the air and then landed writhing on the ground.

"You'd better get out of here. You're a dead man," warned the prisoner.

An ambulance took him to an aid station. I learned from the sergeant that the prisoner had thrown a heavy metal ashtray, striking an officer in the head.

•

Our next ball game was at an air base to the north, on the island of Hokkaido. We lost the game but were consoled by their excellent lunch—especially the bread made from rice flour.

Our coach, an artillery officer, knew very little about baseball. He was very angry about our loss. Because our camp was very small, candidates for the team were limited. The camps we played were substantially larger than ours, with larger pools of players. In spite of this, he wanted to win every game.

The next game was against Camp Drake, a game that should not have been scheduled. This camp received all the men assigned to Japan and Korea. The major league, minor league, and college baseball, basketball, and football players went no further than this camp. Coaches of the respective sports siphoned them off. So here we were, a tiny camp in northern Honshu, playing a baseball team of pros and college all-stars.

The stands were full. The day was bright. The conditions for the game were ideal. But when we saw Camp Drake's pitcher warm up, a dark cloud enveloped the field from our perspective. A wild, angry, blistering fastball exploded from his arm. It sent shivers up my spine and traumatized my knees. He was an outfielder from the Louisville Colonels, a Triple A team, who wanted to try his hand at pitching. How grateful we were when we struck out without being hit by the rocket-propelled grenade he launched from his arm.

In the first inning, he walked the first and the second batsmen. Things were looking up. Then he promptly struck out three in a row. Down we went. In the second inning, he walked one man and burned the baseball past the other three. Meanwhile, our pitcher was being pounded. In the third inning, it was my turn to embarrass myself. I was waiting in the batter's circle when I heard, "Reilly! Reilly!" from the stands. It was Benny Hoover! I ran over and tried to throw my arms around him, but he backed away. He was not of the touchy-feely species. I tried to ask him where he was stationed, but it was my turn to strike out and go into the field. During the next inning, I looked for him. He had disappeared. That was the last I saw of him.

My coach had looked disparagingly on my brief reunion with Benny. The next day, angry at the two losses in a row, the coach told me to hand in my uniform. He said I had "rabbit ears"—that is,

I was paying too much attention to people in the stands. I told him that Benny had been my sergeant in Korea; he'd saved my life and the lives of others in our platoon. This meant nothing to the coach. The jerk wanted to win at all costs, even though he was restricted by his lack of knowledge of the game and his small pool of players.

Reluctantly, I handed in my uniform. At the time, I didn't realize that this was a harbinger of a brighter baseball future for me at Camp Younghans. The coach of the regimental team was eager to have me. We did more traveling and played more games than the division team did.

•

August 1953 was brutally hot. I was reading a magazine in the dayroom (recreation room) when John Sheilds, who had accompanied me from Korea, came in wearing a pile hat and an overcoat with the collar turned up. His eyes were red and glassy. He was trembling. I ran to the command post and called the medics. The next day, Frankie Scudero told me that John had been hospitalized with malaria.

When we were in Korea, we were given large, white, bitter chloroquine tablets once a week. The tablets did not cure or prevent malaria; they merely hid the symptoms. John was a victim. The disease expressed itself when he came to Japan and stopped getting the pills. John returned in two weeks looking like a dropout in a triathlon. He had been depressed from battle fatigue when he arrived in Japan. Malaria completed his agony.

As the months passed, my correspondence continued with Wayne Caton's mother and sister. Their letters were heartwrenching. There was no word either from him or about him. The Department of the Army had no information. I promised I would see them on my return to the United States.

In September 1952, I was on the MSTS *General Mitchell*, heading for the United States.

Nearly Home

Leaving Japan was not as painful as parting with my buddies in Korea. Barracks life had been fun, sometimes tedious, but the men here and I weren't connected for our survival. I was going stateside! Happily I said my farewells to the boys in the barracks and boarded a waiting truck to Camp Drake. I was on my way home! I brought back nothing but a duffel bag filled with GI clothing and my most valuable possession—a mind overflowing with unforgettable experiences.

Camp Drake was close to Tokyo. The port of embarkation was nearby Yokohama. Were we going to sit around camp waiting for our names to appear on the return-home roster? No. A GI bus brought us to the camp gate. From there Frank Scudero, two other GIs, and I took a cab to Tokyo.

We had no idea where we were going, but the cabdriver had an idea: he had GIs in his cab, so we were headed for a bar. First, however, he hopped out to urinate against a wall.

The moment we stepped into the bar, we were surrounded by a bevy of squealing beauties. Beauties? Who knew. It was so dark we tripped over chairs as they escorted us to a table. No, it was too early for beer. The ladies suggested *"whatohmehwenn."* We hadn't seen watermelon since we'd been stateside. Through the darkness, they maneuvered a large plate stacked with watermelon slices. *Okay, let's try one.* It was slick, it was soft, and it was rotten. A wave of nausea overcame me. We ran out with the girls begging for payment at our heels. A nearby outdoor restaurant enabled us to rinse out the rot with beer.

We drowned the rotten "whatohmehwenn" with beer in a Tokyo garden restaurant.

Shipping orders greeted us when we returned to our barracks. I stuffed everything I owned into my duffel and ran to the waiting buses. The speed with which we climbed up the bus' steps was doubled when we scrambled down them at the pier. In the army, a milling crowd eventually evolves into a line. The GIs waiting to board the ship quickly formed queues. The man in front of me had a New York accent—a *landsman*.

"Hey, where were you stationed?" I asked.

"Right here in Tokyo," he replied. "Where were you?"

"First Korea, then near Sendai."

"What were you doing in Korea?"

"Infantry."

"Oh."

An American civilian was distributing pamphlets alongside the queue. He was a member of Jimmy Doolittle's squadron that had bombed Japan on April 18, 1942. This man had been shot down in China and captured by the Japanese. He was placed in solitary confinement and tortured for thirty-four months. While in confinement, he said, he'd found God. This religious experience enabled him to return to Japan after the war to forgive his captors. He wanted us to join him in worshipping the God he had found. I took his pamphlet and moved on.

What next? A large wooden barrel was sitting at the foot of the gangplank. Alongside the barrel, a chaplain's assistant was shouting, "You are leaving your babies here with little food and hardly any clothing. Drop all your scrip and dollars into this barrel to keep them fed and dressed."

I dropped my remaining scrip into the barrel, which filled quickly as the troops passed by. I am sure it was full by the time we were aboard.

I was going home! Familiar food! Real shoes, real sneakers! Dungarees, not fatigues! Would my ankles miss the cold caress of combat boots? There were more important things to consider. Had Pa finally retired? Would Alvin's forthcoming marriage break up a long and cherished friendship? Would the candy store still be the base of operations for the neighborhood? What would I do after I flushed two years of army life out of my system?

I threw my duffel onto a cot and waltzed away, searching for familiar faces. With no work detail, I wandered the decks, enjoying the ocean breeze and sharing it with my newfound buddies. On one of my excursions, I found my *landsman* GI from the queue on the pier. He was talking about the 1951 Brooklyn Dodgers. I told him I'd been at the Camp Kilmer Reception Center the day I heard Bobby Thompson hit a home run off Ralph Branca to win the National League pennant. This GI was the younger brother of Ralph Branca. Whenever he saw me wandering the deck, he called on me to complain about the Giants knowing what pitch his brother was going to throw.

"Ralph would have struck out Bobby Thompson if he'd had no clue as to what pitch was coming." What could I say?

This was a joyride compared to the trip to Japan. The ocean was calm. The breeze was refreshing. The sun was shining. *Why not stretch out and scoop up the pleasure?* I thought. Within a few minutes, I was fast asleep on the deck. The bare skin above my ankles began stinging. A sailor was welding a hook to a hatchet five feet from me. Sparks flying from the tool had landed on my legs.

"Hey! You're burning my legs! Why didn't you tell me to move?"

"I didn't want to wake you up."

Oh, they have these wiseguys in the navy, too.

There were no letters to write. The food was good. I had no details to accomplish. Bingo and movies were the evening's entertainment. *Where's that Branca guy?* I thought. *Maybe he has some new complaints.*

I found a substitute—another New Yorker from Brooklyn. He was a Brooklyn Dodger fanatic who unashamedly told me he'd cried when Bobby Thomson hit the homer off Branca.

"You know, Branca's brother is on this ship," I said.

"Did you see him? Shh, he might hear you. I can't get rid of him and the cheating Giants."

The ship continued plowing through the waves. The PA system scratched out some static, silence, and then

> Pepsi Cola hits the spot.
> Twelve full ounces, that's a lot—
> Twice as much—and better, too.
> Pepsi Cola is the drink for you.

Everyone chimed in on the last line.

When the ship at last sailed under the Golden Gate Bridge, a small speedboat approached and circled us a few times. It held an enterprising photographer snapping the troops with a telephoto lens.

Where was the "Welcome Home" to greet the boys as they carried their duffels down the ramp of the MSTS *Mitchell*? There were no bands, no cups of hot coffee, and no doughnuts. Those treats were props for the photographers who were absent.

For those who hadn't been there—for those who hadn't seen what I had—the Korean War became the Forgotten War. Korea, unlike World War II, was not a priority in anyone's life except its veterans.

Some of the vets planned on reenlisting, while some would blend into factories, farms, and schools, resuming lives interrupted by experiences that had added years to their chronological ages and PTSD to their minds.

By the time we arrived at Camp Stoneman in Pittsburg, California, the speedboat photographer had printed our photos and was selling them at the PX. The next morning, we were flown to New York on nonscheduled Resort Airlines, whose stewardesses resembled retired and weary librarians. After that trip, all of us agreed that the airline's name was appropriate: one took its flights only as a last resort. Tragically, three months later, a Resort plane carrying Puerto Rican vets from Korea crashed in the Midwest, killing everyone aboard.

Near our destination, the plane dipped to one side. A panorama of lower Manhattan appeared in the window. The GIs began a frenzy of jumping and cheering at the sight of the skyline.

Is there something wrong with me? I wondered. I saw the same skyline and was happy to return home, but I couldn't generate that hysteria. Maybe the other guys were trying to ape or outdo the antics in a movie they'd seen.

We landed at an airbase in New Jersey and were bused to Camp Kilmer to be processed for discharge.

There was Dave Sohmer! I hadn't seen him since the night we'd lost one another at Inchon. Mel Winter was not far behind. I joined them. We had no time to talk about our experiences. We were sent quickly from one processing station to another.

"Did you see Bucky?" they asked.

"He should be here, but maybe he was on another ship," I replied.

After the processing, we stepped outside the building, and there was Bucky in the street. He didn't disappoint us; he was standing on a small pile of coal stacked in an open cement bin, talking to someone who had the sense to stand on the sidewalk. The lower parts of his chinos were as black as the coal underneath him.

Three days of processing transformed us into civilians. I was tempted to call my parents, but someone from the candy store would then have had to go two blocks to my apartment to tell them I was on the phone, and they would have had to trek to the candy store to answer. *No, I'll surprise them*, I decided.

Mel, Bucky, Dave, and I boarded a bus for New York City. The Seventh Avenue subway train once again brought me to the East 174th Street station. I was nearly home.

Back to the Old Neighborhood

Like a grimy, dingy, somber creation from an old Erector set, my East 174th Street elevated station was exactly as I had left it. I stepped onto a platform polished throughout the years by an army of shabby shoes worn by poverty-bruised, hopeless, fatigued immigrant sweatshop serfs rushing to work and then dragging their bodies home.

In the past, I never held on to the subway staircase handrails. They were as sanitary as a subway toilet seat. Not this time. The duffel on my left shoulder kept pushing me down the steps as if it were as anxious as I was to get home. The steps reversed direction halfway into the descent, so that they looked like an arrowhead from the street below. The sun's rays never reached the street; the long, broad subway platforms and the rails above me made sure of that. In their shadow, fluorescent lights fought a losing battle with filth and darkness in an attempt to brighten the depressing merchandise of the corner army-navy store. Litter, assembled like platoons under the subway steps and street corners, awaiting the wind's command to scatter and regroup at their new assembly areas.

I gripped my duffel bag and raced through the shadows toward the sunlight reflecting off the Boston Road concrete sidewalk. It was still lit! But sunshine in the Dover Bar window had dulled the red and blue neon gases of the fading Pabst Blue Ribbon sign. The Dover Theater's marquee announced free dishes every Monday night. Two employees on tall ladders were removing a large navy-blue cloth sign hanging from the marquee informing patrons that the theater was fully air-conditioned. This officially ushered in autumn.

I hadn't passed Gitelson's Deli since Dave and I had left to be inducted into the army two years earlier. Its open doors revealed the same worn, faded Formica tables, decorated with small ceramic mustard bowls and Heinz ketchup bottles separated by rectangular chrome napkin dispensers. Tables that had once been crowded with pastrami-on-club sandwiches, french fries, and Cokes, after our quarter-a-man stickball games, now stood as silent as the morning. *Should I step in and say hello? No, I'm on my way home!*

Hermann Ridder Junior High School still rose above and glared down at Gitelson's. Those carefree school days, each a precious jewel, were safely stored in my memory bank. The school's Art Deco building with an inverted-flowerpot tower stood proud and tall, incongruous to its drab surrounding tenements. It dominated the landscape, occupying a whole city block except for the small Tried Stone Baptist Church tucked in on its left and Kehelith Israel Synagogue behind it. In this landmark school, my three years had been punctuated by laughs and friendships that were formed for life.

I crossed Boston Road to Seabury Place, a two-block stretch of concrete and asphalt on which the diary of my youth was deeply etched. I was walking on asphalt again! At the far end of the second block, I pictured my mother trudging home from Jennings Street Market, lugging her shiny black oilcloth shopping bag swollen with the previous day's cut-rate bargains from Miller's fruit stand.

At the far end of the block, next to Nick's Shoe Repair, stood the barber pole. Its red, white, and blue stripes were rapidly spinning as if to say, "Welcome home!" This was a better greeting than I got when I debarked in San Francisco.

What am I doing standing here in the street? I'm home! My heart pounded as I ran up the two-step stoop. I opened the door to 1540 Seabury Place. Passing the mailboxes, I detected the acrid odor of urine diffusing from beneath the stairwell. Ah, yes! The longshoreman was up to his old tricks.

With my duffel bag digging into my shoulders, and my starched, wrinkled, chino uniform damp behind the knees and at the crooks of the elbows, I opened the door to apartment 11. Two aging folks resembling my parents threw their arms around me. We sobbed for a while. I stepped back.

What had happened? I had left two active middle-aged parents two years ago. Had I declined as rapidly?

Two years had had an exponential effect on their aging process. I wasn't prepared for this. It should have been part of the "Return to Civilian Life" orientation at the Camp Kilmer separation center.

"Why didn't you call? I would have made browned chicken and *helzel* [stuffed *derma* or kishkes—a flour, fried onion, and chicken fat mixture stuffed into the skin of the neck]."

"Ma, we don't have a phone."

"So call a neighbor."

"I don't have their phone numbers."

"Ach, you should have called anyway."

While warming the previous day's chicken, she cooked spaghetti and made a spicy sauce from a recipe Nick the Shoemaker's wife had given her. She knew I liked this sauce, but it was guaranteed heartburn for Pa. He joined me in spite of the potential inferno.

I ate very little. Reliable Ma contributed my excuse to Pa: "After eating so much *trayf* [unkosher] food, it will take time."

"Maybe he lost a few pounds, but I don't see where it bothered him."

The dialogue was refreshing and familiar, but the deeper wrinkles, the grayer hair, and the slowness of movement had stopped my digestive juices from flowing.

"Were you wounded anywhere?" Pa asked.

"Pa, I wrote you. I wasn't in combat."

"I saw that picture of you digging a foxhole."

"That wasn't a foxhole, Pa; I was digging a hole for a refrigerator."

"Who digs a hole in a field for a refigerator? A refrigerator is electric. It belongs in a kitchen. What did you do? Plug it into a *pferd's* [horse's] *tuchiss* [rear end]?"

Ma broke in. "Yeah, yeah, a refrigerator. Morris, do you expect him to tell you everything?"

"Sheldon's mother told me they were on the front lines. Get up and walk a little, Danny; I want to see if you were wounded."

While I waltzed around the room, my uncle Shrolleh came home from work. He stopped, he froze, and then we embraced.

"I think you've lost about ten pounds, and your shirt is too big" was his way of greeting me. It was back to the good old days, with comments worth bronzing.

When the after-dinner questions had been exhausted, it was nightfall. I thought maybe some of the boys would be hanging out at the candy store. I hurried down Seabury Place and made a left on East 172nd Street, leading to the store. There was Monty, leaning forward against a tenement wall, his hands pressed against the bricks as two detectives went through his pockets. Across the street, from a second-floor apartment, his mother was calling, "Monty! Monty! Come upstairs! Your supper is getting cold!"

Some words passed between Monty and the detectives. They left. What had changed in the past two years?

I opened the door to the candy store. Winkler was there, along with a couple of new faces. The darkness that had been illuminated by the comraderie and humor was AWOL. I smiled, but the candy store was as stale as the storage room in my tenement.

Lenny Blum asked if I had seen action in Korea. When I replied I had, one of the new faces burst out, "Oh, oh! Wait a minute. I'm going to get my helmet!"

Who is this twerp? I wondered. *Who cares. I'm home!*

Afterword

He Was Our Puppy Too

What if I called Frackville for a visit? I wondered. Would the sight of a survivor from that night add to their pain?

I decided to call, remind them who I was, and learn if a visit would be welcome. Wayne's brother answered. He told me that his mother had passed away a few months before. His father was so bitter about the way the army had handled Wayne's missing-in-action status that a visit to him would be a waste of time. But he gave me the phone number of his sister, who was living in a suburb of Philadelphia. She would appreciate a visit, he said.

How could I get to that suburb? Who had a car? Julius Herman and I had had a few classes together in junior high school. The only thing we had in common was making a minimum effort to achieve a passing grade. On September 27, 1951, we reported for induction into the army. That was the last I had seen of him until we were discharged from Camp Kilmer on September 17, 1953. He lived three blocks from my tenement, and he had a car—an unusual possession for a twenty-three-year-old in our neighborhood. I decided to walk the three blocks to pay him a visit.

"What are you doing? Did you get a job? Will you be going to school? We have the GI Bill. Did you meet any girls?"

After I had dispensed with the trivia, I worked up enough nerve to ask him if he would drive me to visit the sister of a close buddy who was missing in action.

"Why not? It's early in the morning. Where is she? Let's go. My car is in front of the house."

"Hold on. Mrs. Auld lives in Philadelphia. I'll call her."

She knew my name, and she remembered writing to me after Wayne went missing. She'd had no further word about Wayne's status; he was still missing in action. Yes, she would like to see me.

On the Pennsylvania Turnpike, Julius and I reminisced about our crazy days in junior high school. Were we immature or normal in our early teens? No answer. In spite of Korea, I think both of us were still immature, normal teens.

In Korea, Julius had been with the 555th Artillery. "All we did was zero in our 105 mm howitzers and fire for effect. We had no contact with the Chinese."

"If your shells were far enough away, they rocked us to sleep," I replied.

Julius listened while I began to rehearse my conversation with Wayne's sister.

"Hello, I'm Dan Wolfe. Wayne was my bunker buddy. What do I say after these opening lines?"

"Tell her what happened."

"I don't know what happened. Nobody knows."

Julius shook his head. "It's tough. I don't envy you."

We had no difficulty reaching the housing complex where Wayne's sister lived. Gloomy, gray two-family stucco homes were lined up on what appeared to be a wasteland. Trees, bushes, and lawns were absent from the landscaping design. Was there a landscaper? There certainly was no design. I didn't expect a housing project to be built on prime real estate, but this stark area was a candidate for an industrial park.

Mrs. Auld's home was at the end of the street. A weary "come in" responded to the doorbell. She appeared to be prematurely aged and depressed. From Wayne's appearance, I had pictured a short, cute, slim redhead or blond, not the worn-out, dejected woman whose conversation was a monotone delivered with no animation. She mentioned neither a husband nor children. I believe the loss of

Wayne had stolen the joy from her life. Her letters to me in Japan had been intelligent and informative. Anyone reading them would have felt the pain and frustration the family was going through.

After an armistice was signed at Panmunjom in 1953, American POWs returned to the United States for medical evaluation and rehabilitation. Wayne's mother heard that they were being sent to Valley Forge General Hospital in Pennsylvania. She made a few hundred photos of Wayne and sent them to the hospital. She asked if anyone had seen Wayne in the POW camps. No one recognized him. (Two years later, Wayne was listed as killed in action.)

We sat at the kitchen table while Mrs. Auld made coffee. "Please, tell me what you know about Wayne," she said.

Julius faded into the background.

"He was like a puppy dog," I said. "When he approached, everyone wanted to put an arm around him. He was the platoon mascot. He was also our medic—a dedicated medic. We knew we could depend on him. When we were in reserve and received orders to move up to the line, he asked me what would happen if he was so frightened he froze. I told him, 'Everyone is scared shit, yet they do what they have to, and you will, too.' And he did—above and beyond his call to duty. We shared a bunker on the line. My remaining image of Wayne is of him walking ahead of me on a patrol, the strap on his medic bag over his left shoulder and the bag bouncing off his right hip with each stride."

She sobbed as she brought me a photo of him from a shelf in the hallway.

"He was our puppy, too. My mother died heartbroken. Were you there when it happened?"

"It was a raid on Hill 121, occupied by the Chinese. Our platoon was the assault force. Wayne was always in the center so that he could reach a casualty as quickly as possible. We gave each other a thumbs-up sign before we moved up the hill. About halfway up, I fell into a deep trench. By the time I had climbed out to join my squad, Wayne was ahead, on Sergeant Flaherty's left and moving forward. A blinding flash followed by a boom went off in their area. I saw our Korean litter bearers run to gather the wounded. When we were ordered to withdraw, I ran to the area of the blast. There was no trace of him. I ran down the hill and saw Sergeant Flaherty being carried on a litter with his jaw macerated. He was evacuated. The platoon waited for Wayne at battalion headquarters, but he didn't return."

She cried again. I kissed her and left. For a while, we drove home in silence, and then Julius said, "I wish you hadn't asked me to come."

"I wish I hadn't come."

Hill 117

Hill One-One-Seven was only a wart of a hill.
Artillery will level it before we go in for the kill.
We'll cross the Imjin; it'll be a walk in the park.
My vest and my helmet won't be seen in the dark.

Two cartridges and two grenades are enough for this mission.
Let's be off to the chaplain before we head to perdition.
"The Lord is my shepherd ..." was his solemn prayer.
Will these words shield me while I'm a target out there?

What will Ma do if she gets the sad news?
"Your son was a hero, but we have some bad news ..."
Dusk over the Imjin helped our jon boats get through.
We assembled at the Bubble for another review.

With Charley at the point and Sid leading the raid,
I unlatched my safety and secured each grenade.
A trail matted with wire led us along a steep cliff.
It was here Charley whispered, "Come close; have a whiff.

It's kimchi, it's garlic, it reeks in the air."
"Into that ditch," shouted Sid, "artillery will blast 'em."
A round plunged into the Imjin.
Another flew past them.

So much for the shells; we moved up the hill.
I hurled my grenades. Whose blood did I spill?
Bullets from burp gins buzzed overhead.
Some buddies lay wounded; how many were dead?

Down the cliff Sid yelled, "Our ammo is low."
The men skidded and slid to the Imjin below
When I began to descend, Poodles ran up and said,
"Massengale's out there; I think that he's dead."

"Follow me, Poodles, and keep your head down."
I crawled under fire, but Poodles was gone.
Massengale's collar in hand, I dragged him away.
My heart beat like thunder; *Will I see another day?*

I buckled his ankles with my web GI belt.
We tumbled to the Imjin; what a hand I was dealt.
His helmet was gone; his vest was in shreds.
My OD fatigues were a palette of reds.

Bullets pockmarked the Imjin; *Will we ever reach a boat?*
I edged closer to the cliff with Massengale afloat.
They didn't see us; they missed us amid the slaughter.
He was a hero on the cliff, but cold dead in the water.

Ah, there's a jon boat; I towed him across.
Graves Registration was waiting to record Love Company's loss
Swaddled in a body bag; its zipper tolled the knell.
Massengale was at rest after his visit to hell.

Wet in my bunker, I zipped up my sack.
The zip of the zipper zipped; I was back.
I survived through the night; I'll never know why.
Maybe the old adage held true; I was too mean to die.

Dear Ma, dear Pa, nothing's going on here.
I'm far south of Seoul, way back in the rear.
I'll send a few photos, show the guys my great tan.
Tell them it's a picnic for your rear-echelon Dan.

Forty-Three Years Later

Memories of Wayne and the night of the raid on which he disappeared remained vivid in my mind. Completely unaware of the incident's potential impact on my life, I could have shared it, and many others, with friends and family. Or, like King Midas, I could have fondled each flawed jewel in seclusion, in my private vault. Although they had no intrinsic value, unconsciously I squirreled them into a strongbox and slid them deep into a compartment of my memory bank. Like a prehistoric trilobite encased in sedimentary rock, the saga was for years frozen in time.

In 1995, after thirty-five years of teaching biology in New York City, I retired to Florida with my wife, Sheila. Two weeks later, I went to Washington, DC, for the dedication of the Korean War Memorial.

I was sitting in my son Marc's living room in Washington, waiting for him to return from work so we could go to celebrate the dedication and maybe find buddies from Company L.

When he opened the door, his eyes were red, flooded with tears. Marc had learned that my younger son, David, was in a coma in a New York City hospital. We rushed to the airport. David was in the critical care unit, unconscious. After two weeks, he expired without regaining consciousness.

My return to Florida was a nightmare. Wherever I went, whatever I saw, and whatever I heard reminded me of my beautiful, sensitive, and talented David. I suspect I would have been curled in depression to this day had I not had the support of my wife and two other children, Marc and Sharon.

Time was my enemy. It filled the vast spaces between my few distractions. Scenarios of the joy David had given us played in my mind wherever I saw children doing whatever children do. I felt guilty if my thoughts wandered from him. My focus was on David and David alone. My wife's embrace and my children's insistence that we go on sustained my sanity.

One week after we had returned from the funeral, I received a phone call.

"Danny, pick up the phone. This guy scares me."

"Who is this?"

"It's Flaherty, you dummy!"

"Wow! The last time I saw you, you were on Hill 121. You were being carried on a litter by two KATUSAs. Your jaw was skidding on your chest like gelatin. Are you okay?"

Ray told me he had been taken first to an aid station and then to a MASH. They did what they could and sent him on to Tokyo Army Hospital. After partial rehabilitation, he volunteered to return to Sid, our commander of Company L. After the Korean War, Sid had gone to Vietnam as a helicopter pilot and then commanded a helicopter airfield. Ray went with special forces to the mountains of Laos and to two assignments in Vietnam.

"Enough of that," he said. "I remember you in reserve helping the guys write letters to their girls. I'd like to get the men together. If you're willing to write a newsletter, I'll send you their addresses."

"How did you get them?"

It had taken a few years. Ray told me he'd requested the morning reports from the army. He found the names on the reports and then located many of the GIs in their cities' phone books. He also paid a "people finder," who hadn't been very helpful.

Ray sent me seventy-nine addresses. Sid, who had retired as a lieutenant colonel, was living in Coronado Beach, California, and Lieutenant Theiss could not be found. Ray had found several men from my squad, including Charley Kauneckis, Oscar Konnerth, John Hollier, Ken Brockett, and Ed Heister.

I dedicated the first newsletter to my late son, David. It was followed in three months by a second. After the second newsletter, Ray called to say it was time for a Company L reunion. He was living in Merritt Island, Florida, about two hundred miles north of me.

"How about meeting at a seafood restaurant in Fort Pierce to discuss the reunion?" He was as eager as I to meet all the men. We settled on having dinner with our wives in Fort Pierce.

It had now been forty-four years since I'd seen Ray on that litter. I wondered, *Will I recognize him? Will he recognize me? What will I say? What if we have little to say to one another?* These thoughts ran through my mind on the two-hour drive from Boca Raton to Fort Pierce.

Sheila was as apprehensive as I. "He scared me when I answered the phone. Couldn't he be more delicate?"

The restaurant was empty when we arrived. Within a few minutes, a Ford Victoria came into the parking lot. The height was right, the dense shock of hair was right, but the waistline was wrong. Ray had been a superbly conditioned, wiry member of the Rangers assigned to Company L when I knew him. Beer had done a huge number on his waistline. Happily, there was no indication of a pulverized jaw.

Ray came to the meeting with a mission: to plan a reunion for the men of Company L. He had already contacted Fort Stewart, Georgia (the home of the Fifteenth Regiment), inquired about using its Hospitality Room, and made preliminary arrangements for the Company L dinner and some entertainment. We left promising to meet again at Fort Stewart.

A few weeks later, Ray called early in the morning. Sid, our company commander, was visiting his ex-wife, Ava Griffiths, in Orlando. The Flahertys and the Sidneys had a reservation at a restaurant that evening, and Sid wanted Sheila and me to join them. Who would dare disobey an order from Lieutenant Sidney? He had towered above any officer I'd met in both stature and performance. Whenever his name was mentioned, I saw the image of him carrying his M1 in his right hand and pointing to our objective with his left. He had been at the center of every raid and patrol—an inspiring figure.

In spite of meeting Ray, Sheila was still intimidated by him. She wondered what it would be like with the two of them barking at her.

On the trip to Ray's house, I wondered whether Sid actually remembered me. Could he recall our experiences in Korea? I'd known him as a company commander. What was he like as a civilian? Sheila knew as much about him as I did. She was the only person I'd spoken to about Lieutenant Sidney. She knew I admired and respected him. Would he be the man in civilian life that he had been as a commander?

Dan Wolfe, "Sid" Sidney, and Ray Flaherty reunited in 1997 at Flaherty's home in Florida.

We met at Ray's home and immediately began reminiscing about Korea and our lives afterward. How could we squeeze forty-four years into one afternoon? We left for the restaurant leaving many years and many recollections for another time.

At the restaurant, Ray and I grilled Sid about his military experiences. As he described his adventures in Europe, Korea, and Vietnam, chairs from nearby tables edged closer, eavesdroppers not wanting to miss a word. At seventy-one years of age, he still had the bearing of a battlefield commander.

We returned to Ray's house, where planning for Company L's first reunion at Fort Stewart took shape. Ray volunteered to have enlarged photocopies made of maps of Company L's positions on the front line in Korea, and to arrange for a tour of Savannah, Georgia. Sid volunteered to get the alcoholic beverages and secure the Hospitality Room. I volunteered to create posters from photos of the men from Company L.

"I was in awe," said Sheila on our return to Boca Raton. "Remember how you once said that you would follow Sid through a minefield? Well, I might be alongside you." This was quite an accolade from Sheila.

Ray was driven. In addition to the maps and the tour of Savannah, he enlarged his photos of Company L personnel and arranged for familiar Korean folk music to be piped into the Hospitality Room.

Three days before the reunion, I received a phone call from Linda Flaherty. Ray had suffered a heart attack. He needed quadruple bypass surgery, but he insisted that we go ahead with the reunion without him.

Sheila and I flew to Savannah and drove to Fort Stewart. When we arrived, Sid was at the center of the parking lot of the motel. As if we were in Korea, he gathered the men to plan our assault on the fast food and liquor stores. Mission accomplished! The squad returned intact.

We went into the motel anxiously waiting for the moment to assemble at the Hospitality Room.

Reunion

Shoney's was at the bottom of the line among low-budget southern motels, but it was a good choice. It was near Fort Stewart, and it didn't put a strain on the pockets of the vets who were on low-income pensions. Sheila and I signed in at the reception desk.

"Mr. Wolfe, Ed Heister left a message saying he would like to see you when you check in. He's in room 212."

"I'll go to our room; you go to Ed," said Sheila.

As soon as the door to Ed's room opened, my image of tall, slim, and handsome Ed Heister was quickly eclipsed by the sight of a huge man who somewhat resembled the powerful physique I once knew.

"Hello, Dan." Ed was always a man of few words. Turning to his wife, who was unpacking their luggage, he added, "Dan was our BAR man and runner, Flo."

Enveloped in the silence that followed, I wondered why I had received his urgent message. I tried to stuff in a filler to ease my discomfort.

"What have you done for a living since you were discharged?"

"I build cabinets."

"What kind of cabinets?"

"Kitchen mostly."

"I could have used you when I changed the cabinets in the house I sold. The old cabinets were pressboard crap."

"I build only wood cabinets, and I don't travel for my work."

"Well, okay … I'll see you later."

I left hoping this spare exchange would not be a precursor to what was coming later that evening.

Sheila was apprehensive as we dressed to meet the vets.

"What do I have in common with these guys and their wives? What will I talk about?"

"You might learn something about me you don't know."

"I know all I want to know about you," she countered.

Buttoned and zipped, Sheila and I stepped into the Hospitality Room. As we entered, she exclaimed, "Oh my God, they are a bunch of senior citizens!"

There was an alcohol-generated electricity in the air. In spite of the room's dark, depressing faux-wood paneling, we found tongues flapping rapidly in cadence to the recall of our experiences. Glistening beads of perspiration skidded on bare scalps and trickled slowly toward the remaining hummocks of hair. Most of the wiry bodies I had known in Korea had yielded to the ravages of age and gluttony. My buddy Charley Kauneckis, ex-paratrooper, had stood as straight as a redwood when I knew him. Now he was bent over like the handle of a cane, bewildered, and staring at the floor. This was not the Charley I'd known. I left the room quickly to prepare myself, and I then returned to the fray.

Although Oscar Konnerth, John Hollier, Ken Brockett, Hank Klepper, and Dale Knight were forty-five years older, they had not surrendered to the wicked processes of aging; they looked as if they could still fall out on the company street and chug along for a five-mile hike.

Sid was still our company commander—tall, straight, and slim. With Ava, his ex-wife, at his side, he held court with the men who had been his twenty-two-year-old draftees. It was incredible how he could recall the details of every raid and every patrol, as well as the fun we had had in reserve.

Colonel Sidney and his ex-wife, Ava, at the
reunion in Fort Stewart, Georgia.

"What happened to Whitefeather?" asked Brockett.

"Flaherty couldn't locate him," I told him.

"When was the last time you saw him?" he asked me.

"The last time was in the trench outside his bunker. We were saying good-bye; I was leaving the company and going to Japan."

My first recollection of Whitefeather, I said, was of seeing the grenades dangling from a bent sapling outside his bunker, and then I recalled him downing twenty-four cans of beer to the accompaniment of his haunting Indian chants. He would have added his usual unusual excitement to the event.

Benny Hoover was another distinguished member of our platoon whom Flaherty hadn't been able to locate. Everyone agreed that he was probably in a jail for disturbing something, someone—anyone.

Joe Mullen, with a shock of white hair, looked like a corporate executive. He'd been one of our commo men, but, when we returned to the MLR and he discovered he would have to go on more patrols and raids than the riflemen, he passed his radio on to an unsuspecting GI.

Ken Brockett and his brother-in-law Dwight were an item. We badgered them unmercifully about sharing a room at the hotel. Ken tried to deflect the assault by recalling a night when we were returning from a patrol. "I still get nightmares thinking about it. I stepped on a pheasant's nest and nearly had a heart attack when the bird rose up and brushed its feathers over my face. Do you remember that night? Isn't this reunion like Korea—all the action took place at night there, too."

Where was Sheila? I probably wouldn't have recognized her if she'd said "Hello."

Laughing, drinking, shouting, and sweating had set my head spinning to a point where I could hardly nudge the woolly words past my lips.

Most of the questions my buddies asked were left hanging. Each vet tried to pour out all he remembered without any attempt to wait for a reply.

"Flaherty told me that Sid held a dance the night before we moved into the blocking position. He laid out a cardboard dance floor in his tent and had some mooses brought in for a waltz. Did you know about it, Chuck?"

"No, I wasn't invited. Let's go and ask Sid."

"Not me—not with Ava sitting beside him."

A hush spread over the room as a vaguely familiar face appeared at the door entrance. It was Truman Bastin! The last time I'd seen him, he was being carried on Ed Heister's shoulders and gushing blood from his head and his mouth. No one knew what had happened to him after that night. After two years at Walter Reed Army Medical Center, Truman had made it through alive! Ed saw him, he saw Ed, and uncharacteristically, Ed ran over and threw his arms around Truman. They embraced. My heartbeat accelerated, and my throat tightened. I turned to Sheila. Her lips were pursed—she cries at soaps and movies—and a teardrop was balancing on her lower eyelid. She was not alone: some men stood frozen, some wives wept, and even Charley Kauneckis rubbed an eye.

Ed Heister (*left*) and Truman Bastin at the 1997 reunion.

Charley Kauneckis and Dan Wolfe in 1997.

Our throats needed lubrication. We made for the cans of Budweiser congregating below melting ice cubes. The talk turned to Hill 121. Ed had placed Truman in a jon boat to be sent across the river to an aid station. Now we learned that Truman's wounds had left him with a glass eye, a steel plate in his head, a plastic jaw with false teeth implanted in it, and abdominal wounds. His measured Kentucky drawl highlighted his upbeat attitude about his fate and set me wondering, *What would I be like if this had happened to me?* Later in the evening, Truman realized he had forgotten to bring his pills with him on the trip. He left the reunion to return to his home in Sanford, Kentucky.

"Elmer, go to the Lister bag and draw me a pint of beer," demanded Joe.

"Trippi, you call yourself Italian and you talk about beer?" Don Elmer responded. "You should be pushing vino, a slab of cheese, and a loaf of bread."

Don had driven to the reunion with Bill Gardner all the way from Pasa Robles, California. On the way, they'd stopped to visit their buddy Evertie Moore, who was a preacher in Kentucky. All of them were Third Platoon buddies.

Joe Trippi was the self-appointed official greeter. He was slim and tanned with chiseled features when I knew him. Now he resembled a Santa Claus, with a cherry-red face as round as a bowling ball, and a waistline to match. We'd spent hours in reserve exchanging biographies, complaining about Goff's menus, and searching for laughs. Most of the evening, he apologized for not being with us when we returned to the line. He had put in his time. He was entitled to go home. Our slim, dark, handsome twenty-two-year-old GI Joe was now a retired accountant living in Newark, California.

Joe Trippi at the 1998 reunion in Fort Benning, Georgia.

Sheila had heard lots of stories from me about Charley Kauneckis. At the cocktail party, she found him pontificating on the injustices of affirmative action, his service-related injuries, his hip replacement and lung problems, and his planned skirmishes with the Veterans Administration. For a moment, he seemed to have escaped his depression. In the war, Charley, the self-appointed point man, and I, the runner, were in constant contact on patrols. Soon after I left Company L, he and Lieutenant Daly volunteered to scout Jackson Heights, a hill the company had lost earlier. Both were wounded and cited for heroism. Upon returning from Korea, Charley was placed in an army motor repair school. He quickly volunteered for Vietnam, where he was assigned to a motor repair unit for boats patrolling the Mekong Delta.

"Repairing motors in Vietnam was as exciting as repairing motors in the United States," said Charley. Charley volunteered for and was accepted by a rifle company. As an infantryman, he was twice exposed to Agent Orange.

"Why do you call me more often than I call you?" was Charley's way of greeting me.

"You were a memorable part of my life, and I want it to continue." I reminded him of the time we were court-martialed in reserve. Did he remember the incident?

Charley was bewildered. This was a fragile, vacuous image of the ex-paratrooper I had known.

"I don't remember anything about Korea. But it would have been one of the more than twenty-five court-martials in my army career. Why should I remember that one?"

Unfortunately, Charley's memory had moved on, as had his body. The one thing he could recall was my thinning hair. Now a recovering alcoholic suffering from post-traumatic depression and lung problems brought on by Agent Orange and smoking combined, Charley was in a very sad chapter of a life devoted to the military. Sid was trying to use his influence as a retired colonel to get Charley a larger disability pension. Charley lived with his wife in Poquoson, Virginia, where he repaired washing machines, dryers, dishwashers, and refrigerators. He barely eked out a living. When I told him I wasn't happy with the performance of my dryer, he said, "I'll go anywhere for a repair. Just pay the bill and cover my travel expenses."

The VA doctor had diagnosed Charley's chest pain as a muscle strain. I wondered whether it might be more than that.

"Charley," I said, "if your chest hurts and you're not happy with the diagnosis the VA gave you, can't you get a second opinion?"

He brushed me off, saying we'd meet again next year at Fort Benning.

At our second reunion, Sheila said good-bye to Charley and told him she hoped to see him the following year.

He replied, "You're not going to see me again. I have lung cancer." That was the "muscle strain" in his chest.

In December, 1998, my wife and I drove from Chapel Hill, North Carolina, to Poquoson, Virginia, to attend Charley's funeral.

After a member of the American Legion delivered his eulogy, I spoke about my experience with Charley. Needless to say, there were many laughs. But I learned that his family—two sons, a daughter, and his frail wife—knew very little about him. After spending thirty years in the army, how much time did he spend at home? Or did he want to spend time at home? One son told me he was an alchoholic, another son was married to a black woman (Wow! What did Charley have to say about that?), and his wife, who was in a daze, didn't seem to know what was going on. His daughter, a beautiful, young, and personable married woman, lived in Colorado. She thanked me for delivering my tribute to Charley, but she said that as a father, Charley had never been home.

Oscar Konnerth and his wife, Mary Ann, drove in from Erie, Pennsylvania. We had been neighbors on the MLR. His silver-gray hair topped the same quiet, handsome, softspoken Oscar I remembered in the platoon.

Oscar Konnerth, 1997.

"Where were you taken after you were hit on Nori?" I asked.

"I don't remember a thing about that night. I woke up in a MASH. After a week, Mary Ann was waiting for me when I arrived in Erie." He was wearing a plastic leg brace. Shrapnel had torn out part of his buttock.

Charlie Messiar and his wife, Ginny, flew in from Chippewa Falls, Wisconsin. When he told the boys that his burial vault business was doing very well, they lined up to reserve choice spots in his mausoleum. Francis Mette asked if he gave a discount to disabled veterans. Charlie shook his head and left with Ginny to get a beer.

Francis Mette and his wife, Shiloh, joined the reunion from Utica, Michigan, a suburb of Detroit. Francis had been severely wounded in the abdomen on the August 8 ambush. He spent a year and a half recovering in army hospitals, with Shiloh visiting him there, but he claimed he was fine now. "I owe it all to the army doctors," he said. Francis had retired as an auto body mechanic. Shiloh was the cookie baker for the elementary schools of Utica. Whenever the schoolchildren would see her in the street, they'd shout, "Hey, Cookie!"

John Hollier was the same slim, handsome Cajun I knew in Korea. He'd been a machine gunner in our platoon. Full of fun, he had constantly patted my head in Korea, and he continued to pat my bald pate in the Hospitality Room. He and his wife, Anna, drove from Lafayette, Louisiana. Her intelligent and persistent contact with her state senator finally got John the Purple Heart he'd earned when mortar shrapnel sliced across his back. Fortunately the shrapnel had not penetrated his spinal cord.

Hank Klepper came without his wife, Helen; as a teacher in an elementary school, she had to tend to her scholars in Orlando, Florida. We accused him of making a couple of moves toward a pretty young lady sitting opposite him at the regimental dinner, but he denied this. Hank was a retired warrant officer.

Lt. Don Daly, dressed in a blue blazer and with snow-white hair, added class to the reunion. Don was a Yale graduate whose bearing announced he was an Ivy Leaguer. Upon graduation, he had been offered a scholarship to a university in France.

"What were you doing in Korea with those credentials?" I asked.

"I wanted to see what was going on," was his reply.

Although Don was a very modest man, he related a story that happened soon after I left for Japan. He was company commander of L company. Company L was ordered to take back the hill called Jackson Heights that we had recently lost. The operation was a poorly planned daylight attack in which many men were lost. After dark, Don Daly and Charley Kauneckis went to scout the area. They became involved in a firefight, and Don was wounded. He and Charley were awarded Bronze Stars with a *V* for valor for their heroism.

On the night of November 30, 1952, Don led fifty men on a raid. A company-size force of Chinese (twice the size of Don's patrol) encircled them. During the half-hour firefight, Don was disabled by a bullet in his leg, but he managed to call battalion to give the precise coordinates of his location. Battalion directed heavy mortars to ring Don's men, and Don's patrol fought its way back to the MLR. For his action in saving the patrol, Don was awarded the Distinguished Service Cross. He now lives with his wife and son in Bryn Mawr, Pennsylvania, and works as a financial consultant for a major investment firm. After the reunion, while Sheila and I were waiting to board our plane at the Savannah Airport, Don conducted a personal investment seminar for us. Unfortunately it had no effect on the devastating losses we were soon to experience in the stock market.

Dale Knight flew in from Arizona. Although he was not in my platoon, I distinctly remembered hearing his name bandied about in reserve. I therefore concluded that he must have been an eight-ball (goof-off). He agreed. When he wasn't taking time out for a cigarette, he spent the entire reunion doubled over in laughter. Dale and his wife, Lou, were absorbing the sun's rays in Phoenix. Their business was buying and selling antique glass.

"Antique glass!" I was excited. "You're just the man I want to see. When my wife was in Israel, she bought a ring with a stone that the dealer claimed was antique Roman glass. I told her it was a shard from a recently discarded Coca-Cola bottle. Can you look at it?"

"No way," he replied. "I'm not going to start with your wife."

I was happy Sheila wasn't there to hear this; she probably would have intimidated him into giving an overblown estimate of the value of her unseen ring.

It was quite a night. Faded memories were retouched in living color, carrying a group of old men back to the terror and fun they'd found on the hills and in the valleys of Korea.

The following day, the vets were given a tour of Savannah. On the bus, our beautiful tour guide, dressed in a costume from the Civil War era, lectured about Savannah's history and architecture. She ended by singing "Georgia on My Mind." During her rendition, I could see the World War II vet sitting alongside me squirming in his seat. As soon as she finished her last note, he stood up and loudly crowed, "Nothing could be finer than to be in Carolina in the morning," to the amusement and applause of the Carolinians.

On the final day, the Fort Stewart personnel gave us a tour of their weaponry. We crawled through monstrous tanks that were controlled by using computers. In Korea, we had used tanks as self-propelled artillery pieces. Those vehicles would have looked like toys next to these monsters.

Charley and I checked out the light weapons. The present M16's firepower was what we had desperately needed in Korea. Our M1 was no match for the burp gun in close combat. The modern machine gun was the size of my BAR and appeared to weigh less. Recalling the incident with Charlie and the Sniperscope, I asked one of the GIs if the army still used that equipment.

"A Sniperscope? What's that?" he asked.

After I described it, he brought us a standard-issue M16 rifle with a viewing screen attached to it. Remembering how Charley's back had been burned by sulfuric acid spilling out of the battery, I asked, "Where's the battery?"

Somewhere near the screen, the soldier removed a disc a bit larger than my thumbnail. That was the battery!

That evening, we had our company dinner. I opened the dinner by reading the names of our men who had been killed or wounded or were missing in action. This was followed by a tribute to Sid, our heroic company commander.

A roast beef dinner was served. Had I been given the choice, I would have opted for a can of C-rations—ham and lima beans—for old times' sake. The men maintained that Sergeant Goff had somehow gotten into the kitchen of the reunion's kitchen to exact his revenge for the wisecracks we'd made about his delicacies. The cutlery should have included a scalpel rather than a steak knife to dissect the roast beef.

Forty-five years before, we had depended upon one another for survival; now this group of aging vets were Company L again, with Sid as our leader. Our good-byes were followed by a promise to meet the following year at Fort Benning, Georgia.

Epilogue

Following are brief accounts of what has happened to some of the men of Company L since Korea.

Charley Kauneckis at the 1998 reunion at Fort Benning, Georgia.

Colonel "Sid" Sidney at the Fort Benning reunion.

Truman Bastin: After a year and a half of rehabilitation at Walter Reed Army Hospital, Truman was released with a steel plate in his head, a glass eye in his orbital, inset teeth in a plastic jaw, and bits of shrapnel in his abdomen. Since then he suffered both cancer and heart trouble, requiring bypass surgery that replaced three valves in his heart. In spite of all these afflictions, he was the most positive and optimistic man I have known.

Truman passed away on January 11, 2009.

Chuck (Charlie) Messiar: Chuck and his wife, Ginny, came to the first reunion from Chippewa Falls, Wisconsin. He had become a successful businessman building burial vaults. Throughout the first reunion, he was bursting with laughter. Ginny said he was eagerly looking forward to the second reunion when he had a fatal heart attack.

Sgt. Ray Flaherty: After twenty years of military service in Korea, Vietnam, and Laos (with special forces), Ray retired to Merritt Island, Florida. He spent three years researching the whereabouts of the men of Company L and organized our first reunion, although a heart attack prevented him from attending it. With a pacemaker and two defibrillators installed in his chest, he had been writing a novel about his military experiences. His wife, Linda, passed away in January 2004.

At one of our company reunions, I told Flaherty that if he predeceased me I would deliver the eulogy no matter where he passed away. Flaherty passed away in September 2005. My wife and I flew from Raleigh, North Carolina, to Bushnell Military Cemetery in Florida to attend his funeral. After my eulogy, four men introduced themselves. They told me that as a team, they and Flaherty were flown as civilians on a secret mission to Laos. They were to get information on the combined Laotian and Vietnamese Communists who were attempting to overthrow the Laotian government—a government that was friendly to the United States. They lived in the jungles of Laos, making tents from their ponchos and sleeping on their backpack in case they had to bug out. They killed water buffalo, monkeys, and snakes for food. After that mission was completed, they were to leave Laos by antique aircraft. It crashed upon takeoff, but no one was hurt. Johnny McCallum who told me this story, weighed 175 pounds when he left for Laos. He weighed 135 pounds upon his return. Sergeant Flaherty passed away in 2006.

Oscar Konnerth: After his discharge, Oscar spent time in the hospital to repair the wounds he had received on Outpost Nori.

His wife, MaryAnn, helped speed his recovery by making sure he was receiving the proper care. Oscar became a bus mechanic in Erie, Pennsylvania. Upon retiring, he was assigned daily KP duty in the kitchen of his son's pizza parlor.

Joseph Mullen: Joe attended many of our reunions. He originally lived in Michigan but later moved to Hurst, Texas. Walter Garceau (a Korean vet from another company who met us at our first reunion and continued to attend our gatherings from then on) continually distracted Joe at the Camp Stewart and Fort Benning golf competitions. Their verbal jousting in the evening had us rolling on the floor. At the third reunion, in Washington, DC, Walter was confined to a wheelchair, and Joe spent the days wheeling Walter around Arlington National Cemetery and other points of interest. A year or two later, Joe suffered kidney failure and had to undergo dialysis. Although his prognosis was poor, his wife, Joan, was undeterred; she tenderly brought him back to good health. He and Hank Klepper were the only ones who showed up at the 2004 reunion.

Hank Klepper: Hank, a twenty-year man, retired as a warrant officer and moved to Orlando, Florida. When his giant avocado tree toppled over in a storm there, he moved with his wife, Helen, to Melbourne, Florida, where all the greenery is tended by landscape personnel. Hank hasn't missed a single reunion. Despite his aches and pains, he did not complain.

Hank passed away on December 26, 2010, and is buried in Arlington National Cemetery.

Francis Mette: Francis received severe abdominal wounds in the ambush on the night of August 8. After commuting to hospitals for more than a year, he bounced back to become an auto body mechanic. He is now retired but is active with the Disabled War Veterans, which makes his wife, Shiloh, very happy because she can watch the soaps without being harassed.

Dale Knight: Dale and his wife, Lou, travel throughout the United States for their antique glass business. I think Dale enjoyed our reunions more than anyone else. Whenever I saw him, he was doubled over in laughter. He was wounded on the night of the ambush, and while recovering, he was sent to battalion headquarters to help write awards for valor. He distinctly recalled writing citations for Wayne Caton, Ed Heister, and Sgt. Fostine Rutledge. He is now recovering from a heart problem. Dale claims that the hundred-plus-degree weather in Phoenix has accelerated his recovery. Easterners claim that the weirdest people were the ones who left and took off for the West.

Sgt. Don Staszewski: Don lives in Santa Fe, New Mexico, with his wife, Becky. He led one of our platoon's machine gun teams. The output from his men was instrumental in preventing more casualties from the ambush on August 8, 1952. Poor health prevented Don from coming to our early reunions, but he and Becky made it to the Las Vegas reunion. Now Don is suffering from vertigo, which interferes with his sense of balance. He was recovering from the removal of his gallbladder when I spoke to him at the end of June 2004. Company L could form a pretty long line for sick call these mornings. (Don't forget to bring your duffel bag with all of your clothing.)

Don Elmer: Don is a retired police officer who originally lived in Milwaukee, Wisconsin. After his wife passed away, he moved near his platoon buddy, Bill Gardner, in Pasa Robles, California. Our reunions have been enlivened by the humor they brought with them all the way from California. Now Don is living with a lady friend in Creswell, Oregon. He makes a yearly visit to Germany to ensure that the hands that make the beer haven't lost their skill.

Bill Gardner: Bill was wounded on a patrol near the base of Hill 317 and then became a clerk/typist pecking out the vital data on dog tags. Now retired in Pasa Robles, California, he has discovered that golfing is an impossible sport, but he continues to dream that he will one day qualify for the US Open.

Joe Trippi: After Joe returned to the United States, he and his wife settled in Newark, California. With the help of the GI Bill, he graduated college as an accountant. In the area behind his home, he grows almost every fruit and vegetable one can find in a supermarket. With wine purchased from Trader Joe's, he made sure that Bill Gardner's blood met at least the legal alcohol limit for inebriation at all times. Joe was the dedicated financial secretary of Colonel Sidney Outpost 52 (the name we've given to our band of Company L vets) and was very active in keeping our group together.

Joe passed away on January 12, 2002.

Ed Heister: Ed lives in Norman, Oklahoma. He and his wife, Florene, attended the first reunion, but Florene later was diagnosed with cancer and passed away. Ed is now working part-time while his son runs the business. His major occupation now is restoring old cars and presenting them at auto shows.

Dan Wolfe: With financial aid from the GI Bill, I graduated with a degree in education from City College of New York and taught biology for thirty-five years at Jane Addams High School in the South Bronx. There I met my wife, Sheila, then a librarian at the school. We had three children, a girl and two boys. Unfortunately we lost our son, David when he was 29 years. We presently live in Bronxville, New York.

Col. "Sid" Sidney: In section 66, site 5912, Arlngton National Cemetery, rests Lt. W. A. "Sid" Sidney (Lt. Col., retired). He was an airborne paratrooper and highly decorated commander of Company L, Fifteenth Regiment, Third Infantry Division. In the face of danger, he was fearless. Unfortunately, many details regarding this man, who saved numerous lives in our platoon, are buried with him.

Sid was cited three times for the Combat Infantry Badge (WWII, Korea, and Vietnam). This indicated that he was exposed to enemy fire for at least thirty days for each citation. Among his many awards, he received two Silver Star Medals, seven Bronze Star Medals, the Distinguished Flying Cross, the Legion of Merit, the Purple Heart, eight Air Medals, the Bravery Gold Medal from Greece, the Master Parachute Badge, the Glider Badge, and the Order of St. Maurice Medallion.

When Company L was sent into reserve, Sid replaced Captain "Command Post" Smith, who never ventured out of his bunker (i.e, command post).

Sid was a role model fit for a US Army recruiting poster. Such a poster would have drawn many recruits into the service. He was tall, he was handsome, and he was brazen. It seemed as if his fatigues had been customized by a tailor from London's Savile Row. He was a standout wherever he went.

In every raid, he presented optional paths for withdrawal. On August 8, 1952, while patrolling over a cliff overlooking the Imjin River, the Second Platoon was caught in an ambush at Hill 117. After a fierce firefight, the Chinese apparently withdrew. Lieutenant Sidney, aware that the enemy might be lying in ambush along our return path, decided that we would scale down the ninety-foot cliff overlooking the Imjin with our casualties in hand. The platoon waded safely back to their bunkers on the MLR.

On August 12, 1952, artillery and supporting cannon fire from a British Centurion tank and its heavy machine guns bombarded Hill 121. It was now ready for attack. The hill was rubble as we made our way toward the entrenched Chinese. During this action, we heard screams from our rear that overwhelmed the din of combat. Sid, who anticipated an attempt to encircle our company, stationed our 57 mm recoiless rifle team on a knoll behind us. Three white phosphorus rounds incinerated their attempt.

Forty-five years after the end of the Korean War, Company L began their reunions. The men of Company L had been reunited once again. Sid was able to attend two more reunions. Sid passed away on January 18, 2000. With Sid gone and age slowing us down, there were no more reunions. He was the glue that kept us together.

We were young. We did what we were ordered to do. Some returned. Some were crippled; others were lost or died in battle. Someone said that wars should be fought by the old men who plan them. If they survive, let them come home and write their their memoirs.

All wars are planned by old men
In council rooms apart,
Who call for greater armament
And map the battle chart.

But out along the shattered field
Where golden dreams turn gray,
How very young the faces were
Where all the dead men lay.

Portly and solemn in their pride,
The elders cast their vote
For this or that or something else,
That sounds the martial note.

But where their sightless eyes stare out
Beyond life's vanished toys,
I've noticed nearly all the dead
Were hardly more than boys.

—Grantland Rice

A Follow-Up on Wayne Caton

In March 2004 (fifty-two years after I left Korea), I received an e-mail from Holly Miller, Wayne Caton's niece; her father, Howard, was Wayne's brother. Holly had located a website that carried a description of Wayne Caton's action on the nights of August 8 and 12, 1952, before he was listed as missing in action. She noted that I had contributed the information, and she contacted me to learn what I knew about her uncle. She had no information about him except that he was listed as killed in action. Another brother had received some information about Wayne but had never passed it on to the rest of the family. After an exchange of e-mails and phone calls, my wife, Sheila, and I decided that it would be the compassionate and the right thing to visit the family. But what could I say that I hadn't already said?

Yes, he was my bunker buddy. Yes, he was always at the center of the action and was always available on raids and patrols. Yes, I definitely saw him to the left of Sergeant Flaherty and myself at the base of Hill 121. Yes, I saw him through the dust and rubble when we reached the top of 121. But what happened after a concussion grenade exploded to my left, pulverizing Sergeant Flaherty's jaw?

"What do I say to the family? They know all this."

Sheila replied, "I'll speak to them, and you join in. I'm sure they want to hear it from you in person."

We pulled up to a modest house in Allentown, Pennsylvania, and were wamly welcomed by Holly, her father, Howard (Wayne's brother), and his wife, Kate.

Thank goodness for Sheila. She began our meeting by expressing her appreciation for this unfortunate but unusual experience.

Holly, a beautiful and appealing young woman, wanted know every detail about her uncle. Her father was a duplicate of Wayne fifty-two years later.

I told them all I could remember about Wayne and brought some photos and letters. It was a sad and emotional affair. We left for lunch and then went home without discovering anything new about Wayne's disappearance.

Spent from the draining experience we drove home with few words passing between us.

Holly is a determined young woman who will not be denied. When she was in Washington, DC, she went to the Department of the Army to get whatever information they had about Wayne. Their records confirmed Ed Heister's story about Wayne returning to Hill 121 to find more casualties. Wayne was awarded a Bronze Star with a *V* for valor. Although this citation is noted in the Department of the Army files, the citation paper itself has not yet been found. Holly has asked her congressional representative's office to investigate.

I called Ed Heister one day because I was determined to uncover any new information about Wayne. I knew he was the one who carried the severly wounded Truman Bastin to the jon boats before I arrived. I wondered if he saw Wayne Caton at the jon boats the night he had cartried Truman Bastin. He related the following incredible story to me.

"When I arrived with Truman, I placed him in a jon boat and told the GI in charge of the boats to get Truman quickly across because he was hemorrhaging. The GI said that his orders were to fill the jon boats with four men before they could be pulled across the river. Wayne, standing alongside me, pulled out his .45 pistol, placed it into the gut of the GI, and said, 'If he doesn't get across now, you're a dead man.'"

Wayne returned to Hill 121 "to look for men who were wounded and not found." He never returned.

Truman was immediately pulled across, and after one and a half years at Walter Reed Army Medical Center, he survived. Whe appeared at Company L's first reunion, he embraced Ed Heister. Truman was a funny and engaging personality. He passed away on June 11, 2009.

Acknowledgments

The passage of time sometimes erodes recall. It has been more than sixty five years since I fought in Korea, but the events in this memoir have been permanently imprinted on my psyche. I would like to thank my friend Dave Sohmer, who filled in the gaps of our experience in basic training at Indiantown Gap, Pennsylvania. For the events in Korea, I am deeply indebted to my late company commander, Col. "Sid" Sidney, Sgt. Ray Flaherty, and my heroic buddies in Company L, who were kind enough to relate their experiences during our many reunions: Truman Bastin, Kenneth Brockett, Don Daly, Don Elmer, Bill Gardner, Ed Heister, John Hollier, Charley Kauneckis, Hank Klepper, Dale Knight, Oscar Konnerth, Chuck Messiar, Francis Mette, Joe Mullen, Charley Nunns, Don Staszewski, and Joe Trippi. If I have neglected to mention anyone who played a role in this memoir, please accept my apology.

I could not have written this without the critique and guidance I received from my wife, Sheila—a critic, a taskmaster, and a stress-relieving companion—my son Marc, and my daughter, Sharon. I must also thank my teachers—Maudy Benz and Ruth Messinger at Duke University, Cathy Switzer at Sarah Lawrence College, and Joan Potter at the Hudson Valley Writer's Center, and Zipporah Collins, our dear friend and editor of the first edition, who should have been awarded the Bronze Star with a *V* for valor for poring over my writing without the benefit of a helmet or an armored vest. All have been invaluable in the publication of this memoir.

Finally I thank my parents, whose humor, pathos, and guidance contributed to my full life, which turned out to be much fuller than the life they achieved for themselves.